NUCLEA

Untangling the Societal Enigma

NUCLEAR WEAPONS

Untangling the Societal Enigma

Kishore Kumar Khera
Dr U C Jha

Vij Books India Pvt Ltd
New Delhi (India)

First Published in India in 2022

Published by

Vij Books India Pvt Ltd
(Publishers, Distributors & Importers)
2/19, Ansari Road
Delhi – 110 002
Phones: 91-11-43596460, 91-11-47340674
Mob: 98110 94883
e-mail: contact@vijpublishing.com
web : www.vijbooks.in

ISBN: 978-93-90917-19-8 (HB)

ISBN: 978-93-90917-78-5 (PB)

ISBN: 978-93-90917-82-2 (ebook)

Cover Photo:
Atomic Bomb Dome, the Hiroshima Peace Memorial Park
Courtesy:
Puneet Jha

Contents

List of Tables and Figures

Preface

Societal order is intricate. The intertwining of material possessions and the psychological outlook of all players play a pivotal role in order matrix. Among the possessions, military power and specifically weapons are significant data points. Weapons symbolise power. And effective use of weapons often pays dividends much higher than the destructive power of the weapons used. Some weapons not only cause physical damage and destruction but have a disproportionate psychological impact. And nuclear weapons epitomise this category. Mere possession of such a weapon can alter the geostrategic balance and its usage can have a devastating effect. Unfortunately, human greed led to avoidable and unnecessary usage of nuclear weapons in the Second World War but luckily it has not happened again, so far. But the threat remains with thousands of nuclear weapons with multiple states and possible access to non-state actors.

Cold War between NATO and Warsaw Pacts in the 20th Century witnessed nuclear brinkmanship. It was a norm to keep aircraft armed with nuclear weapons airborne for a retaliatory strike in case of a nuclear attack by the opposing side. The risk of the accidental nuclear conflagration was very high. Fortunately, the human race survived that period. With the breakup of the erstwhile USSR, the Cold War practically ended. The risks have come down but still, prevail. With the US-China competition for strategic space, access of nuclear weapons to not so stable states and the possibility of falling of nuclear weapons with non-state actors, gradually we are moving higher on the risk matrix. According to an estimate, China will more than double its nuclear arsenal and will reach 1000 nuclear warheads by 2030.[1] Will the human race survive this uncertain period with nuclear weapons?

Several publications are available on technical aspects of various types of nuclear weapons covering both fission and fusion aspects. This book

1 Military and Security Developments Involving the People's Republic of China 2021, Annual Report to Congress, Office of the Secretary of Defence, USA, p. VIII.

focuses on the impact of nuclear weapons on a society looking at it through procedural, processes and legal prisms. This book is divided into seven chapters. It begins with estimating the human cost of nuclear weapons with specific reference to the psychological impact on nuclear weapon attack survivors. Scars of such an attack and its implication last much longer and well beyond the life span of the survivors.

The second chapter covers various aspects of nuclear weapon testing and nuclear facilities and their impact on humanity. While testing is an important aspect of any new system but in the nuclear domain, it has a multi-faceted impact on the environment. And the same is true for nuclear weapons storage facilities as well. Besides physical hazards, a threat of a nuclear accident, a possibility, enhances the level of uncertainty among the residents of that area. Lack of authentic information and widespread misinformation makes a discomforting combination and disturb the psychological balance.

The next chapter dwells on the ongoing modernisation of the nuclear weapons arsenal, specifically of the US. It has a huge economic cost. Should the states continue in a nuclear weapons race? Or the states can better utilise their resources. These are nearly a trillion-dollar questions.

Rules, regulations and laws exist to keep order and deliver justice. Various aspects of international laws and their relevance concerning nuclear weapons are discussed in chapter four. Can non-binding and discriminatory rules and regulations mitigate the threat of nuclear weapons? It is time for all stakeholders to move consciously to create a new framework for the elimination of nuclear weapons. In case nuclear weapons remain, the threat of their use remains.

Some bright spots exist in an otherwise gloomy scenario. These are nuclear-weapons-free zones. Chapter five covers the concept, process and implementation of Nuclear-Weapons Free Zones. It also encompasses the advantages and shortcomings of various models adapted for this process. The penultimate chapter encapsulates various aspects of the Nuclear Weapons Treaty and its ramification for humanity. The concluding chapter charts out a likely future path for the role and place of nuclear weapons for the survival of the human race. Hopefully, humanity will triumph.

New Delhi
January 2022

Kishore Kumar Khera
U C Jha

Abbreviations

ALBM	Air-Launched Ballistic Missile
CASD	Continuous At-Sea Deterrent
CMC	Central Military Commission
CNS	Centre for Nonproliferation Studies
CTBT	Comprehensive Test Ban Treaty
FMCT	Fissile Material Cut-off Treaty
GBSD	Ground-Based Strategic Deterrent
HEU	Highly Enriched Uranium
IAEA	International Atomic Energy Agency
ICBM	Intercontinental Ballistic Missiles
ICRC	International Committee of the Red Cross
IPFM	International Panel on Fissile Materials
IPPNW	International Physicians for the Prevention of Nuclear War
ISPR	Inter-Services Public Relations
KSSR	Kazakh Soviet Socialist Republic
LOW	Launch-On-Warning
MOD	Ministry of Defence
NASIC	National Air and Space Intelligence Centre
NFU	Nuclear No-First-Use
NPT	Nuclear Non-Proliferation Treaty

NWFZ	Nuclear Weapon Free Zones
NWS	Nuclear Weapons States
PLA	People's Liberation Army
PRC	People's Republic of China
PTBT	Partial Test Ban Treaty
SLCM	Sea-Launched Cruise Missiles
SNTS	Semipalatinsk Nuclear Test Site
SSBN	Submersible Ship, Ballistic missile, Nuclear powered
START	Strategic Arms Reduction Treaty
TNT	Trinitrotoluene
TNW	Tactical Nuclear Weapons
USAF	United States Air Force
UV	Ultraviolet
WMD	Weapons of Mass Destruction

Chapter 1

Human Cost of Nuclear-Weapons

In a single stroke, Hiroshima was devastated. It was August 6, 1945, a black day of human history. On that day, during World War II (1939-45), a United States Air Force (USAF) B-29 bomber dropped the world's first atomic bomb over the Japanese city of Hiroshima. The explosion immediately killed an estimated 80,000 people, including 20 US soldiers held as prisoners of war in a camp in Hiroshima.[1] Weapons do not discriminate. Three days later, a second B-29 dropped another atomic bomb on Nagasaki, killing an estimated 40,000 people. Japan's Emperor Hirohito announced his country's unconditional surrender in World War II in a radio address on August 15, citing the devastating power of "a new and most cruel bomb." Thc nuclear bombs destroyed about 60,000 buildings, snapped all communications including radio, television, and telegraph facilities and left thousands homeless. Those who survived the immense heat and high-pressure blast had injuries from collapsing buildings and flying debris. Survivors fled to nearby villages, where they found overcrowding and food shortages. Within the next two weeks, even those who appeared to be uninjured suddenly fell ill and died of radiation sickness. By the end of 1945, the bombing had killed an estimated 140,000 people in Hiroshima, and a further 74,000 in Nagasaki.[2] In the years that

1 The Commander in Chief, US Army Forces, Pacific, had received information that about twenty American airmen from the crews of airplanes shot down over Japan were killed in the bombing of Hiroshima. Subsequent information provided by Japanese officials confirmed the presence of the US airmen in Hiroshima on August 6, 1945. Jones Vincent C, 1985, *Manhattan: The Army and the Atomic Bomb*, Centre of Military History, US Army, Washington DC, p. 547.

2 Greenwell John, The atom bombing of Hiroshima and Nagasaki: Were they war crimes? *ISAA Review*, Vol. 12 (2), 2013, pp. 35-44; Lewis, Jonathan and Stelle Ben., 2001, *Hell in the Pacific: From Pearl Harbour to Hiroshima and beyond*, London: Channel 4 Books; O'Malley, Gerald F., The grave is wide: The hibakusha of Hiroshima and Nagasaki and

followed, many survivors faced leukaemia, cancer, or other side effects from the radiation and died within five years.

In late 1946, when criticisms of the nuclear bombings were beginning to mount, a small group of high-level US atomic policymakers (US President Harry S. Truman, President of MIT James Conant, President of the Carnegie Institution Arthur Compton, States Secretary of War Henry S Stimson, among others) crafted a version that the bombs were dropped exclusively to end the war as soon as possible, and were the product of a rational, deliberative process that took into account a delicate moral calculus, and had, on balance, a positive effect. However, the most important critics from the time of the necessity of the bombings were high-ranking officers of the US military, who felt their military accomplishments were being overshadowed by a technological marvel. The various alternative positions have argued that the bombs were dropped to satisfy geopolitical concerns were unnecessary (since the Japanese were on the verge of surrender), or were inhumane to the point of being war crimes (the deliberate massacre of tens of thousands of noncombatants).[3] Indeed, deliberately killing noncombatants is criminal.

Impact of Nuclear Weapons on Humanity

The atomic bombs were airdropped over the cities of Hiroshima and Nagasaki. The destructive effects in each case were on a scale that far exceeded that of previous air raids. Light at the epicentre was 10 times brighter than the sun (Lewis & Steele, 2001) with the temperature near the hypocenter reaching 3000 to 4000 degrees Celsius. In Hiroshima, more than nine square kilometres of the city were destroyed. In the smaller city of Nagasaki, about 2.5 square kilometres were destroyed.[4] In areas within 1 km of ground zero, the blast pressure forced human beings without any shielding, namely in the open air on the roads and ground, against walls, causing multiple fractures of skeletons and ruptures of the abdominal cavity causing escape of colons. Many people in open roads and grounds were carbonised by the direct effect of heat rays within a kilometre from

the legacy of the atomic bomb casualty commission and the radiation effects research foundation, *Clinical Toxicology*, Vol. 54(6), 2016, pp. 526-530; Wainstock Dennis D., 2010, *The Decision to Drop the Atomic Bomb: Hiroshima and Nagasaki: August 1945*, USA: Enigma Books.

3 Wellerstein Alex, Manhattan Project, *Encyclopedia of the History of Science*, April 2019, p. 29.

4 The Effects of the Atomic Bombs at Hiroshima and Nagasaki: Report of the British Mission to Japan, NP-1156, United States Atomic Energy Commission, p. vi.

ground zero.[5]

The nuclear destruction in the two cities was so extensive that entire neighbourhoods were obliterated, often with few survivors to recall them. By one standard calculation, 60 percent of the deaths came from burns, 20 percent from trauma from the blast, and 20 percent from radiation sickness. Many deaths, however, also took place between 1946 and 1950. Over the decades that followed, small numbers of survivors continued to die from bomb-related injuries or illnesses.[6] Those who survived have suffered many difficulties. As of March 2017, there were more than 164,000 hibakushas (atomic bomb survivors)[7] living in Japan, suffering from thyroid, breast, lung and other cancers at higher-than-normal rates. The effects of the bombings have also been passed down through generations to children and grandchildren. Children exposed to radiation (in the womb) were more likely to suffer from developmental disabilities 'and have smaller brains and impaired growth, as well as increased risk of developing cancer.' The exact death tolls from the bombing of Hiroshima and Nagasaki remain unknown even today.[8]

---

5 Tomonaga M., The atomic bombings of Hiroshima and Nagasaki: A summary of the human consequences, 1945-2018, and lessons for *Homo sapiens* to end the nuclear weapon age, *Journal for Peace and Nuclear Disarmament*, Vol. 2(2), 2019, pp. 1-27.

6 The Commander in Chief, US Army Forces, Pacific, had received information that about twenty American airmen from the crews of airplanes shot down over Japan were killed in the bombing of Hiroshima. Subsequent information provided by Japanese officials confirmed the presence of the US airmen in Hiroshima on August 6, 1945. Jones Vincent C, 1985, *Manhattan: The Army and the Atomic Bomb*, Centre of Military History, US Army, Washington DC, p. 547.

7 As a result of the atomic bombings of Hiroshima and Nagasaki new identifier categories emerged. The term, genbaku-shi was used to describe those killed by the atomic bombings, risaisha was used for the victims, and genbakushogaisha referred to those who were injured from the atomic bombing. In contrast, the term hibakusha is used for an explosion-affected or atomic bomb-exposed person. Hibakusha did not emerge as a category directly after the atomic bombings, and it was not until more than ten years later that the word was used in the 1957 Atomic Bomb Survivors Medical Care Law. Over time, hibakusha came be to defined as someone who has directly received injurious effects from an atomic bombing, rather than all who suffered as a result. Shimasaki Olivia, Seventy-Five Years on: An Ethnographic Exploration of Oral Histories on the Atomic Bombing of Hiroshima, Unpublished Master of Arts dissertation, University of Canterbury, January 2021, p. 20. Also see: Naono Akiko., The Origins of '*Hibakusha*' as a Scientific and Political Classification of the Survivor, *Japanese Studies*, Vol. 39(3), 2019, pp. 333-352.

8 There has been great difficulty in estimating the total casualties in the Japanese cities as a result of the atomic bombing mainly due to fires which ravaged the cities, destruction of official records, displacement, trouble identifying the dead, and mass cremations

One of the reasons for the non-availability of the accurate impact of the bombing was US-imposed censorship (commonly known as the Press Code) in Japan from September 19, 1945, until the end of the US occupation in 1952. This censorship prevented reporting on topics such as the occupation, the atomic bombings, and effects of radiation ostensibly to maintain 'public tranquility'. Under this Code, the US occupation authorities prohibited even Japanese medical researchers from publishing scientific articles on the effects of the atomic bombing. It also inhibited the public from learning about atomic bombs, their impacts, and prevented the open flow of sharing experiences with others. As a result, photographs could not be published. The public had virtually no access to graphic images of bombings and devastation of Hiroshima and Nagasaki until seven years after the bombs were dropped.

On August 29, 1945, Fritz Bilfinger, delegate of the International Committee of the Red Cross (ICRC) arrived in Hiroshima. He was the first outsider to witness the devastation caused by the atomic bomb. The next day, he sent a telegram to the ICRC delegation in Tokyo describing the horrific conditions and calling for immediate relief action. Bilfinger made a detailed report on the effects of the atomic bomb in Hiroshima as he witnessed them three weeks after the bomb was dropped. His report was kept confidential till it was made public in January 1996.[9]

Power of Nuclear-Weapons

A single thermonuclear weapon[10] can have the destructive power of a

---

of bodies which were charred beyond recognition. The extensive destruction of civil installations (hospitals, fire and police department, and government agencies) the state of utter confusion immediately following the explosion, as well as the uncertainty regarding the actual population before the bombing, contribute to the difficulty of making estimates of casualties.

9 ICRC report on the effects of the atomic bomb at Hiroshima, *International Review of the Red Cross*, Vol. 97, No. 899, 2015, pp. 859–882.

10 Nuclear weapons that release a large portion of their energy in fusion reactions are called thermonuclear weapons or, more popularly, hydrogen (H) bombs. The dominant fusion reactions are between isotopes of hydrogen-deuterium and tritium. The fusion reaction cannot be triggered by a conventional charge alone. To get hydrogen isotopes to fuse in sufficient quantities rapidly enough to produce an explosion requires very high temperatures, like those in the interior of the sun. Therefore, thermonuclear weapons use a fission component with plutonium-239 or uranium-235 to trigger the fusion reaction. The main radioactive contaminants from thermonuclear weapons come from the fission triggers and any uranium-238, uranium-235, or plutonium-239 close enough to the fusion portion of the weapon to be split by neutrons from the

million times the largest conventional weapon. The detonation of a nuclear weapon produces a blast wave, a thermal wave, instantaneous radiation, radioactive fall-out and an electromagnetic pulse.[11] This results in incinerating heat, powerful shock waves, overpressures, ionising radiation, and massive amounts of smoke and soot. Nuclear weapons have the power to produce such devastation that the apparent unreality of the detonation's aftermath may differentiate a nuclear battle from a conventional battle. No conventional weapon ever invented can cause so much death and destruction so quickly, on such a catastrophic scale, or leave such widespread and persisting toxicity in the environment. The GBU-43/B Massive Ordnance Air Blast (MOAB colloquially known as the "Mother of All Bombs") is the largest conventional bomb ever used dropped from MC130H of the USAF in Achin in Afghanistan on April 13, 2017, had a yield of approximately 11 tons of TNT equivalent. However, a modern nuclear warhead can produce an explosion measured in megatons. Two megatons are roughly equal to the explosive output of all bombs dropped during World War II. Unlike conventional weapons or other weapons of mass destruction (i.e. chemical and biological), nuclear weapons instantaneously wipe out entire populations, level cities, and devastate the environment. A small number of nuclear explosions over modern cities would kill tens of millions of people. A nuclear war with weapons in existing arsenals could kill many more people in a single day than were killed during the entire Second World War. These weapons produce radioactive contamination that remains active for millennia, causing cancers and other illnesses that can persist across generations. Moreover, the environmental consequences of nuclear war, including severe climate disruption, can lead to global

fusion reaction. In the case of a 1-megaton H-bomb, the fission trigger contributes only about 3 percent of the radioactive contamination; the rest comes from the uranium-238 tamper.

11 An electromagnetic pulse disrupts the electricity supply grid and electronic equipment and systems, including computers, medical equipment and satellite communications. In the aftermath of a nuclear war, all forms of international travel, including planes and trains, would likely be disrupted for an indeterminate time. Electronic communications could fail worldwide as a result of nuclear electromagnetic pulse (NEMP) effects. There is no evidence that NEMP is a physical threat to humans. However, electrical or electronic systems, particularly those connected to long wires such as power lines or antennas, can undergo damage. Nuclear EMPs are characterized by a range of spectrum of frequencies, pulse waveform shape, duration, and amplitude. For instance, a nuclear weapon detonated between 40 and 400 kilometers can generate an EMP that could affect up to 70% of the US electric power grid, depending upon intensity. Available at: https://www.chds.us/ed/resources/uploads/2010/05/2017_HS_Summit_Lane_Electromagnetic_Pulses.pdf

famine and, in the most extreme case, human extinction. No meaningful medical or disaster relief response to the detonation of nuclear weapons is possible.[12] If several powerful weapons are used at the same time, global environmental disturbance and climatic changes may take place. Exposure to radiation—including fallout from nuclear tests—causes acute and long-term illnesses that are often deadly, as well as genetic and inter-generational health effects. The effects of nuclear weapon detonation will have serious prolonged effects on human beings and their surrounding environment. The entire global economy would be severely impacted.

Immediate Effects. The detonation produces three major sources of death, injury and destruction - the blast, the heatwave and instantaneous radiations including electromagnetic pulse (EMP). Overpressure results in death and injury directly or through the collapse of buildings and structures. Heat and the resultant fire causes death and injury by burns and, and EMP results in impairment of electronic devices. But the greatest impact is for the release of radioactive substances and human exposure to them. An exposure to instantaneous radiation (gamma rays and neutrons) produces radiation syndrome with sickness and, possibly, death. At relatively low doses, it impairs bone marrow. At higher doses, damage occurs to the gastrointestinal tract, and at very high doses injury to the brain.[13]

Radiation Effects. Survivors of a nuclear explosion will be confronted by protracted non-healing wounds, suppurating extensive burns, skin infestations, gastrointestinal infections and psychic trauma. Suppression of the body's immune system is recognised as a consequence of radiation overexposure. Ionising radiation reduces the helper T-lymphocytes and increases the suppressor T-lymphocytes, thus increasing the victims' vulnerability to infection and cancers. Other effects of the explosion, such as bums, trauma and psychic depression can also influence the immune response.[14] Long-term effects such as cancer induction and genetic damage will result from instantaneous radiation during the explosion and the longer-term radiation contamination of the environment. The survivors

12 United Nations conference to negotiate a legally binding instrument to prohibit nuclear weapons, leading towards their total elimination, Working Paper, Submitted by International Physicians for the Prevention of Nuclear War, World Medical Association, World Federation of Public Health Associations, International Council of Nurses, Doc. A/CONF.229/2017/NGO/WP.11, dated March 28, 2017.

13 Health and Environmental Effects of Nuclear Weapons, World Health Organization, A46/30, April 26, 1993.

14 Effects of nuclear war on health and health services, 1987, Second Edition, Geneva, World Health Organization.

of the nuclear explosion and the populations of contaminated areas will be at risk of such effects. The risk from instantaneous radiation will vary depending on the quantum of the dose received. Radiation exposure also causes birth defects and genetic damage. Subsequent generations can suffer both because of genetic damage they inherited, as well as exposure to radioactivity from lingering radioactive contamination and fallout. Exposure to dangerous ionising radiation has become a persistent global problem because of continuing fallout from atmospheric tests and contamination of land and water around the former test sites, nuclear weapons production facilities, and radioactive waste storage sites. In addition to the acquired health risk for survivors from high-dose external radiation, the longer-lived radioisotopes (particularly strontium-90 with its 28.8-year half-life and caesium-137 with its 30.2-year half-life), would lead to a risk for the population over a large area and long periods. An impaired immune system would contribute later to an increased incidence of cancer.[15]

Environmental Impact. Nuclear weapons detonations have extreme and long-lasting environmental consequences, including disruption of the Earth's climate and agricultural productivity. The thousands of nuclear weapons possessed by the US and Russia could bring about a nuclear winter, destroying the essential ecosystems on which life depends. A regional nuclear conflict involving only 100 Hiroshima-size nuclear weapons would severely disrupt the global climate and agriculture for two decades or more. Estimated more than two billion people would face starvation from a nuclear war-induced famine, primarily in the Global South. Famines are also potent triggers of social unrest and violent conflict, both within and between nations. These factors are likely to significantly increase the toll of food shortages and famine induced by a regional nuclear war, especially as the effects would be both widespread and prolonged over many years.

In Hiroshima, large trees in the centre having a diameter of up to two meters were uprooted and some of the heavy branches of at least 60 cm in diameter were broken like matches by the force of the concussion.[16] Evergreen trees are especially vulnerable to radiation; coniferous forests are

15 Radioactive Heaven and Earth: The health and environmental effects of nuclear weapons testing in, on, and above the earth, A Report of the IPPNW for the International Physicians for the Abolition of Nuclear War, New York: Apex Press, 1991, p.193.

16 ICRC report on the effects of the atomic bomb at Hiroshima, *International Review of the Red Cross*, Vol. 97, No. 899, 2015, pp. 859–882.

liable to suffer most, whereas weeds are more resistant and will proliferate. Radiation is notably harmful to crops and the food chain; it is harmful to livestock and will contaminate milk and meat products. Plant pests are particularly resistant and would abound. The marine ecosystem would become contaminated and suffer similarly. It would lead to a severe shortage of edible and sustaining substances. In addition to the direct agricultural impacts, stratospheric ozone depletion would result in large increases in the ultraviolet (UV) radiation—30 to 100% increases in summer outside the tropics, endangering human and animal health, and further damaging crops and marine ecosystems.

Disruption of Health Services. Nuclear weapons will also destroy the physical and social infrastructure required for recovery. In the aftermath of nuclear detonation, doctors and health care workers would be killed or severely injured along with the general population. Hospitals, clinics, and other medical facilities would be destroyed or rendered unusable. Medicines, blood for transfusions, diagnostic equipment, and all other essential supplies would be unavailable. Power supplies that are important for the operation of hospitals would be interrupted and would severely interfere with the treatment and care that could be provided.[17] There would be no water, no electricity, no transportation, and no communication systems. Roads would be impassable and the terrain would be unrecognisable. Corpses would be everywhere, strewn among the injured and the dying. Surviving health care workers would be unable to find, let alone treat, other survivors. Dangerous levels of radiation would prevent emergency responders from entering affected areas in search of survivors. In Hiroshima, 90% of physicians and nurses were killed or injured, and 42 out of 45 hospitals became non-functional. The few outside physicians who arrived in Hiroshima and Nagasaki had to work without equipment, blood supplies, medicines, and other resources needed for effective treatment. Any meaningful medical and humanitarian response to aid the immediate survivors of the use of nuclear weapons is nearly impossible. The drastic fall in available health services on account of the small number of remaining health personnel, health centres, supplies or functioning ambulances and the immense logistical difficulties will render care inadequate.

Impact on Infrastructure. Within the extensive destruction of the built environment, a nuclear explosion will destroy public health and sanitary facilities, thus opening the way for the spread of disease. Water supplies

17 Clarke, R., 1986, *London under attack: the report of the Greater London Area War Risk Study*. Oxford: Blackwell.

would be contaminated not only by radioactivity but also by pathogenic bacteria and viruses. Sewage treatment and waste disposal facilities would have almost completely disappeared. A large number of putrefying human bodies and animal carcasses as well as untreated waste and sewage would provide an easy breeding ground for flies and other insects. Diseases like salmonellosis, shigellosis, infectious hepatitis, amoebic dysentery, malaria, typhus, streptococcal and staphylococcal infections, respiratory infections and tuberculosis would occur in epidemic form over vast areas.

The Socio-economic Bearing. The socioeconomic impact of the use of nuclear weapons would be devastating. Besides the extensive breakdown of health facilities, attendant social structures, the economic system, communication lines and the very fabric of society would be severely disrupted. Evacuation of large numbers of people to uncontaminated areas in the same country or mass exodus to neighbouring countries would lead to serious health problems and several associated social and economic difficulties for both the abandoned area and the receiving regions. Shortages of food, the possibility of inter-communal strife, disarray due to lack of work, societal disorganisation, poverty, dependence and apathy, or revolts, all converge to create complicated social and economic problems that are likely to be of some duration. Environmental degradation will create poverty and shortages of food. Future generations will also experience the ongoing depletion and degradation of aquifers, rivers and other bodies of water, the decline of fisheries, further stratospheric ozone loss and, perhaps, significant climatic change. This in turn, will exacerbate social friction, conflict and disorganisation of authority, which may lead to violence and societal disintegration.[18]

Hibakusha – Survivors of the Holocaust

Those who lived through the atomic bomb are referred to as 'Hibakusha', meaning 'a person affected by an atomic bomb'. Their offspring are referred to as second-generation Hibakusha (or Hibakusha Nisei). Fears of genetic and chromosomal effects exist among the people surrounding the Hibakusha, creating a stigma for the Hibakusha and their families. Arranged marriages and preservation of the family name through children remain important in Japan. The knowledge that an individual comes from a Hibakusha family raises the unpleasant feeling that there may be "bad blood" (i.e., blood contaminated by radiation). As a result, the Hibakusha

18 Homer-Dixon Thomas F., et al., Environmental Change and Violent Conflict, *Scientific American*, Number 268, February 1993, pp. 38-45.

Nisei may be socially rejected out of fear that their genes will taint marriages and families. The social stigma stemming from fears of continued radiation effects among subsequent generations engenders additional psychological consequences.

Invisible environmental contamination from radiation can have traumatic psychological effects that are not related to radiation dose. These fears may be widespread, as contaminated radioactive particles from atmospheric nuclear detonations can travel over long distances in patterns that can be difficult to predict.[19] The psychological impact of nuclear weapons radiation in Japan was manifold: (i) There was always the threat to their health from delayed radiation effects; (ii) There was the fear that their children would be unhealthy or malformed; (iii) Economic instability threatened if delayed radiation effects decreased their ability to work or care for themselves and also required increased medical expenses; (iv) Death, sickness, and decline or loss of ability to work and manage could further accelerate the disintegration of their families; (v) Discrimination against them by non-victims added to difficulties in social life, especially the burned victims whose suffering and distress was intensified by the appearance of keloid scars. The psychological impacts of radiation contamination may be more serious for women. These multiple effects on health, life, and livelihood imposed a great psychological burden on the victims.[20]

The Hibakusha and their families tend to avoid being open about their history as atomic-bomb survivors, aware of the potential rejection that might result from such a disclosure. This further increases their feelings of isolation within the community and creates an additional burden of trying to maintain secrecy and silence about their suffering. Many of the scientific investigations on the consequences of the atomic bomb have focused on the biological transmission of long-term effects of radiation. The Hibakusha and Hibakusha Nisei feel socially stigmatised as well, and may be blocked from marital and social opportunities that are open to non-Hibakusha.[21]

19 Dimmen Anne Guro, Gendered Impacts: The Humanitarian Impacts of Nuclear Weapons from a Gender Perspective, Paper 5, ILPI-UNIDIR, 2014, pp. 7.

20 Harwell Mark A. and Hutchinson Thomas C., 1985, *Environmental Consequences of Nuclear War Volume II: Ecological and Agricultural Effects*, Scientific Committee on Problems of the Environment (SCOPE), pp. 427-467.

21 Tatara Mikihachiro, The Second Generation of Hibakusha, Atomic Bomb Survivors: A Psychologist's View, pp. 6, available at: https://icmglt.org/wp-content/uploads/2019/09/8-The-Second-Generation-of-Hibakusha-Atomic-Bomb-Survivors-.pdf.

Although numerous first-hand accounts have been written to describe the damage to the people exposed to the destructive forces of the nuclear bombs, it would be difficult to quantify specific medical effects given the chaotic circumstances; the confounding effects of burns, infections, physical injuries and trauma, and contaminated food and water; and the overall magnitude of the damage. Medical facilities were destroyed, the infrastructure and resources of the two cities were disrupted, and a large percentage of trained medical personnel were among those killed.[22] The narration of the first-hand experiences of four survivors of the Holocaust to understand the horrors of the use of atom bombs on Hiroshima and Nagasaki gives an insight. These individuals and their families have suffered and witnessed the horrific suffering of others caused by atom bombs. These individuals and thousands of others and their families continue to suffer medical problems for generations.

Mr Hiroshi Sawachika, an army doctor, was 28 years old when the bomb was dropped. He was stationed at the army headquarters in Ujina. When he was exposed, he was inside the building at the headquarters, about 4.1 km from the hypocenter. Being rather far from the hypocenter, he was not seriously injured. He was engaged in providing medical treatment to the survivors. His testimony:[23]

> I was in my office. I had just entered the room and said "Good morning" to colleagues and I was about to approach my desk when the outside area suddenly turned bright red. I felt very hot on my cheeks. Being the chief of the room, I shouted to the young men and women in the room that they should evacuate. As soon as I cried, I felt weightless as if I were an astronaut. I was then unconscious for 20 or 30 seconds. When I came to my senses, I realised that everybody including myself was lying at one side of the room. Nobody was standing. The desks and chairs had also been blown off to one side. At the windows, there was no window glass and the window frames had been blown out as well. I went to the windows to find out where the bombing had taken place. And I saw the mushroom cloud over the gas company. The sound and shock somehow suggested that the bomb had been dropped right

22 Douple Evan B., Mabuchi Kiyohiko, et. al., Long-term Radiation-Related Health Effects in a Unique Human Population: Lessons Learned from the Atomic Bomb Survivors of Hiroshima and Nagasaki, *Disaster Med Public Heath Prep*, Vol. 5, March 2011, pp. S122-S133.

23 Testimony of Hiroshi Sawachika, available at: https://www.inicom.com/hibakusha/hiroshi.html.

over the gas company. I still had no idea what had happened. And I kept looking towards the gas company. After a while, I realised that my white shirt was red all over. I thought it was funny because I was not injured at all. I looked around and then realised that a girl lying nearby was heavily injured, with lots of broken glass stuck all over her body. Her blood had splashed and made stains on my shirt.

In a few minutes, I heard my name called. I was told to go to the headquarters where there were lots of injured persons waiting. I went there and I started to give treatment with the help of nurses and medical course men. We first treated the office personnel for their injuries. Most of them had broken glass and pieces of wood stuck in them. We treated them one after another. Afterwards, we heard a strange noise. It sounded as if a large flock of mosquitoes were coming from a distance. We looked out of the window to find out what was happening. We saw that citizens from the town were marching towards us. They looked unusual. We understood that the injured citizens were coming towards us for treatment. But while we thought that there should be Red Cross Hospitals and another big hospital in the centre of the town. So why should they come here, I wondered, instead of going there. At that time, I did not know that the centre of the town had been so heavily damaged. After a while, with the guide of the hospital personnel, the injured persons reached our headquarters. With lots of injured people arriving, we realised just how serious the matter was. We decided that we should treat them also.

Soon afterwards, we learned that many of them had badly burned. As they came to us, they held their hands aloft. They looked like they were ghosts. We made the tincture for that treatment by mixing edible peanut oil and something. We had to work mechanically to treat so many patients. We provided one room for the heavily injured and another for the slightly injured. Treatment was limited to first aid because there were no facilities for the patients to be hospitalised. Later on, when I felt that I could leave the work to other staff for a moment, I walked out of the treatment room and went into another room to see what had happened. When I stepped inside, I found the room filled with a smell that was quite similar to the smell of dried squid when it has been grilled. The smell was quite strong.

It's a sad reality that the smell human beings produce when they are burned is the same as that of the dried squid when it is grilled. It

> was a strange feeling, a feeling that I had never had before. I can still remember that smell quite clearly. Afterwards, I came back to the treatment room and walked through the roads of people who were either seriously injured or waiting to be treated. There I felt someone touch my leg, it was a pregnant woman. She said that she was about to die in a few hours. She said, "I know that I am going to die. But I can feel that my baby is moving inside. It wants to get out of the room. I don't mind if I had died. But if the baby is delivered now, it does not have to die with me. Please help my baby live." There was no obstetrician. There was no delivery room. There was no time to take care of her baby. All I could do was to tell her that I would come back later when everything was ready for her and her baby. Thus I cheered her up and she looks so happy.
>
> But I had to return to the treatment work. So I resumed my work, taking care of the injured one by one. There were so many patients. I felt as if I was fighting against the time. It was late in the afternoon towards the evening. And the image of that pregnant woman never left my mind. Later, I went to the place where I had found her before, she was still there lying in the same place. I patted her on the shoulder, but she said nothing. The person lying next to her said that a short while ago, she had become silent. I still recall this incident because I was not able to fulfil the last wish of this dying young woman and I had a chance to talk with her, however short it was.

Mr Isao Kita was 33 years old when the bomb fell. He was working for the Hiroshima District Weather Bureau 3.7 km from the hypocenter. He was the chief weatherman and his shift fell from August 5 to 6. He kept observing the weather even after he was exposed. His testimony:[24]

> Well, at that time, I happened to be receiving the transmission over the wireless. I was in the receiving room and I was facing northward. I noticed the flashing light. It was not a big flash. But still, it drew my attention. In a few seconds, the heatwave arrived. After I noticed the flash, white clouds spread over the blue sky. It was amazing. It was as if blue morning glories had suddenly bloomed up in the sky. It was funny, I thought. Then came the heatwave. It was very very hot. Even though there was a window glass in front of me, I felt really hot. It was as if I was looking directly into a kitchen oven. I couldn't bear the heat for a long time. Then I heard the cracking sound. I don't know what

24 Testimony of Isao Kita, available at: https://www.inicom.com/hibakusha/isao.html.

made that sound, but probably it came from the air, which suddenly expanded in the room. By that time, I realised that the bomb had been dropped. As I had been instructed, I pushed aside the chair and lay with my face on the floor. Also as I had been instructed during the frequent emergency exercises, I covered my eyes and ears with hands like this. And I started to count.

You may feel that I was rather heartless just to start counting. But for us, who observed the weather, it is a duty to record the process of time, of various phenomena. So I started counting with the light flash. When I counted to 5 seconds, I heard the groaning sound. At the same time, the window glass was blown off and the building shook from the bomb blast. So the blast reached that place about 5 seconds after the explosion. We later measured the distance between the hypocenter and our place. And with these two figures, we calculated that the speed of the blast was about 700 meters per second. The speed of sound is about 330 meters per second, which means that the speed of the blast was about twice as fast as the speed of sound. It didn't move as fast as the speed of light but it moved quite rapidly.

There is a path that leads by here over there. And on that day, a large number of injured persons walked this way along the path toward the Omi Hospital. They were bleeding all over and some of them had no clothes. Many of them were carrying people on their shoulders. Looking at the injured, I realised how seriously the town had been damaged. The fire was at its peak at around that time. It thundered ten times between 10 and 11 o'clock. The sound of thunder itself was not so great but still, I could see the lightning over the fire. When I looked down at the town from the top of that hill, I could see that the city was completely lost. The city turned into yellow sand. It turned yellow, the colour of the yellow desert. The town looked yellowish.

The smoke was so thick that it covered the entire town. After about 5 minutes, a fire broke out here and there. The fire gradually grew bigger and there was smoke everywhere and so we could no longer see towards the town. The cloud of smoke was very tall, but it didn't come in this direction at all. The cloud moved in that direction from the ocean towards Hiroshima Station. It moved towards the north. The smoke from the fire was like a screen dividing the city into two parts. The sun was shining brightly just like it was the middle of the summer over here on this site. And behind the cloud on the other side, it was completely dark. The contrast was very much. So about

> 60 or 70 % of the sky was covered by the cloud and the other 30 % was completely clear. It was a bright clear blue sky. The condition had remained like this for some time. From Koi, looking towards Hiroshima Station, you could see the black rain falling. It was black and sticky rain. It stuck everything. When it fell on trees and leaves, it stayed and turned everything black. When it fell on people's clothing, the clothing turned black. It also stuck on people's hands and feet. And it couldn't be washed off. I couldn't be washed off. I couldn't see what was taking place inside the burning area. But I was able to see the extent of the area which was on fire.

Mr Sadao Yamamoto was born in 1931 and was 14 years old when the atomic bomb was dropped on Hiroshima on August 6, 1945. He was approximately 2.5 km away from the hypocentre when the bomb exploded. His testimony:[25]

> We did not have major air raids in Hiroshima before the atomic bomb. At night sometimes we had air-raid warnings and we would have to cover the lights with black cloth and go into the air-raid shelters. During the daytime, we had ordinary, regular lives.
>
> When the bomb was dropped, I was in the second year of junior high school. 140,000 people died because of the atomic bombing, including many students like myself. At that time, the population of the city of Hiroshima was about 350,000, including the military personnel stationed there and those who came from outside of the city; as much as 40% of the total population died in the bombing.
>
> At that time, students from elementary school in the third through sixth grades were evacuated to the countryside because of the air raids. First- and second-grade students were considered too young to be separated from their families. There were only three schools left in Hiroshima: one was the two-year high school, another was the boys' junior high school, and the third was the girls' junior high school. When they were not at school, the junior high school students were mobilised to work at the munitions factories and other military

25 Mr Yamamoto has given testimony for the Hiroshima Peace Culture Foundation, which can be read on the organization's website. Sadao Yamamoto, "1st and 2nd Year Students at Hiroshima Second Middle School – A Difference of Life or Death", Peace Culture English Newsletter, No. 72, January 2015. Also see: After the atomic bomb: Hibakusha tell their stories, *International Review of the Red Cross*, Vol.97, No. 899, Autumn 2015, pp. 513-518.

facilities. The third-year to the fifth year of the junior high students mainly worked at the munitions factories.

There were many small munitions factories in the city, but the major ones were located relatively far from the hypocentre. The first-year and second-year junior high school students, like myself, were engaged in building demolition, which was carried out in the centre of the city. We would tear down buildings to make fire lanes to prevent fire from spreading after air raids. It was tough work. Adults tore down the buildings, and students would clear the debris.

These building demolitions were carried out in the centre of Hiroshima, and the students were mobilised from almost all over the city. This meant that a lot of students in the first and second year of junior high were victims of the atomic bomb because they were working in the area directly surrounding the hypocentre. Concretely, 8,187 students were mobilised in building demolition work with 176 teachers from thirty-five schools in the city. Out of these, 6,295 students and 132 teachers were killed by the bombing. This means that almost 77%, or three out of four, of the total mobilised students, were killed.

All of the older students from the schools who were mobilised to work in the demolition works near the hypocentre were killed. The location where the first-year students were working was on the riverbank, behind a building about 600 metres from the hypocentre of the explosion. The eastern drill grounds where the second-year students had gathered were about 2.5 km from the hypocentre, near the Hiroshima station. This difference in distance from the hypocentre was the difference between life and death. All 321 of the first-year students were killed. The second-year students were burned all over our bodies, but none of us was killed.

On August 6, 1945, at 8:15 a.m., the time of the bombing, I was in the east drill ground, and at that time we noticed three B-29 bombers were flying over the sky from the southeast. There had been an air-raid warning, but it had been cancelled and there were only three planes, so we thought they must be doing reconnaissance.

We looked up into the sky and noticed that suddenly, after flying over the city, those planes turned around and flew away, which was strange. At that moment, we heard a roaring explosion and all of us were blown back onto the grass by a shocking wave of heat. I was knocked unconscious. After I came to and stood up, I noticed that in the direction of the Hiroshima train station, there was a huge, pink pillar of fire. We thought the station must have been bombed.

The left sides of our faces were burned. Those burns were treated with vegetable oil because in those days it was believed that applying vegetable oil would prevent bacteria from entering our bodies. After we received that treatment, we fled with our friends to the shrine on the nearby mountain because we were afraid that another bomb would be dropped. There were already some adults at the shrine, and they told us not to go outside because it was too dangerous, so I hid inside with some of my classmates. When there was no sign of another bomb we went outside to see the city, but all we could see was white smoke. Then gradually we could see that the houses and buildings were burning down, including the elementary school.

By around three or four in the afternoon, the fire had died down. I decided to go back to my house. It was about a kilometre from the evacuated area. Everything was burning in that area. I saw the house destroyed. The tatami mats covering the floor were lifted, and it was all messy. Fortunately, my family was all right. My elder sister, who had been mobilised, also came home. My father was lucky because he was at work at the time of the explosion inside a building only about 680 metres from the hypocentre, but fortunately, he was on the other side of a thick concrete wall inside the building so he was not injured. The building then caught fire and burned down. He was one of the few survivors.

I was astonished to learn that of the 321 first-year students, about a third were killed on the spot and some of them drowned in the river, but the rest of them, some of them severely burned all over their bodies, walked several kilometres to attempt to get back to their homes out of an ardent desire to see their parents. Some twenty students instead tried to go back to the school, led by a teacher. Some died on the way. Others jumped into the river, singing war songs together for encouragement.

After the bomb, all the people who were able to flee had fled. Many of those who could not escape died in the burning city. My aunt, one of my mother's younger sisters, was in the Hondori Street area, about 400 metres from the hypocentre. On the day after the bomb was dropped, my mother told me to go there to see what was happening to her family. The house was still on fire. There had been some people

> there, but now all that was left were charred bones. One person I saw was just a skeleton, but the bones were on fire.

Mr Yoshiro Yamawaki was just 11 years old when the atomic bomb was dropped in Nagasaki. He and his twin brother were about 2.2 km from the hypocentre. His experience:[26]

> On the morning of the atomic bombing, my father, my brothers and I woke up at home. My mother had already evacuated to the countryside with my four younger siblings. After getting breakfast, our father went to work as usual. My older brother, who was in junior high school, went to the weapons factory where he was working as part of the mobilised student forces. The two of us twins stayed at home because it was summer vacation and there was no school.
>
> Until just before 11 o'clock, we were out on the veranda. Then we got hungry and went into the sitting room in the back of the house. While we were sitting there at the table, a whitish-blue light shot across the room. Then came a roar that seemed to shake the whole house. The two of us got down on the tatami mat and covered our eyes, ears and noses with our fingers, just like we had been taught to do. In that position, with plaster from the walls and other debris falling on top of us, I remember thinking that a bomb had directly hit our property and that we would probably be buried alive there.
>
> The falling debris didn't continue falling for long, however. After a few minutes, I heard the voices of people in the neighbourhood, screaming and crying. Remaining on the ground, I lifted my head and looked around to find that everything had completely changed. Almost all the furniture had been mangled and tossed around. The walls had come crumbling down, and in every room, the tatami-mat floors were covered with dirt and debris. If my twin brother and I had not moved from the veranda to go to the sitting room five minutes before, we most likely would have suffered horrible wounds from the heat rays and the blast.
>
> The roof had been blown off, and we could see the sky. The pillars and walls were embedded with large numbers of sharp-edged fragments of broken glass. The other houses in the neighbourhood were in the

26 Yoshiro Yamawaki, "The Unforgettable Experience of the Atomic Bombing", available at: https://nagasakipeace.jp/en/search/survivors/yoshiro_yamawaki.html.

same state of destruction. Across the harbour, the central part of the city was covered in clouds of dust.

My twin brother and I evacuated to the bomb shelter in our yard, where we waited for our father and our older brother to come home. About an hour had passed when our oldest brother arrived home from his factory. He told us that it was too dangerous to stay in that small bomb shelter and that we should move to a larger one nearby.

The bigger bomb shelter, which was like a tunnel carved into the cliff-side, was filled with mothers and their children. Children who were outside when the bomb detonated had been showered with heat rays and had suffered burns on any exposed skin. Other children were crying because they had been injured by shards of glass and other fragments that had been thrown by the blast. We spent that entire night waiting anxiously for our father to come back. By the next morning, however, he still hadn't returned. At that point, the three of us went to find him.

The primary concern of survivors was to look for family members. Right after the bombing, people began to look for their relatives. In terms of medical needs, as you can imagine, the hospitals were destroyed, but a relief centre had been established in an elementary school. The medical workers were also injured and there was no medicine, so they fetched water from the ocean and boiled it to put on the injuries. It was the best that they could do. More sophisticated medical assistance was not available. There was a hospital set up by the Japanese army in the late afternoon of August 9 that had some medicine and a few medical workers, but it was not a very sophisticated hospital.

The second thing that the survivors were concerned about was a shortage of food. There was no allocated food delivered by the government, so survivors ate whatever they happened to have in the house or asked their relatives to send food.

Another thing that survivors suffered from was the lack of shelter. With their houses destroyed, people did not know where to go. The northern part of Nagasaki city was destroyed. Some people lived underground in bomb shelters. Others collected pieces of wood from the ground and built makeshift shelters.

The damage we saw grew worse and worse as we continued to look for our father. The houses near the roadside had all burned to the ground. Even those trees and electric poles that remained standing were scorched. The factories on the other side of the river now looked like masses of crushed wire, with only the largest of their columns left standing.

There were many dead bodies amongst the debris littering the roads. The faces, arms and legs of the dead had become swollen and discoloured, causing them to look like black rubber dolls. As we stepped on the bodies with our shoes, the skin would come peeling off like that of an over-ripe peach, exposing the white fat underneath.

Many dead bodies were floating in the river as well. We were drawn to one that belonged to a young woman of about 18 or 19, from which a long white belt was dragging behind. When we got closer, we saw that this white belt was her intestines, which were protruding from the side of her abdomen. Feeling nauseous, we turned our eyes away and hurried off in the direction of our father's workplace.

When we had come within about 100 metres of the factory where our father worked, my brother suddenly screamed out and stood paralysed with fear. I looked over his shoulder to see a boy of 6 or 7 who had died with something white hanging out of his mouth. At first glance, it seemed to me that he had been vomiting up noodles when he died. Looking closer, however, I realised that the roundworms that had been living inside his body had come shooting out when he died. We ran away, fighting back our nausea.

Our father's factory had been reduced to nothing but scorched metal framing. Through the demolished walls we saw three men working with shovels. We called out, "Our name is Yamawaki. Where is our father?" One of the men glanced over and said, "Your father is over there." He pointed in the direction of the demolished office building.

The three of us dashed off in the direction he had pointed to. What we found there was our father's corpse, swollen and scorched like all of the others. As we stood there stunned, the men with the shovels told us that if we wanted to take our father back home, it was better to cremate him there first. The crematories had also been destroyed in the bombing and could not be used. Not knowing what else to do, we went around the scorched ruins of the factory and gathered up smouldering pieces of wood so we could perform the cremation. We put our father's body on top of a bed of burned posts and then piled up the pieces of wood on top of him. When we lit it on fire, the flames rose high in the air. We put our hands together to say prayers for him. When we looked up again after finishing our prayers, we saw both of our father's feet were sticking out from the fire. That was an unbearable thing to see. Our feelings must have shown because the man from the factory told us we had better go home for the day and come back the next day to collect the remains.

The next morning we looked around the kitchen area of our demolished house for a pot to put our father's remains in. We found one and the three of us took it along with us as we went to collect our father's remains. It was very strange but we were not scared at all by the corpses that we saw anymore. We thought of them as no more than objects that blocked our way as we walked. When we arrived at the place where we had cremated our father's body, however, a shock awaited us. The body remained as it had been the day before, in a half-cremated state and covered over with ash. There was no one from the company around. We three brothers only wanted to collect our father's cremated bones, but his half-burned body was lying exposed. The only parts of his body that had been cremated were the tips of his hands and feet and part of his stomach. We could only pick out a few of his bones. This body, which was like a skeleton covered in ash, was far more gruesome than the corpse of someone just deceased. It was even more unpleasant when we thought about how this body belonged to the same father we had always talked to and eaten meals with. It got so that I could no longer bear to look at our father's body and I said to my brother, "Let's go home now and leave his body here."

My brother looked at our father's body for a while longer and then said that there was nothing more we could do except to take his skull home. My brother had brought tongs, but when the tongs touched our father's skull it crumbled apart like a plaster model and the half-burned brains came flowing out. Letting out a scream, my brother threw down the tongs and darted away. The other two of us ran after him. There were the circumstances under which we forsook our father's body. I think that all people who lost family members and others close to them in the atomic bombing went through experiences similar to this. There were approximately 74,000 people who were killed in an instant by that one, single atomic bomb.

These are scenes from the atomic bomb that will never leave my mind. I still have those images and visions, and I am still suffering from them. When I see something like an image of a skull, it reminds me of my father's skull, and when I see something like a long, white cloth, it reminds me of the dead woman floating in the river.

Gestalt

The use of atomic weapons in 1945 has been one of the most dreadful events in the history of mankind. Atom bombs changed people's lives in two Japanese cities completely even if they were able to survive. People struggled with pain from their keloid scar,[27] illness, appearance, discrimination, poor health, anxiety for their descendants, and inferiority complex. Thousands suffered various combinations of symptoms, including unexplained bleeding, sudden purple sores, hair loss, inflamed gums, high fever, diarrhea, loss of appetite, nausea, headaches, and dizziness. In some cases, within the first few days of the initial appearance of these symptoms, the infected lost consciousness, spoke deliriously, and succumbed to their illness in extreme agony.

Nuclear weapons are the most terrifying weapons ever invented. No weapon is more destructive, no weapon causes such unspeakable human suffering; there is no way to control how far the radioactive fallout will spread and how long the effects will last. A nuclear weapon detonated in a city would immediately kill tens of thousands of people, and tens of thousands more would suffer horrific injuries and later die from radiation exposure. A nuclear war will cause long-term damage to our planet; severely disrupting the earth's ecosystem, reducing global temperatures causing a food shortage.[28] The recent Covid-19 pandemic has taught us a lesson that we do not have effective capacity at the international level

27 Most survivors received burns so severe their wounds formed hard growths of scar tissue known as keloids. These keloids were permanent disfigurements, which could only be removed by extensive corrective surgeries. Unfortunately, Japanese surgeons often lacked the tools, funds, and training to perform these procedures. A few *hibakusha* found generous sponsors who paid for their travel to US for the corrective surgeries; yet even American doctors, with their extensive knowledge of plastic surgery, could never fully restore their patients to their pre-bomb state. Keenan Meghan, Survivors' Hardships Following the Atomic Bombing of Nagasaki; History: Student Scholarship & Creative Work, Elizabethtown College, 2019, p. 15.

28 Nuclear Weapons-an intolerable threat to humanity, August 7, 2018, available at: https://www.icrc.org/en/nuclear-weapons-a-threat-to-humanity.

to deliver appropriate humanitarian assistance to survivors if a nuclear weapon were ever to be used.

Decades of atmospheric and underground nuclear testing have led to cancers, birth defects, and other radiation-related illnesses among millions of people worldwide. The mining and processing of uranium that provides the fuel for nuclear weapons have serious and long-lasting health consequences for workers, local communities and their environment. Workers at nuclear weapons facilities have sustained severe and debilitating damage to their health as a result of occupational exposure to fissile materials and toxic chemicals involved in the production and maintenance of nuclear weapons. The issue of nuclear testing has been discussed in detail in the next chapter.

Chapter II

Nuclear Weapons: Testing and Facilities

Nuclear weapons' testing plays a central role in the design of nuclear weapons. These tests were primarily devised so that scientists could learn more about the engineering and physics principles of the weapons. These tests also yielded information on the effects of nuclear weapons on living creatures, the environment, military equipment, and personnel. In some cases, the intention was also political - with tests designed as much to instil fear in other states by demonstrating a country's nuclear superiority and furthering military and scientific research. In a few tests conducted by the states, military personnel were deliberately exposed to the tests and then monitored throughout their lives to study the effects on their bodies.[1] Civilians, mostly indigenous peoples, living in the vicinity

1 From 1946 to 1962, the US conducted about 200 atmospheric nuclear tests--more than the other nuclear states put together at that time. Approximately 400,000 servicemen in the US Army, Navy, and Marines were present during these atmospheric tests, whether as witnesses to the tests themselves or as post-test cleanup crews. At that time, many of these servicemen did not know about the effects of radiation exposure and did not question if their health was at risk. After leaving the armed services, many developed serious health complications, including cancer. For years, these veterans tried to seek assistance and compensation from the Veterans Administration (VA). However, the VA denied some of these claims for assistance because the US government has asserted that the veterans were not exposed to unsafe levels of radiation. In 1994, President Bill Clinton established the Advisory Committee on Human Radiation Experiments to investigate the US government's role in radiation experiments on US servicemen and American civilians from 1944 to 1974. This committee not only investigated the cases of the atomic veterans but also cases of people being injected with plutonium without their consent. The committee eventually released its report and concluded that many of the test subjects, including the atomic veterans and civilians, were unaware that they participated in these tests and therefore did not give consent. A year later, Clinton apologized to all people involved with US nuclear radiation testing, including the atomic veterans. Atomic Veterans 1946-1962, Atomic Heritage Foundation, June 17, 2019, available at: https://www.atomicheritage.org/history/atomic-veterans-1946-1962.

of test sites were similarly monitored. Some such groups were permanently displaced from their lands, with devastating consequences. In the early days of nuclear testing, little consideration was given to its devastating effects on human life, let alone the dangers of nuclear fallout from atmospheric tests. To date, eight countries have conducted over 2,000 nuclear tests in the atmosphere, underwater, or in space since the first nuclear test explosion on July 16, 1945, almost a month before the bombings of Hiroshima and Nagasaki.[2][3]

The US' decision to use nuclear weapons against Japan forced the rest of the major powers to follow suit, unleashing a wave of nuclear proliferation. Immediately after the bombing of Hiroshima, the erstwhile Soviet Union doubled down on its nuclear program and conducted its first successful test in August 1949. Soon afterwards, the UK developed nuclear weapons in 1952, France in 1960, and China in 1964. Thus, all permanent members of the United Nations Security Council managed to test and

2 A worldwide public concern over the danger posed by atmospheric radioactive fallout produced by the aboveground testing of nuclear weapons led to the ratification of the 1963 Treaty Banning Nuclear Weapon Tests in the Atmosphere, in Outer Space and Under Water, also called the Limited Test Ban Treaty or the Partial Test Ban Treaty. Within three months of the treaty became effective it was signed by over 100 countries. So far, it has been ratified by 123 states, whereas 10 states have signed but not ratified it. The Nuclear Test-Ban Treaty banned nuclear-weapons tests in the atmosphere, in outer space, and underwater but permitted underground testing and required no control posts, no on-site inspection, and no international supervisory body. It did not reduce nuclear stockpiles, halt the production of nuclear weapons, or restrict their use in time of war. The US, Soviet Union, and the IK, all signatories to the treaty, then moved their tests underground. France and China continued atmospheric tests after 1963-France until 1974 and China until 1980.

3 In the early 1950s, the Prime Minister of Australia, Robert Menzies, received a request from the Prime Minister of England, Clement Attlee, requesting if Britain could conduct their nuclear weapons testing in Australia. Without discussing to the politicians in his cabinet or requesting any information or reports on the possible health or environmental risks, Menzies gave his concurrence and even committed Australian servicemen to help the British carry out their tests. Thus, began the testing in Monte Bello Islands off the coast of Western Australia, and the 2 sites in South Australia, Emu Field and Maralinga. In the mid-1950s, seven bombs were tested at Maralinga in the south-west Australian outback. The combined force of the weapons doubled that of the bomb dropped on the Japanese city of Hiroshima in World War Two. Locals around Maralinga reported a black mist of radioactive dust over their communities following the explosions. It resulted in sickness, lung disease, liver and kidney problems. The indigenous communities involved in the clean-up operation also got sick. Donnison Jon, Lingering impact of British nuclear tests in the Australian outback, BBC News, December 31, 2014. Available at: https://www.bbc.com/news/world-australia-30640338.

develop nuclear weapons by 1964 and this group retained exclusivity for another decade till India forced its entry of nuclear testing in 1974. The details of the nuclear test explosion are shown in Table 2.1.[4]

Table 2.1
Number of Global Nuclear Weapons Tests

Country with period of Tests Type of Test	US [1945-1992]	USSR/ Russia [1949-1990]	UK [1952-1991]	France [1960-1996]	China 1964-1996]	India [1974-1998]	Paki-stan [1998]	North Korea [2006-2017]	Total
Atmo-spheric	215	219	21	50	23	Nil	Nil	Nil	528
Under-ground	815	496	24	160	22	03	02	06	1,528
Total	1,030	715	45	210	45	03	02	06	2,056

Notes:

A. The total number and yearly listing of the US nuclear test explosions listed here are based on the figures published in US Nuclear Tests: July 1945 through September 1992 DOE/NV-209 (Rev. 14), December 1994. The Department of Energy has since published two revisions of the publication that slightly revise these numbers and reassign the purposes originally described for certain nuclear test explosions.

B. In accordance with the definition of a nuclear test contained in the 1974 Threshold Test Ban Treaty and to allow accurate comparison with other countries' figures, India's three simultaneous nuclear explosions on May 11, 1998, are counted as only one nuclear test, as are the two explosions two days later. Likewise, Pakistan's five simultaneous explosions on May 28, 1998, are counted as a single test.

While no country has used nuclear weapons since 1945, many people have nevertheless died because of associated occurrences such as nuclear

4 The Nuclear Testing Tally, Arms Control Association, Fact Sheets and Brief, July 2020, available at: https://www.armscontrol.org/factsheets/nucleartesttally.

tests, radiation, and nuclear accidents. From South Asia to Kazakhstan, to Nevada, to the Sahara and Australia, to the Marshall Islands, Kiribati, and French Polynesia, nuclear weapons tests above and below ground over decades have devastated lives and brought environmental contamination which continues even today.[5] The list of countries affected by atmospheric and underground nuclear-weapon tests includes Algeria, Australia, China, North Korea, French Polynesia, India, Kazakhstan, Kiribati, Marshall Islands, Pakistan, Russia, Turkmenistan, Ukraine, United States, and Uzbekistan. These tests caused immediate and long-term health problems, including thyroid cancer and birth defects. According to a few estimates, nuclear tests since 1945 have resulted in tens of thousands of deaths around the world, along with displacement and environmental degradation that long remained secret and continues to affect communities today. In addition, radiation exposure from testing has been associated with cancer. Accidents at nuclear power plants in Chernobyl, Ukraine, in 1986 and Fukushima, Japan (following a tsunami), in 2011 have led to 110 deaths. The number of deaths caused by long-term radiation exposure in both Ukraine and Japan is being determined to date. This chapter covers the impact of nuclear weapons tests, nuclear weapons facilities on the people and the surrounding environment.

Beginning of Nuclear Weapons – The Manhattan Project

Prof Albert Einstein identified the prospects of applying then-emerging developments in nuclear physics to weapon technologies. He sent a letter to the US President Franklin D Roosevelt on August 2, 1939, stating that, "…. the element uranium may be turned into a new and important source of energy in the immediate future….and it may become possible to set up a nuclear chain reaction in a large mass of uranium, by which vast amount of power and large quantities of new radium-like element would be generated. This new phenomenon would also lead to the construction of bombs, and it is conceivable---though much less certain---that extremely powerful bombs of a new type thus may be constructed. A single bomb of this type, carried by boat and exploded in a port, might very well destroy to whole port with some of the surrounding territories."[6] Einstein was successful in getting President Roosevelt's attention. After some internal deliberations,

5 Pollock Nancy, Nuclear contamination of food in the Pacific: Lifting the veil of secrecy, *Pacific Ecologist*, Issue 22, Summer 2013, p. 21.

6 Letter from Albert Einstein to President Franklin D. Roosevelt (August 2, 1939), US National Archives, available at: https://www.docsteach.org/documents/document/letter-from-albert-einstein-to-president-franklin-d-roosevelt.

the US Army was directed to establish the "Manhattan Engineer District," better known today as Manhattan Project.[7]

The Manhattan Project [8] has been one of the largest scientific research programs the US has ever seen. It was commissioned by President Roosevelt by executive order in June 1941. At its height, the project employed 130,000 people. The project was headed by Major General Leslie Groves of the US Army Corps of Engineers and scientist Dr J. Robert Oppenheimer. The scientists worked for over three years on methods to extract plutonium from Uranium-235 and then to harness plutonium's natural fission into a controllable bomb. Eventually, they settled on an implosion method, where a critical mass of plutonium would be condensed by surrounding explosions to create a supercritical mass which would then be triggered to create fission.

On July 16, 1945, a test was conducted of the implosion bomb, code-named Trinity by Oppenheimer as an allusion to a poem by John Donne. Test planners chose a flat, desert scrub region in the northwest corner of the isolated Alamogordo Bombing Range in southern New Mexico for produced a yield of 31 kilotons. The site was several hundred miles from Los Alamos, and the nearest off-site habitation was twenty miles away. Detonated from a platform on top of a 100-foot high steel tower, the Trinity device used about 13.5 pounds of plutonium. At 05:29 am the device exploded with an energy equivalent to around 21 kilotons of TNT.[9] The blast, which temporarily blinded the nearest observers 10,000 yards away, created an orange and yellow fireball about 2,000 feet in diameter from

7 Pennington Todd W. "Weapons of Mass Destruction: Issues and Implications for National Security Lawyers," in Corn Geoffrey S. (ed.), 2016, *US Military Operations: Law, Policy and Practice*, Oxford: Oxford University Press, p. 762.

8 The Manhattan Project (for the engineering corps' Manhattan district) started in 1940. By 1942, the first dedicated office was on the 18th floor of a federal building on the corner of Broadway and Chambers Street in Manhattan, New York. The project had been called "the Laboratory for the Development of Substitute Materials," but that was thought to be too transparent. At the time, Columbia University had a concentration of people working on the concept of atomic bombs, New York was a hub of work in the subject, and the bulk of America's supply of uranium ore was stored in warehouses and on docks in New York Harbour. The 18th floor of the building was occupied by the Army Corps of Engineers, and the location gave its name to the project. Headquarters was quickly moved to Oak Ridge, Tennessee when it was felt New York was too crowded and too vulnerable to attack for such a secret and sensitive programme.

9 Fehner Terrence R. and F.G. Gosling, The Manhattan Project, US Department of Energy April 2012, p. 11.

which emerged a narrow column that rose and flattened into a mushroom shape.

The desert sand, largely made of silica, melted and became a mildly radioactive light green glass, which was named trinitite. It left a crater in the desert 10 feet deep and 1,200 feet wide. At the time of detonation, the surrounding mountains were illuminated brighter than daytime for one to two seconds, and the heat was reported as being as hot as an oven at the base camp. The observed colours of the illumination changed from purple to green and eventually to white. The roar of the shock wave took 40 seconds to reach the observers. The environmental contamination that resulted was severe in some locations.

The test was a success. Three weeks after the Trinity test, on August 6, Little Boy, the untested uranium bomb, was dropped at Hiroshima, Japan.[10] The plutonium weapon, Fat Man, followed at Nagasaki on August 9, 1945. The Manhattan Project was one of the largest and most ambitious scientific ventures of all time, and it brought the power of the atom to humanity. Two of its direct and indirect outcomes were the destruction of Hiroshima and Nagasaki and the development of nuclear power.

The US Nuclear Weapons Testing

The US has conducted more nuclear weapons tests, both atmospheric and underground, than any other country. It has conducted 1,030 nuclear tests; of which 5 were underwater, 815 underground, and 210 in the atmosphere or on the surface of the land.[11] These conducted nuclear tests were conducted at 11 locations within the 50 states, at four island locations in the Pacific, in the open ocean in the Pacific, and over the open ocean in the Atlantic. Since July 1962, all nuclear tests conducted in the US have been underground, and most of them have been at the Nevada Test Site. Some tests were conducted on the Nellis Air Force Range (NAFR); in central and

10 From the US point of view, the mission was a success by the standards of the project: the Hiroshima city was completely disabled and about half of its occupants were killed, around 90% of them civilians. A coordinated "publicity" campaign was immediately launched by Manhattan Project officials to inform the world about the new weapon, including a Presidential press release and numerous newspaper stories written by a *New York Times* science journalist, William L. Laurence, who was "embedded" in (co-opted by) the project. Wellerstein Alex, Manhattan Project, *Encyclopedia of the History of Science*, April 2019, p. 22.

11 United States Nuclear Tests: July 1945 through September 1992, US Department of Energy, Navada Operations Office; DOE/NV-209-REV15, December 2000, p. xi.

northwestern Nevada; in Colorado, New Mexico, and Mississippi; and on Amchitka, one of the Aleutian Islands off the coast of Alaska.

Nuclear Tests in Pacific

After the initial testing of nuclear weapons and dropping of two bombs over Japan, the subsequent 106 tests were conducted at five locations in the Pacific, the major being in the Bikini, Marshall and Christmas Islands. The Marshall Islands were selected for nuclear weapons testing because of their remoteness, the government control of the territory, and evading the attention of the US public.[12] In the selection of the Marshall Islands, public health considerations were disregarded in favour of other advantages.[13]

Between 1946 and 1958, the US detonated 67 nuclear bombs on, in and above the Marshall Islands — vaporising whole islands, carving craters into its shallow lagoons and exiling hundreds of people from their homes.[14]

12 Following the Trinity test and the bombings of Hiroshima and Nagasaki, officials still knew very little about weapon effects, especially on naval targets. Accordingly, the Joint Chiefs of Staff requested and received presidential approval to conduct a test series during summer 1946. Experience with the radiological hazards of Trinity and the two bombs dropped on Japan strongly influenced the decision to locate Crossroads at Bikini Atoll in the Marshall Islands, which was far from the US and population centres in the middle of the Pacific. Jones Vincent C, 1985, *Manhattan: The Army and the Atomic Bomb*, Centre of Military History, US Army, Washington DC, p. 660.

13 Radioactive Heaven and Earth: The health and environmental effects of nuclear weapons testing in, on, and above the earth, 1991, Report of the IPPNW International Commission to Investigate the Health and Environmental Effects of Nuclear Weapons Production and the Institute for Energy and Environmental Research, New York: The Apex Press, p. 72.

14 The military governor of the Marshall Islands used Christian parables to convince the paramount chief of Bikini to abandon the atoll. On the understanding that experimenting with nuclear devices would "with God's blessing, result in kindness and benefit to all mankind," the chief told the governor that his people would be pleased to go elsewhere. The Bikinians were led to believe that they would be returned to their atoll after the tests were concluded. They chose to move to Rongerik Atoll, 200 kilometers to the east. This previously uninhabited atoll with only a quarter of Bikini's land mass failed to support an adequate diet, and by 1947 there were obvious signs of malnutrition among the people. After a period of dietary rehabilitation at Kwajalein military base, the Bikinians were moved to Kili Island. Although somewhat more suitable for growing staple foods, Kili has no lagoon and is frequently isolated from shipping by rough seas. The most seriously affected atolls have been evacuated and resettled a number of times. The fears and controversies about residual radiation and contamination of waters and fish remain and, for some groups of Islanders, have intensified over the years as more information has become public. Radioactive Heaven and Earth: The health and environmental effects of nuclear weapons testing in, on, and above the earth, 1991, Report of the IPPNW International Commission to

The US authorities later cleaned up contaminated soil on Enewetak Atoll, where the US not only detonated the bulk of its weapons tests but, also conducted a dozen biological weapons tests and dumped 130 tons of soil from an irradiated Nevada testing site. It then deposited the atoll's most lethal debris and soil into the dome.

The extreme shortage of land, the fragility of the environment on which people depend for a living and the weather also made the Marshall Islands an unsuitable place to test nuclear weapons. As a result of testing, the Marshall Islands sustained severe physical damage and radiological contamination. The people of Bikini and Enewetak were placed in exile by the US government so that their atolls could be used to explode nuclear weapons. Other Marshallese were occasionally evacuated temporarily but for the most part, were left on their atolls.

Unplanned Hydrogen Bomb. 'Bravo' was part of Operation Castle, a nuclear test series designed to develop an aircraft-deliverable thermonuclear weapon. On March 1, 1954, bomb 'Bravo' using solid lithium deuteride was tested by the US on Bikini Atoll in the Marshall Islands as part of the Castle test series. The bomb was about 1,000 times more powerful than the bomb that exploded over Hiroshima in 1945. By missing an important fusion reaction, the scientists had grossly underestimated the size of the explosion. Within seconds the fireball was nearly 4.8 km in diameter. Its cloud raised 40 km and after 10 minutes had a diameter of over 120 km. The predicted yield was 5 megatons, but, in fact, 'Bravo' yielded 14.8 megatons, making it the largest US nuclear test ever exploded. The blast gouged a crater more than 2.4 km wide and several hundred meters deep and ejected several million tons of radioactive debris into the air.

Effects on Islanders. No one was living on the Bikini atoll at the time of the Bravo blast. However, a total of 236 people were living on the atolls of Rongelap and Utirik, 100 and 480 km east of Bikini, respectively. The residents of Rongelap were exposed to as much as 200 rems of radiation.[15] They were evacuated 24 hours after the detonation. The residents of Utirik, which were exposed to lower levels of radiation, were not evacuated until

---

Investigate the Health and Environmental Effects of Nuclear Weapons Production and the Institute for Energy and Environmental Research, New York: The Apex Press, pp. 73-74.

15 These are large doses of absorbed radiation. To give some idea of dose magnitude, the whole-body radiation from an extensive X-ray survey of the large intestine with contrast media would rarely exceed 0.5 rems. The dose from one chest X-ray is about 0.01 rems.

at least two days later. After their evacuation, many experienced typical symptoms of radiation poisoning: burning of the mouth and eyes, nausea, diarrhoea, loss of hair, and skin burns. Ten years after the blast, the first thyroid tumours began to appear. Of those under twelve on Rongelap at the time of Bravo, 90% have developed thyroid tumours. In 1964, the US Government admitted responsibility for exposing the islanders to radiation and appropriated funds to compensate them.

Runit Island is one of 40 islands of the Enewetak Atoll of the Marshall Islands in the Central Pacific. A massive, concrete dome called "Runit Dome", was constructed by the US authorities which holds more than 3.1 million cubic feet (or 35 Olympic-sized swimming pools) of US-produced radioactive soil and debris, including lethal amounts of plutonium.[16] Nowhere else has the US saddled another country with so much of its nuclear waste, a product of its Cold War atomic testing programme. There are ongoing concerns around the deterioration of the waste site and a potential radioactive spill. A recent study conducted by a team of Columbia University scientists showed levels of radiation in some spots in Enewetak and other parts of the Marshall Islands that rival those found near Chernobyl and Fukushima.[17]

Some of the US army personnel who participated in the dome construction and transport of radioactive materials claim that illnesses that developed years later are a result of unprotected exposure. Some of these have died of cancer and others have become sick. The US government denies that there is any connection between the work on the island and the health problems and has so far refused to offer any compensation for the illnesses associated with the construction of Runit Dome.

---

16 The Runit Dome, also called Cactus Dome or locally *The Tomb*, is 46 cm thick dome of concrete coffin, which is at risk of collapsing from rising seas and other effects of climate change. Tides are creeping up its sides, advancing higher every year as distant glaciers melt and ocean waters rise. Officials in the Marshall Islands have lobbied the US government for help, but American officials have declined, saying the dome is on Marshallese land and therefore the responsibility of the Marshallese government. To many in the Republic of the Marshall Islands, Runit Dome is the most visible manifestation of the American nuclear legacy, a symbol of the sacrifices the Marshallese made for US security, and the broken promises they received in return. They blame the US and other industrialized countries for global climate change and sea level rise, which threaten to submerge vast swaths of this island nation's low-lying atolls.

17 Maveric K. I. L. A., Monica Rouco Molina, et. al., Background gamma radiation and soil activity measurements in the northern Marshall Islands, *Proceedings of the National Academy of Science of the USA*, Vol. 116(31), July 2019, pp. 15425-15434.

A *Times* review of documents, and interviews with US and Marshallese officials, found that the US government withheld key pieces of information about the dome's contents and its weapons testing programme before the two countries signed a compact in 1986 releasing the US government from further liability. One example: The United States did not tell the Marshallese that in 1958, it shipped 130 tons of soil from its atomic testing grounds in Nevada to the Marshall Islands. The US authorities also did not inform people in Enewetak, where the waste site is located, that they conducted a dozen biological weapons tests in the atoll, including experiments with an aerosolised bacteria designed to kill enemy troops.[18] Marshallese leaders acknowledge that the US doesn't bear full responsibility for their nation's distress. But they say the US has failed to take ownership of the environmental catastrophe it left behind, and they claim US authorities have repeatedly deceived them about the magnitude and extent of that devastation. The tribunal, established by the two countries in 1988, concluded the US should pay $2.3 billion in claims, but Congress and US courts have refused. The US position is that it has already paid more than $600 million for the resettlement, rehabilitation and radiation-related healthcare costs of communities affected by the nuclear testing.[19]

Effects on Fishermen. The *Fukuryu Maru* (Lucky Dragon) was a small Japanese tuna boat, fishing about 145 km east of Bikini at the time of the test. About two hours after the explosion a 'snow' of radioactive ash composed of coral vaporised by Bravo began to fall on the ship. Within hours, 23 Japanese fishermen aboard the crewmembers began to experience burning and nausea. Within a few days, their skin began to darken and some crewmember's hair started to fall out. Upon returning to

18 Rust Susanne, How the US betrayed the Marshall Islands, kindling the next nuclear disaster, *Los Angeles Times*, November 10, 2019.

19 The dome was never meant to last. According to the World Health Organization, the $218m plan was designed as temporary fix: a way to store contaminated material until a permanent decontamination plan was devised. In 2012, when the UN special rapporteur on human rights and toxic waste, Calin Georgescu, visited the Marshall Islands, he criticized the US, remarking that "the islanders feel like 'nomads' in their own country. Nuclear testing has left a legacy of distrust in the hearts and minds of the Marshallese". Locals, scientists and environmental activists fear that a storm surge, typhoon or other cataclysmic event brought on by climate change could tear the concrete mantel wide open, releasing its contents into the Pacific Ocean. The US has never formally apologized to the Marshall Islands for turning it into an atomic testing ground. Jose Coleen, Kim Wall and Jan Hinzel, Marshall Island: This dome in the Pacific houses tons of radioactive waste – and it's leaking, *The Guardian*, February 3, 2015, available at: https://www.theguardian.com/world/2015/jul/03/runit-dome-pacific-radioactive-waste.

Japan, many were hospitalised and one eventually went into a coma and died. The incident resulted in a diplomatic crisis between Japan and the US and gave rise to international criticism of nuclear testing. Though the US denied responsibility, it sent the widow a check for 2.5 million yen "as a token of sympathy."[20]

US Testing in North America

After the first nuclear weapons test at the Alamogordo site in New Mexico, the US planned a new nuclear weapons test site in Nevada. Testing at the Nevada Test Site began during the Korean War, but planning for the selection of a site in the continental has been stated much earlier.[21] A total of 100 atmospheric and 814 over-ground nuclear weapons tests were held in Nevada.[22] At the Nevada site, nuclear wastes have accumulated underground, and recent studies of a nearby location as a possible long-term high-level waste repository raise doubts about the geological

20 The US government has officially maintained that the Bravo fallout tragedy was an unfortunate accident due to an unexpected shift in the winds. It had been planned that the bomb cloud would be blown to the west and north, however, for unexpected reasons, the wind blew to the east. Radioactive Heaven and Earth: The health and environmental effects of nuclear weapons testing in, on, and above the earth, 1991, Report of the IPPNW International Commission to Investigate the Health and Environmental Effects of Nuclear Weapons Production and the Institute for Energy and Environmental Research, New York: The Apex Press, p. 78.

21 The Korean War accelerated the planning efforts, especially because the US Amy and Navy wanted weapons they could use in battle. Until that time, the Air Force had dominated the nuclear weapons scene. It was realized that there would be resistance to having a test site in the US because of the public's fear of radioactivity. The're-education' of the public to take a more realistic and less fearful attitude was considered necessary in order to locate a test site in the US. Radioactive Heaven and Earth: The health and environmental effects of nuclear weapons testing in, on, and above the earth, 1991, Report of the IPPNW International Commission to Investigate the Health and Environmental Effects of Nuclear Weapons Production and the Institute for Energy and Environmental Research, New York: The Apex Press, pp.50-53.

22 The Nevada Test Site consisted of approximately 1,375 square miles of remote desert and mountain terrain owned and controlled by the Department of Energy and located in the southern part of the Great Basin northwest of Las Vegas. The Nevada site also held other advantages. Immediately to the south of the bombing and gunnery range was a government airfield at Indian Springs, with runways 6,600 feet in length and housing to accommodate 1,000 people. Despite the harsh climate, the Nevada Test Site has been home to a variety of flora and fauna. The animal species include Kit fox, the sidewinder rattlesnake, the striped whip snake, mule deer, coyotes, golden eagles, wild horses, mountain lions, bighorn sheep and antelope. The Test Site played a vital and central role in the development and maintenance of the Cold War nuclear arsenal. Gowin Emmet, 2019, *The Nevada Test Site*, Princeton University Press, p. 160.

suitability of the site and its ability to contain wastes over thousands of years. Communities downwind of the Nevada Test Site received large amounts of fallout.

The US federal government also recognises that people in 12 western states (Arizona, Colorado, Idaho, Nevada, New Mexico, North Dakota, Oregon, Utah, Washington, Wyoming, Texas and South Dakota) have 'developed serious illnesses after radiation exposure' as a result of the tests. Between 1992 and March 2016, the US Department of Justice has approved 3,963 Radioactive Exposure Compensation claims[23] for 'onsite participants' in nuclear tests and 19,555 claims from 'down-winders' (exposed to fallout from the Nevada Test Site) who had 'contracted certain cancers and other serious diseases as a result of their exposure.'[24] Nevada test site was selected against public health considerations, resulting in contamination locally and across the continent. There is a 'high risk of groundwater contamination with several radioactive isotopes in the Nevada Test Site.[25]There is a strong possibility that in future, some of the inventory of long-lived radioactive

23 The US conducted nearly 200 atmospheric nuclear weapons development tests from 1945 to 1962 which were considered essential to the nation's nuclear weapons development and uranium mining and processing. These tests were carried out by tens of thousands of workers. Following the conclusion of these activities, lawsuits were filed against the government's alleged failure to warn of exposures to known radiation hazards. These suits were dismissed by the appellate courts. Congress responded by devising a programme allowing partial restitution to individuals who developed serious illnesses after presumed exposure to radiation released during the atmospheric nuclear tests or after employment in the uranium industry. The Radiation Exposure Compensation Act was passed on October 5, 1990 and its scope of coverage was broadened on July 10, 2000. The Act has established an administrative system for claims relating to atmospheric nuclear testing and uranium industry employment. The Act has delegated authority to the Attorney General to establish procedures and make determinations regarding whether claims satisfy statutory eligibility criteria. The Act covers three categories of individuals: (i) Uranium Miners, Millers, and Ore Transporters may be eligible for one-time, lump sum compensation of $100,000; (ii) 'Onsite Participants" at atmospheric nuclear weapons tests may be eligible for one-time, lump sum compensation of up to $75,000; and (iii) Individuals who lived downwind of the Nevada Test Site who may be eligible for one-time, lump sum compensation of $50,000.

24 Radiation Exposure Compensation System: Awards to Date, US Department of Justice. Information as on March 17, 2016. Available at: https://web.archive.org/web/20160318033248/https://www.justice.gov/civil/awards-date-03172016.

25 Pravalie Remus, Nuclear Weapons Tests and Environmental Consequences: A Global Perspective' *Ambio*. Vol. 43(6), October 2014, pp. 729-744.

wastes from over 700 underground explosions will eventually reach the human environment, endangering people's health.[26]

Nuclear Weapons Tests by the Soviet Union

The US dropping of nuclear weapons over the Japanese city in August 1945 completely changed the balance of power in the world and the Soviet Union had no choice but to develop its nuclear weapons. To test the planned atomic weapons, a designated test site was necessary. On August 21, 1947, the Soviet government decided to establish a test site in the north-eastern part of the Kazakh Soviet Socialist Republic (KSSR). The Semipalatinsk Nuclear Test Site (SNTS) occupied territory of 18,300 km sq, to the west of Semipalatinsk city.[27] The Soviet Union started nuclear testing in 1949.

Between 1949 and 1989, it has conducted 715 nuclear weapons tests at many locations far from Moscow. It detonated 456 nuclear explosive devices at the SNTS in Kazakhstan, 130 on Novaya Zemlya, a Russian Far North archipelago, and an additional 129 at other locations in Russia, Kazakhstan, Turkmenistan, Ukraine and Uzbekistan.[28] There are 50 other sites at which the Soviet Union has conducted nuclear tests; most of these tests have been labelled as peaceful and civilian rather than military. The Soviet Union's atmospheric nuclear tests include the largest nuclear explosion ever, 58 megatons, conducted at Novaya Zemlya in 1961 about four times larger than the largest US test in 1954. This was the largest-yield device ever exploded. The largest underground explosion by the Soviet Union was of a 3.5-megaton weapon, exploded at the southern site in Novaya Zemlya. At least three of the Soviet explosions have been underwater, two off the coast of Novaya Zemlya and one in the Barents Sea.

Semipalatinsk Nuclear Test Site

The Soviet Union exploded 456 atomic and thermonuclear devices at the SNTS between 1949 and 1989. Explosions were conducted on the surface and in the atmosphere. Five of the surface tests were unsuccessful; which

26 Radioactive Heaven and Earth: The health and environmental effects of nuclear weapons testing in, on, and above the earth, 1991, Report of the IPPNW International Commission to Investigate the Health and Environmental Effects of Nuclear Weapons Production and the Institute for Energy and Environmental Research, New York: The Apex Press, pp. 67-68.

27 The city was renamed Semey in 2007.

28 Nuclear Explosions: 1945-2016: World Nuclear Force, SIPRI. p. 467, Available at:https://www.sipri.org/sites/default/files/SIPRIYB17c11sXI.pdf.

resulted in the dispersion of plutonium into the environment, with the first test on August 29, 1949 unexpectedly contaminating villages to the northeast of the SNTS. The approximate cumulative explosive yield of the tests conducted before 1963, when the Soviet Union signed the Partial Test Ban Treaty (PTBT), was 6.4 Mt. This was about six times greater than the explosive yield of the above-ground tests at the Nevada Test Site. More than 300 test explosions were conducted underground after 1961. Semipalatinsk's Degelen Mountain nuclear test facility was the largest underground nuclear test site in the world, consisting of 181 separate tunnels. Between October 1961 and October 1989, 224 tests were conducted there.[29]

The last test took place on February 12, 1989 and resulted in a leakage of large amounts of the radioactive noble gases xenon and krypton at the SNTS. It resulted in environmental contamination causing benign and malignant thyroid disease in the East Kazakhstan region of the Republic of Kazakhstan. A commission appointed by the government estimated that nearly 10,000 residents of the region received excessive doses of radiation.[30]

The Soviet government paid virtually no attention to the impacts of nuclear tests on the local population. In fact, until 1956 the government did not even conduct studies about nuclear testing's effect on the population living close to the test site. There are no clear statistics available about the acute effects of the testing.[31] The first impetus for health studies was initiated in connection with an emergency caused by a surface nuclear detonation on March 16, 1956, when the radioactive cloud from the explosion reached the city of Ust-Kamenogorsk, 400 km from the explosion epicentre. The city's population was exposed to nuclear fallout with radiation doses so high as to cause acute radiation poisoning. In response, the Soviet leadership established a special medical institution and hospitalised 638 persons suffering from radiation poisoning. However, no information about the fate

29 The Soviet Union's Nuclear Testing, Comprehensive Nuclear-Test-Ban Treaty Organization, available at: https://www.ctbto.org/nuclear-testing/the-effects-of-nuclear-testing/the-soviet-unionsnuclear-testing-programme/, accessed September 20, 2021.

30 In May 1989, the Soviet Council of Ministers appointed a commission consisting of 70 government scientists to examine the health and ecological situation at the Kazakhstan test site. The commission, known as 'Tsyb Commission' was headed by Academician A.E Tsyb, Director of the Scientific Research Institute of Medical Radiology of the USSR Academy of Medical Sciences.

31 Roman Vakulchuk, Kristian Gjerde, et.al., Semipalatinsk nuclear testing: the humanitarian consequences, Norwegian Institute of International Affairs Report No. 1, 2014, p. 35.

of these people is available.[32] According to the government of Kazakhstan, over one million people have been recognised as having suffered from nuclear tests. The government has officially recognised 1,323,000 people as having been negatively affected by the nuclear tests. Out of these, 1,057,000 have received 'radiation passports' officially confirming their status.

Health Impact. Several genetic defects and illnesses in the region, ranging from cancers to impotency to birth defects and other deformities, have been attributed to nuclear testing. There were reports of an epidemic of babies born with severe neurological and major bone deformations, some without limbs. There have also been many cases of leukaemia and other blood disorders. There is even a museum of mutations at the regional medical institute in Semey, the largest city near the old nuclear testing site. It consists of a room filled with jars containing monstrosities caused by nuclear testing such as deformed fetuses and human organs, and animal carcasses barely recognisable as potential living beings. According to the director of the Oncology Hospital in Semipalatinsk, at least 60,000 people in the region have died from radiation-induced cancers.

In December 1997, a joint mission of the United Nations and the Government of Kazakhstan travelled to Semipalatinsk to investigate the economic, environmental and social consequences of the Soviet nuclear testing at the SNTS. The mission found that the psycho-social effects of the testing had been profound. The population felt victimised and deceived by the government. The local economy had been affected by the negative image of the region, which discouraged major domestic and international investors. Agricultural land had been contaminated during the years of testing and underground water cycles had been disturbed.[33]

32 In 1957, a permanent research institute was established in Semipalatinsk to carry out research on the impact of the activity at the SNTS on the population's health. It was given the neutral designation 'Dispensary No. 4' in order not to draw attention to its real activity. With the break-up of the Soviet Union, this 'dispensary' was succeeded by the Institute of Radiation Medicine and Ecology (IRME). IRME is a part of Kazakhstan's Ministry of Health and is responsible for studying the health consequences of nuclear testing. Roman Vakulchuk, Kristian Gjerde, et.al., Semipalatinsk nuclear testing: the humanitarian consequences, Norwegian Institute of International Affairs Report No. 1, 2014, p. 10.

33 People living near the Polygon near SNTS were exposed not only to acute bursts, but also to low doses of radiation over the course of decades. Kazakh researchers have been collecting data on those who lived through the detonations, as well as their children and their children's children. The effects aren't always obvious or easy to trace. But researchers are now starting to see some subtle impacts that linger 30 years after the Polygon closed. The nuclear sins of the Soviet Union live on in Kazakhstan, *Nature*,

In a statement to the UN in October 1998, the Permanent Representative of the Republic of Kazakhstan to the UN stated that the underground tests destroyed ecological linkages, and this, in turn, accelerated the process of desertification of the territory of the region, which is continuing to take place up until the present time.

Specialised studies have shown that currently the Semipalatinsk region is heavily contaminated with radioactive isotopes and the radio-nuclides present especially in the soil and the vegetation. It was also found that the local water bodies feature high concentrations of radioactive uranium isotopes, well above the maximum value allowed by the World Health Organization.[34]Harm from Soviet tests was also not limited to the areas of the former Soviet Republics. An earlier study found higher risks of thyroid cancer in subjects exposed to fallout in Norway and Sweden.[35] Radioactive contamination from the Russian nuclear weapons explosion also spread to Canada and Alaska.[36]

The British Tests of Nuclear Weapons

The US maintained complete secrecy over its nuclear weapons projects and did not collaborate on nuclear weapons with any other country. The US prohibition on international collaboration was contained in a clause of the McMahon Act of 1946, which set up the US Atomic Energy Commission to develop nuclear weapons. The British therefore decided to build nuclear weapons independently for which they needed a test site. The first test was conducted in Australia,[37] which had been an independent commonwealth

April 3, 2019.

34 Remus Pravalie, Nuclear Weapons Tests and Environmental Consequences: A Global Perspective, *Ambio*, Vol. 43(6), 2014, pp. 729-744.

35 Lund E. and M.R. Galanti, Incidence of thyroid cancer in Scandinavia following fallout from atomic bomb testing: an analysis of birth cohorts, *Cancer Causes Control*, Vol. 10(3), pp. 181-187.

36 The Soviet Union's Nuclear Testing Programme, Comprehensive Nuclear-Test-Ban Treaty Organization, available at: https://www.ctbto.org/nuclear-testing/the-effects-of-nuclear-testing/the-soviet-unionsnuclear-testing-programme/.

37 The first British nuclear explosive was brought from Britain on the *HMS Plym* and detonated on the ship on October 3, 1952, near the Monte Bello Islands, off the northwest coast of Australia. One of the attractions of the Monte Bello site for the British nuclear establishment was that it resembled an estuary and thus would yield information about the effects of nuclear weapons on many of Britain's major cities, which are located on estuaries. The Australian Government had agreed to the test on the understanding that the British would have executive control. The Australians

since 1901 but was still under British influence.[38]

The UK conducted 12 major atmospheric tests between 1952 and 1957 on Australian territories at Maralinga, Emu Field and Monte Bello Island. From 1957 to 1958, nine atmospheric tests followed over Christmas Island (Kiritimati) and Malden Island in the central Pacific Ocean. A set of four nuclear weapon test series were also carried out by the UK in 1957 and 1958 at Malden Island and Christmas Island as part of the British hydrogen bomb program. In total nine nuclear explosions were initiated as part of this series. The remaining 24 UK nuclear tests were conducted jointly with the US at the Nevada Test Site.[39] During the testing period, roughly 16,000 Australian civilians and servicemen were involved in the tests and 22,000 British servicemen were exposed to nuclear fallout. The UK is responsible for the radioactive pollution of vast areas of the Australian continent, as a result of the 12 atmospheric nuclear tests conducted at Emu Field, Maralinga and Montebello.[40]

Emu Field.[41] A major nuclear test was detonated at Emu Field in the South Australian desert on October 15, 1953, sending a radioactive cloud known as the "Black Mist" over a 250 km sq area; resulting in a sudden outbreak of sickness and death experienced by Aboriginal communities exposed to the Black Mist. It was later found that the test had been detonated under wind conditions that produced unacceptable levels of fallout and that the

provided logistical support, but there was no technical collaboration. Three Australian scientists were present as observers only.

38 On February 18, 1952, the Australian Prime Minister, Robert Gordon Menzies, made the following brief announcement: In the course of this year, the UK Government intends to test an atomic weapon produced in the UK. In close cooperation with the Government of the Commonwealth of Australia, the test will take place at a site in Australia. It will be conducted in conditions that will ensure that there will be no danger whatever from radioactivity to the health of the people or animals in the Commonwealth.

39 The United Kingdom's Nuclear Testing Programme, Comprehensive Nuclear-Test-Ban Treaty Organization, available at: https://www.ctbto.org/nuclear-testing/the-effects-of-nuclear-testing/the-united-kingdomsnuclear-testing-programme/.

40 Pravalie Remus, Nuclear Weapons Tests and Environmental Consequences: A Global Perspective *Ambio*, Vol. 43, 2014, p. 737.

41 The need for a land test site had been recognized in 1950 and a place had already been selected. A long-range reconnaissance party from the rocket range at Woomera, in the South Australian desert, had found a section of desert scarred with clay pans, covered in red bush spinifex, mulga, and she-oak. The terrain contained large expanses of sand dune and drift, but in places was hard enough to allow landings of large transport planes. It was called Emu Field and was used for two explosions in 1953.

firing criteria did not take into account the existence of people downwind of the test site.

Associated logistical problems prompted the search for another site closer to the transcontinental railway line, and eventually, Maralinga, about 80 kilometres north of the railway, was chosen. Maralinga, meaning "Field of Thunder" in the local Aboriginal language, was intended to be a more permanent test site. While it was being set up, two more explosions took place at Monte Bello in 1956.

Maralinga Test Site. The first explosion at Maralinga occurred on September 27, 1956, the last on October 9, 1957. Altogether seven nuclear tests were carried out at Maralinga in South Australia between 1956 and 1957 (Operation Buffalo and Operation Antler) at various sites. Maralinga saw the first test launches of atomic weapons from aircraft in 1962. The temporary ban on atmospheric nuclear tests in the late 1950s reduced Maralinga's usefulness for major tests, but it was still used for what was called "minor trials." Considerable contamination resulted from the minor trials at Maralinga. The trials were designed to test the safety and security of British nuclear weapons in case of an accident and to improve the trigger mechanisms, which were subjected to chemical explosions, heat and other tests. The resultant destruction produced plumes of radioactive material in the form of fine particles. These particles fell to Earth over a wide area of thc test range and in some cases, beyond it. There were up to 600 minor trials, which contaminated Maralinga with approximately 8,000 kg of uranium, 24 kg of plutonium, and 100 kg of beryllium. Plutonium, one of the most toxic radionuclides with a half-life of 24,000 years remains scattered around a huge area. The effects were not only radiological: restrictions on the indigenous population's access to their traditional lands also caused psycho-social and cultural problems. The relocation of indigenous communities from Ooldea, near Maralinga, occurred before and for reasons unrelated to the British nuclear test programme. However, the tests did have a significant impact on indigenous people seeking to return to their lands and follow traditional migration routes. Many of the Maralinga Tjarutja indigenous population continued to move throughout the region at the time of the tests. It was later discovered that a traditional Aboriginal route crossed through the Maralinga testing range.

An initial cleanup operation was conducted at Maralinga in 1967. This merely involved burying radioactive debris, including plutonium, in pits that were later covered with concrete. Radioactive fragments scattered over the terrain were ploughed into the earth or covered with topsoil to reduce the likelihood of dispersion and subsequent inhalation or ingestion.

Montebello Islands. The nuclear tests conducted at the Monte Bello Islands off the coast of Western Australia spread radioactivity across large portions of mainland Australia. Considerable publicity in Australia in the early 1980s about the health and environmental impacts led to the setting up of the McClelland Royal Commission in 1984. The Commission concluded: "The presence of Aborigines on the mainland near Monte Bello Islands and their extra vulnerability to the effect of fallout was not recognised by either the Atomic Weapons Research Establishment of the UK or the Safety Committee. It was a major oversight that the question of acceptable dose levels for Aborigines was recognised as a problem at Maralinga but was ignored in setting the fallout criteria for the Mosaic tests", which were conducted in mid-1956 and involved the detonation of two weapons at the Monte Bello site.

Christmas and Malden Islands. The British also considered eight places in the Indian Ocean and four in the Atlantic Ocean for nuclear weapons testing. These were rejected because they were too populated or conditions were thought unsuitable. With impending test ban treaties, Britain was determined to test the hydrogen bomb before it was too late. The British government finally settled upon Christmas Island, located at the equator midway between Tahiti and Hawaii. "Operation Grapple" consisted of nine detonations over Christmas Island and Malden Island in the South Pacific Ocean between May 1957 and September 1958.[42] The first was the 1.8 megaton test on May 15, 1957. The weapons were many times more powerful than those discharged at Hiroshima and Nagasaki and included a bomb with a yield of three megatons - the largest British nuclear test ever conducted. Britain's first thermonuclear bomb was detonated during this testing period. Over 500 naval personnel from New Zealand also took part in Operation Grapple.

The US-UK joint testing programme at Christmas Island consisted of Operation Dominic, a series of 24 explosions between April and July 1962. Nearly 300 hundred British servicemen and 3,200 from the US were

42 The first series, Grapple 1-3, were high air burst H-bombs off uninhabited Malden Island, 600 km to the south of Christmas Island. The second series, Grapple x-24, involved four more ocean air-bursts and two smaller atomic bombs balloon-suspended at 450 meters over the end of Christmas Island. Most of these tests were in the megaton range. By 1958 the major British tests were completed. Smaller trials continued until 1963.

involved. In return for the US use of the base, the British negotiated access to the American data. The island was vacated in 1964, and survey and clean-up operations continued until 1967.

Nuclear fallout and the dangers from ingested radioactive particles were not taken seriously after the tests. Servicemen were free to move around the island, drinking local water, eating local fruits, bathing in the lagoons and breathing in dust, all of which could have been contaminated. Ingested radioactive particles from fallout can remain in the body and continue to cause harm for many years. Some veterans were allegedly too close to the epicentre of the blast and witnesses described their experiences of a heatwave of extraordinary intensity, leading in some cases to temporary blindness or a sensation of blood boiling within their bodies.

The health impacts of the tests were highlighted by the British Nuclear Veterans Association in a 1999 survey of 2,500 veterans, many of whom had been at Maralinga. The survey found that 30 percent of the men had died, mostly in their fifties. In addition, more than 200 skeletal abnormalities were reported; and over 100 veterans' children reported reproductive difficulties. In addition to British personnel, thousands of Australians and Aboriginal people living downwind of the test sites were also exposed to airborne radioactivity.

Vulnerability of Indigenous Populations. Authorities paid little or no attention to the vulnerability of indigenous people to the radiological effects of the tests. While major test explosions were announced in the media, the general public had little specific knowledge about the British nuclear testing programme since it was confidential. Factors such as inadequate clothing, ingestion of food contaminated with radioactive material, movement patterns, language barriers (many indigenous people could not read the English warning signs), and general health status rendered them susceptible to the effects of nuclear testing. In addition, Aboriginal people usually lacked amenities such as piped water, hard permanent dwellings with dust proofing, and bathroom and drainage facilities, which would have afforded them more protection from the fallout.

Compensation. The Compensation (Commonwealth Government Employees) Act 1971 permitted ex-service personnel to receive compensation if they could prove that their disability resulted from exposure to radiation from the tests. The Royal Commission recommended that eligibility be extended to civilians at the test sites and Aborigines and others exposed to the 'Black Mist'.

On January 21, 2009, a group of just over 1,000 British ex-servicemen who had served in the South Pacific in the 1950s brought a case against the Ministry of Defence.[43] The veterans were seeking compensation for illnesses, including cancer, skin defects and fertility problems, which they claim are the result of exposure to radiation during nuclear bomb testing. On July 28, 2011, veterans of Britain's 1950s nuclear bomb tests got relief from the Supreme Court for the award of compensation. A revised departmental policy statement on claims for radiation-related disorders was published in December 2017. Veterans, including Nuclear Test Veterans, who believe they have suffered ill health due to service can apply for no-fault compensation under the War Pensions Scheme, which has no time limits and a low standard of proof. Decisions are medically certified and follow consideration of available service and medical evidence, where the evidence supports a causal link to service, entitlement will be given.

The people of the Pacific region have suffered widespread and persisting radioactive contamination, displacement and trans-generational harm from nuclear tests undertaken by the few nuclear-weapon states. It has been reported that radiation exposures for service personnel (soldiers from the British, New Zealand and Fiji) as well as locals were not systematically monitored, and personal protection was minimal. British military documents reveal that one of the purposes of the tests was to study the effects of a nuclear explosion on people, equipment and stores. A medical study of 2,500 men who participated in the UK tests (2,200 UK, 238 New Zealand and 62 Fijian) found that two-thirds of those who had died had cancers.[44] Further, clean-up operations included disposing of thousands of seabirds maimed, blinded or killed by the nuclear explosions, as well as dumping drums of nuclear waste into the ocean.[45]

43 Unfortunately during this time the British Government continue to claim that safety preparations and the conduct of the tests minimized radioactive fallout. A 2008 fact sheet released by the UK Ministry of Defence (MoD) argued that: "Almost all the British servicemen involved in the UK nuclear tests received little or no additional radiation as a result of participation. If personnel who served at Christmas Island at that time had been stationed in the UK in an average location, their dose of naturally-occurring ionising radiation would have been three times greater than it was at Christmas Island." UK atmospheric nuclear weapons tests: UK programme', Factsheet 5, UK Ministry of Defence, June 2008.

44 Roff S.R., Mortality and morbidity of members of the British Nuclear Tests Veterans Association and the New Zealand Nuclear Tests Veterans Association and their families, *Medicine, conflict and survival*, Vol. 15(Suppl.1), Jul-Sep 1999, pp. 1-51.

45 Ruff Tilman A., The humanitarian impact and implications of nuclear test explosions in the Pacific region, *International Review of the Red Cross.*, Vol. 97, No. 899, 2016, pp.

French Nuclear Weapons Testing

France was the fourth nation to join the "Nuclear Club" when it successfully detonated a large nuclear device in Algeria on February 13, 1960, when Algeria was still a colony.[46] In all, 14 nuclear weapons tests were conducted at the two Algerian locations--four atmospheric and 10 underground between 1960 and 1965. This resulted in significant environmental contamination, particularly high in the desert sand.[47] The French Ministry of Defence claimed that local people were not adversely impacted by the tests, but the Algerian government has believed that radiation in some areas near the test sites is 20 times higher than the norm. People continue to be exposed to radiation through inhalation and ingestion of contaminated dust particles.[48]

From the beginning of nuclear tests in Algeria, France set up a policy of burying all waste in the sands. France buried everything that may have been contaminated by radioactivity including planes and tanks. France has never revealed where exactly this waste was buried, or how much of it was buried. In addition to these contaminated materials, voluntarily left on site to future generations, there are two other categories: non-radioactive waste (resulting from the operation and dismantling of the sites) and radioactive materials emitted by nuclear explosions (vitrified sand, radioactive slabs and rocks). Most of this waste was left in the open, without being secured in any way, and is accessible to the local population, creating a high risk for health and environmental damage.[49]

775-813.

46 After a war that killed hundreds of thousands of people, Algeria won independence in 1962. But under the treaty signed by French President ending rule from Paris, the tests were allowed to go on until 1966.

47 Remus Pravalie Remus, Nuclear Weapons Tests and Environmental Consequences: A Global Perspective, *Ambio*, Vol. 43(6), 2014, pp. 729-744.

48 Radioactive material is seeping out from Sahara desert mountain where French scientists conducted nuclear tests in the 1960s, contaminating the soil and poisoning relations between France and Algeria. Algerian officials say France is refusing to give them access to archives about the tests, leaving them in the dark about the extent of the threat from radiation and preventing them from taking effective measures to contain it. Lamine Chikhi, French nuclear tests in Algeria leave toxic legacy, *Reuters*, March 4, 2010, available at: https://www.reuters.com/article/idINIndia-46657120100304.

49 Collin Jean-Martin and Patric Bouveret, Radioactivity Under the Sand; The Waste From French Nuclear Tests in Algeria: Analysis with regard to the Treaty on the Prohibition of Nuclear Weapons, Heinrich Boll Foundation, July 2020, p. 5.

The independence of Algeria in 1962 threatened further testing at the Algerian sites. The French government, therefore, searched for other suitable test sites. The decision was in favour of the uninhabited islands in the Pacific, Moruroa and Fangataufa, two atolls in the southeastern area of the Tuamotu Archipelago, French Polynesia. France caused intense radioactive pollution of marine ecosystems in its 179 tests in the Moruroa Atoll and 14 in the Fangataufa Atoll, French Polynesia. There have been several reported cases of rain-out i.e. fallout by rain formed by the particles of a nuclear explosion during the testing period. One such incident occurred in Samoa, 3,610 km from Moruroa, on September 12, 1966. This was a consequence of the test Betelgeuse the previous day, in which a 120 kiloton bomb hanging under a balloon was exploded at a height of 600m in difficult wind conditions. After two tests within 17 days in 1966, radiation was measured on the nearby Gambier Islands at five times the permitted annual dose. This caused an increased incidence of thyroid cancer in the local population mainly as a result of contamination of the food and water supply.[50] Indigenous workers employed in the clean-up of Moruroa atoll received less protection than those in the French government's Radiological Safety Service. Medical studies have shown that risks of inheriting thyroid cancer as a result of familial exposure to nuclear testing in French Polynesia were particularly high in Maohi populations.[51]

From 1975, all nuclear blasts were carried out underground, causing both short-term and long-term environmental damage. At the time of the explosion, the fracturing of the atoll surface triggered landslides, tsunamis and earthquakes. It was reported that radionuclides vented into the environment. France dumped a total of 3,188 tons of nuclear waste (packed in concrete drums or bulk form) in the Pacific, close to the Moruroa and Hao atolls, between 1972 and 1982.[52] Possible long-term effects include leakage of fission products to the biosphere and transfer of dissolved plutonium from the lagoon to the ocean and the food chain. Several scientific missions to Moruroa described severe impairment to the

50 Pravalie Remus, Nuclear Weapons Tests and Environmental Consequences: A Global Perspective, *Ambio*, Vol. 43, 2014, pp. 729-744.

51 Brindel P. et. al., Family history of thyroid cancer and the risk of differentiated thyroid cancer in French Polynesia, *Thyroid*, Vol. 20 (4), 2010, pp. 393-400.

52 Collin Jean-Martin and Patric Bouveret, Radioactivity Under the Sand; The Waste From French Nuclear Tests in Algeria: Analysis with regard to the Treaty on the Prohibition of Nuclear Weapons, Heinrich Boll Foundation, July 2020, p. 54.

atoll. The damage included fissures in the limestone which are propagated by the testing and surface subsidence of large areas of the atoll.[53]

Until 1974, France's Pacific nuclear tests were atmospheric, detonated at ground level, dropped from an aircraft or suspended from a balloon. This was despite the establishment of the Partial Test Ban Treaty in 1963 by the UK, USA and USSR, which banned atmospheric testing. Atmospheric tests are more likely to disperse radioactive material over wide areas. Radioactive particles were dispersed over much of French Polynesia, including its most populated island, Tahiti. However, the impact of French nuclear weapons testing extended far beyond French Polynesia.[54]

Accidents. On July 21, 1966, a nuclear bomb broke apart on the surface of Momma, dispersing plutonium-239. This plutonium-239 was confined to the area by fixing it in place with a layer of bitumen. Another major test-related landslide and consequent tsunami occurred in Moruroa on July 25, 1979. The report on the Environmental Effects of Nuclear Testing claims that a 120 kiloton weapon, which was supposed to be lowered into an 800m shaft, got stuck at a depth of 400m and could not be dislodged. The French authorities decided to explode the device anyway. The explosion resulted in a major underwater landslide of at least one million cubic metres of coral and rock and created a vast cavity. The underwater landslide produced a major tidal wave comparable to a tsunami, which spread through the Tuamotu Archipelago and injured people in the southern part of Moruroa. French authorities initially denied that any mishap had occurred and declared that the tidal wave was of natural origin. However, in a publication in 1985 they did acknowledge the "accident of July 25, 1979". Cyclones hit Moruroa in 1981, washing radioactive waste from the coral rim into the lagoon, including the plutonium-impregnated bitumen. Reportedly, radioactive materials deposited on Momma have found their way into the lagoon. There is evidence that plutonium-239 is accumulating in the food chain. A mission in 1983 to Moruroa comprising scientists from Australia, New Zealand and Papua New Guinea identified unusual concentrations of

53 France's Nuclear Weapons Testing Programme, Comprehensive Nuclear-Test-Ban Treaty Organization, available at: https://www.ctbto.org/nuclear-testing/the-effects-of-nuclear-testing/frances-nuclear-testing-programme/.

54 Fallout on Countries Downwind from French Pacific Nuclear Weapons Testing: Aotearoa New Zealand, Australia, Cook Islands, Fiji, Niue, Samoa, Tokelau, Tonga and Tuvalu, Addressing Humanitarian and Environmental Harm from Nuclear Weapons, PACE University, Submission of Fiji, Nauru, Palau, Samoa and Tuvalu to 2016 UN meeting on nuclear disarmament, p. 30.

iodine-131 in marine organisms.[55] France conducted its last nuclear test in 1996.[56]

Following a request by the Government of Algeria, the International Atomic Energy Agency (IAEA) conducted an expert mission in late 1999 to sites in Algeria that had been used by France in the early 1960s for the testing of nuclear weapons. The overall findings and conclusions from the fact-finding mission were: that most of the areas at the test sites have little residual radioactive material except (i) At the ground zero localities of the Gerboise Blanche and Gerboise Bleue atmospheric tests at the Reggane test site; and (ii) At Taourirt Tan Afella in the vicinity of the E2 tunnel.[57]

Although some of the facilities used for the tests in Algeria were dismantled before and after the programme's shutdown, waste is still present both above and below ground. At the end of the Algerian War, the two parties failed to negotiate a clause that would have forced France to decontaminate the sites or provide Algerians with archives and documentation related to the nuclear tests.[58] Unfortunately, the nuclear past of Algeria remains buried deep in the sand. The sites are not subject to checks for radioactivity and are even less the subject of campaigns to raise awareness among residents about the health risks. Since France has not

55 Radioactive Heaven and Earth: The health and environmental effects of nuclear weapons testing in, on, and above the earth, 1991, Report of the IPPNW International Commission to Investigate the Health and Environmental Effects of Nuclear Weapons Production and the Institute for Energy and Environmental Research, New York: The Apex Press, pp. 145-149.

56 After its last nuclear test in 1996, the French government requested the International Atomic Energy Agency (IAEA) to conduct a study to assess the radiological impact of the tests. This study was carried out between 1996 and 1998, and a full report was published in 1998 under the title, "The Radiological Situation of the Atolls of Moruroa and Fangataufa." The objectives of the study were to determine whether as a consequence of the tests, radiological hazards exist now or will exist in the future and to make recommendations of any monitoring, follow-up or remedial action that might be required.The study concluded that no remedial action was justified on radiological protection grounds and that there was no need for further monitoring at the atolls for the purposes of radiological protection. However, the study recommended that a programme of measurement of radioactivity in the environment could be useful, not only scientifically but also in assuring the public about the continuing radiological safety of the atolls.

57 Radiological Conditions at the Former French Nuclear Test Sites in Algeria: Preliminary Assessment and Recommendations, International Atomic Energy Agency, Vienna, 2005, p. 60.

58 Alilat Farid, Algeria: France urged to reveal truth about past nuclear tests, *The Africa Report*, September 10, 2020.

been sharing information about nuclear explosion tests in Algeria, many residents of the Sahara feel they are still being treated like guinea pigs.[59]

Compensation. The French nuclear test veterans' association, Aven, in 2008, surveyed more than 1,000 veterans and found that 35 percent had one or more types of cancer and one in five were infertile. According to Aven, veterans have suffered a range of illnesses, including cancers of the blood and cardiovascular problems, and their children and grandchildren are also suffering health complications. For several decades, the soldiers and civilians who worked on France's nuclear testing programme fought for compensation for cancer and long-term health effects they blame on the state's failure to protect them.

For four decades, the official view expressed by the French government and the military was that the nuclear tests in the Pacific had not had any detrimental effects. However, in November 2008, France announced the introduction of a bill to compensate those suffering illnesses related to nuclear testing among the 150,000 military personnel and civilians who had worked on the tests in Algeria and the Polynesian atolls. The French government has also clarified that it would no longer appeal when courts ruled against the state in cases brought by nuclear test veterans suffering health problems who complained that they had been denied disability pensions. On January 9, 2009, France agreed to spend over US$ 80 million to rehabilitate the atoll of Hao, which was a key military base during the 30 years of nuclear weapons testing in the South Pacific. On March 25, 2009, the French Ministry of Defence offered 10 million Euros (US$13.5 million) as compensation to victims of its nuclear testing programme. The treaty signed between Algeria and France in 2012 included the establishment of a Franco-Algerian commission dedicated to the issues of compensation for victims of nuclear tests.[60]

Chinese Nuclear Weapons Testing

After its first test on October 16, 1964, China exploded 45 nuclear bombs at the Lop Nor site, approximately 265 km south-east of Urumqi in the Xinjiang region in western China. The Xinjiang region is the largest Chinese administrative division and spans over 1.6 million square kilometres. It is

59 The long legacy of France's nuclear tests in Algeria, *The Economist*, June 24, 2021.

60 Collin Jean-Martin and Patric Bouveret, Radioactivity Under the Sand; The Waste From French Nuclear Tests in Algeria: Analysis with regard to the Treaty on the Prohibition of Nuclear Weapons, Heinrich Boll Foundation, July 2020, p. 13.

home to 20 million people from many different ethnic groups including Uyghur, Han, Kazakh, Hui, Kyrgyz, and Mongol. China is not a signatory to the treaty banning atmospheric nuclear weapons tests, and it conducted its last one in 1980. In 1986 it announced that it would refrain from further atmospheric testing.[61]

The 23 atmospheric and 22 underground tests ranged in yield from about 1 kt to about 4 Mt. China's largest atmospheric test was 4Mt, conducted on November 17, 1976; its largest underground test was 660 kt. conducted on May 21, 1992. The effects of China's nuclear testing on human health, animals and the environment are largely unexplored owing to the lack of publicly available official data. It has been reported that a few hundred thousand people may have died as a result of radiation from at least 40 nuclear explosions carried out between 1964 and 1996 at the Lop Nur site in Xinjiang. Most damages to Xinjiang locals came from detonations during the 1960s and 1970s, which rained down a mixture of radioactive material and sand from the surrounding desert. According to an estimate, the peak radiation dose in Xinjiang exceeded that measured on the roof of the Chernobyl nuclear reactor after it melted down in 1986.[62]

According to International Physicians for the Prevention of Nuclear War (IPPNW), the following amounts of radioactivity as having been released from Lop Nor:

> The total amount of plutonium-239 released to the atmosphere as a result of the 23 atmospheric nuclear tests is estimated at 3,300 curies, assuming 150 curies per test. One-millionth of a gram of plutonium-239 can cause cancer if inhaled. The amount of plutonium-239 still contained within the Lop Nor site in 1991 as a result of underground nuclear testing. In addition, two million curies of caesium-137 and 1.3 million curies of strontium-90 were released into the atmosphere. Roughly 60 percent of the caesium and strontium still remain in the atmosphere, on the ground, and in bodies of water.[63]

---

61 Radioactive Heaven and Earth: The health and environmental effects of nuclear weapons testing in, on, and above the earth, 1991, Report of the IPPNW International Commission to Investigate the Health and Environmental Effects of Nuclear Weapons Production and the Institute for Energy and Environmental Research, New York: The Apex Press, p. 151.

62 Zeeya Merali, Did China's Nuclear Tests Kill Thousands and Doom Future Generations? *Scientific American*, July 2009. Available at: https://www.scientificamerican.com/article/did-chinas-nuclear-tests/.

63 Radioactive Heaven and Earth: The health and environmental effects of nuclear

Currently, the former Soviet region of Semipalatinsk (Semey) is the most heavily contaminated among the Soviet nuclear test sites. Following detailed investigations, it was found that radioactive pollution is not only due to Soviet nuclear tests but also to the nuclear tests conducted by China in the Tarim Basin.[64] China, however, claims that atmospheric testing did not cause any radioactive harm to the neighbouring countries downwind of China, or the regions of Beijing, Lanzhou, or Dunhuang, based on over 20 years of surveys. According to senior Chinese military officials, no large disasters have happened due to nuclear weapons testing in China.[65] China has not permitted any independent assessment of the environmental or health impacts of its nuclear testing program.

Nuclear Weapon Testing: India, Israel, Pakistan and North Korea

India has conducted underground tests for nuclear weapons. India's choice of plutonium technology was determined by economic and practical reasons. Plutonium is highly radioactive and the dangers of radioactive contamination can be very serious. As little as 0.6 millionth of a gram taken into the body can cause death. However, India has an excellent record for nuclear safety and ensured a minimum likelihood of any contamination affecting the local population.[66] The tests conducted were with a fission device, a low-yield device, and a thermonuclear device.[67] Given the relatively lower number of tests, which have occurred underground, little is currently known about the impact of nuclear testing in Pakistan (six underground tests) and North Korea (six underground tests). While experts agree that Israel possesses nuclear weapons, no open-source exists

---

weapons testing in, on, and above the earth, 1991, Report of the IPPNW International Commission to Investigate the Health and Environmental Effects of Nuclear Weapons Production and the Institute for Energy and Environmental Research, New York: The Apex Press, p. 153.

64 Pravalie Remus, Nuclear Weapons Tests and Environmental Consequences: A Global Perspective, *Ambio*, Vol. 43, 2014, pp. 729-744.

65 How the Chinese military defines a "large disaster" is not known. However,this statement indicates that, at the very least, there have been some deaths attributable to nuclear testing, pointing to the possible occurrence of serious contamination or of accidents. *Ibid*, pp. 151-152.

66 Gosling David, India's Nuclear Explosion: Its Effects upon Environment, *Economic and Political Weekly*, Vol. 9, No. 26, June 29, 1974, pp. 1002-1004.

67 Burns John F., India sets 3 nuclear blasts, defying a worldwide ban; tests bring a sharp outcry, *The New York Times*, May 12, 1998.

on the nuclear weapons testing by Israel.[68]

South Africa is suspected to have conducted a nuclear test as part of a nuclear weapons development program undertaken with possible Israeli collaboration. As reported, on September 22, 1979, the US surveillance satellite detected a signal in the South Atlantic, southwest of the Cape of Good Hope that appeared to be from a nuclear explosion. The flash resembled a two-kiloton explosion of a weapon designed to be fired from field artillery. There is no official confirmation of this test and is subject to considerable controversy.[69]

Nuclear Weapons Facilities

A nuclear weapon facility would constitute the nuclear weapons complex producing nuclear materials, fabricating nuclear and non-nuclear components, assembly and disassembly of nuclear warheads, conducting scientific research and maintaining the reliability of existing warheads, integrating components with nuclear weapons delivery vehicles, and conducting support operations.[70] The transportation of nuclear weapons material places workers and residents living near weapons facilities at grave health risks.[71] There is evidence of major health, safety and environmental problems at nuclear weapons complexes around the world. This is most apparent in the US and Russia, which hold approximately 95% of the world's nuclear weapons. Accidental leakage of liquid radioactive waste

68 Cochran Thomas B., The Relevance of Mordechai Vanunu Disclosures to Israel's National Security, Presented at the International Conference Democracy, Disarmament and Human Rights: The Case of Mordechai Vanunu, 14-15 October 1996, Natural Resources Defence Council, Inc, Washington D.C., pp. 8.

69 Burr William, et. al., Blast from the Past, *Foreign Policy*, September 22, 2019.

70 The US Nuclear Weapons Complex: Overview of Department of Energy Sites, Congressional Research Service, R45306, March 31, 2021, p. 35.

71 In March 1990, there was a federal criminal inquiry into allegations that the US Department of Energy and Rockwell International Company, former operator of the Rocky Flats Weapons facility near Denver, had dumped hazardous wastes illegally and had lied to cover up violations. Rockwell subsequently pleaded guilty to charges of illegally storing and disposing of radioactive and other waste. Rockwell settled out of court in 1992, paying an $18.5 million fine, then the largest environmental penalty ever imposed. Dismantling of the plant and cleanup of the highly contaminated site was undertaken in the mid-1990s and declared completed in 2005. In 2007, most of the site was designated a national wildlife refuge, with areas set aside for eventual recreational use, while the remainder was permanently closed to the public. *Rockwell to Plead Guilty and Pay Large Fine for Dumping Waste, The New York Times*, March 26, 1992; Also see; https://www.britannica.com/place/Rocky-Flats.

at Hanford, the former plutonium production complex in Washington, has contaminated soil and underground water resources.[72] The US Department of Energy has estimated that minimal remediation of the nuclear weapons complex will cost $230 billion over 75 years. Even at this level of expenditure, many sites and buildings will remain out-of-bounds for humans for the foreseeable future. The situation in Russia is even worse. While the US and the former Soviet Union, due to the sheer number of nuclear weapons produced, present by far the most disturbing pictures of radioactive contamination from weapons facilities, the problem is not confined to those two countries alone. Radioactive contamination from nuclear weapons facilities across the world will take an incalculable but heavy human and environmental toll for a very long time. As the nuclear power reactors and weapons facilities age they will get more and more contaminated, releasing greater amounts of long-lasting, active radioactive materials to the biosphere, increasing the radiation to human beings and the environment.

Radiation affects all living things—genetic material, cells, individual animals and plants, biological systems and the environment in general. When radiation hits a tissue or cell, it can kill the cell or damage it. If damaged, the cell can repair correctly; it can repair incorrectly but not reproduce, or it can repair incorrectly and reproduce. If a damaged cell reproduces it passes on the defects to future generations of cells. Furthermore, radiation can reduce immunity, making the animal more susceptible to other diseases that would have been fended off. Studies on both plants and animals have repeatedly shown that exposure to ionising radiation causes genetic mutations. It can also lead to cancer in humans and animals. However, attributing with certainty specific cancer to a specific episode of radiation exposure may not be possible because: (i) cancers may occur decades after the exposure; (ii) there is no way of distinguishing cancer caused by radiation from any other cancer; (iii) cancer is a common illness, with many other possible triggers; (iv) there are some difficulties in assessing the biological effects of low-level radioactivity; and (iv) radiation can spread over large distances, depending on weather patterns, and be

72 At Hanford, the former plutonium production complex in Washington, approximately 800 billion litres of low-level liquid radioactive waste were discharged directly into the soil over a 50-year period. Groundwater at Hanford has been contaminated with caesium-137, iodine-129, plutonium-239, heavy metals and other radioactive or toxic substances. High-level radioactive waste at Hanford is stored in 177 underground tanks, 70 of which have leaked. Hanford is possibly the most contaminated site in the US nuclear weapons complex. Sue Wareham, Nuclear weapons, nature and society, Medical Association for Prevention of War (Australia), November 2008.

dispersed in such a fashion that determining the dose received by specific people or animals is very difficult.[73] Relatively recent research indicates that radiation behaves in unexpected ways. Some radiation effects are not immediately visible and thus cannot be observed or quantified as indicators of damage.[74]

Animals in the vicinity of nuclear facilities unavoidably take up some radioactivity through water and nutrient cycles. The continuous creation and release of radioactive materials into the air, water, food webs, organisms and gene pools of our planet are a dangerous experiment by the nuclear power and weapons industry. The result of these continuous releases is what has been called "a thickening of the radiation environment." Ionising radiation effects are multiple, additive, cumulative and synergistic. The impacts on the present and future generations, but no major efforts have been made to assess these effects. Radioactive contamination of the environment and the organisms in it is a double whammy. It weakens the gene pool, thus reducing the ability of organisms to prevent or overcome environmental threats, and simultaneously increases the environmental stresses to which the organisms are exposed. This is especially disturbing when we realise that all future generations of species are in the genetic material of this generation of organisms.

Dismantling of Nuclear Weapons. In pursuant to the signing of disarmament treaties and unilateral decisions to reduce the number of nuclear warheads have resulted in the dismantling of surplus weapons and

---

73 Hard statistical evidence of genetic damage from radiation exposure being passed on to progeny in humans has long been lacking, despite overwhelming evidence of radiation-induced mutations in plant and animal experiments. Specifically, such damage in the descendants of Hiroshima and Nagasaki survivors has not been demonstrated thus far. However new evidence from New Zealand on survivors of the 1957-58 UK Operation Grapple nuclear tests in the Pacific shows three times the frequency of total chromosome changes (translocations) in the test veterans as in a control group. R. E. Rowland, et al., Elevated chromosome translocation frequencies in New Zealand nuclear test Veterans, Vol. 121, *Cytogenetics and Genome Research*, 2008, pp. 79-87.

74 Examples are cancer with a latency period that makes it difficult or impossible to attribute the cause. In addition, the mechanisms that cause cancer are multiple and interdependent. Radiation exposure to an organism that has already been exposed and stressed could be the final straw to result in a cancer. If an organism has greater immunity or few other factors present that cause cancer it might not get cancer, at that point. Diane D'Arrigo, Ionising Radiation from Nuclear Power and Its Impact on Animals, June 2004, p. 3, available at: http://www.nirs.org/radiation/radstds/radiationandanimals.pdf, accessed September 21, 2021.

other military equipment.[75] Nuclear disarmament is a complex process that includes many interrelated elements, from creating political conditions for disarmament and institutional structures to support the process to the actual dismantlement of nuclear warheads. A very large amount of weapon-related material produced during the Cold War has been eliminated or disposed of in the last few years.[76] The dismantling of surplus nuclear weapons generates large quantities of plutonium and highly enriched uranium (HEU), the two key ingredients of bombs. Both pose a hazard to human health, the environment and international security. Keeping these materials from contaminating the environment and from being used in future weapons poses a great challenge. Of the two, plutonium poses a greater problem[77] because of the relative ease with which it can be used in

75 The dismantling and disposal challenge can be broken into a number of categories: (i) The weapon platform (such as a tank, warplane, or intercontinental missile), which provides the carrier system for an array of nuclear, chemical, or conventional warheads, bombs, projectiles, and munition; (ii) The key materials (such as fissile materials in nuclear arms) contained in the different weapon systems; and (iii) An assortment of fuels and propellants, many of which have been specifically developed for military purposes and therefore are quite distinct from civilian-grade fuels. Susanne Kopte, Michael Renner, and Peter Wilke, The Cost of the Disarmament: Dismantlement of Weapons and the Disposal of Military Surplus, The Nonproliferation Review, Winter 1996, pp. 33-45.

76 Podvig Pavel and Ryan Snyder, Watch them go: Simplifying the elimination of fissile materials and nuclear weapons, The United Nations Institute for Disarmament Research (UNIDIR), 2019, p. 56.

77 Radioactive materials in nuclear warheads require measures to control health risks from occupational or environmental exposures for thousands of years. The radioactive half-lives (i.e., the time required for one-half of the material to undergo radioactive decay) of uranium-235 (the principal isotope in highly enriched uranium), plutonium-239, and plutonium-240 (the principal isotopes of plutonium in weapons) are approximately 700 million, 24 thousand, and 6.5 thousand years, respectively. The actual risk posed by a radioactive material is a combination of the material's half-life, the radiation emitted during decay, and its quantity. If ingested with food or water, most plutonium is poorly absorbed by the stomach and excreted. If inhaled, the amount remaining in the lungs depends on the particle size and form. Forms that dissolve easily may be absorbed and move to other parts of the body. Forms that dissolve less easily are often coughed up and possibly swallowed. Plutonium may remain in the lungs or move to the bones, liver, or other organs. It generally stays in the body for decades and continues to expose the surrounding tissues to radiation, which may eventually cause cancer. Cancer risks due to enriched uranium are not known; however, there is some evidence that very long-term, low-level exposure to insoluble uranium causes increased risk of lung cancer. The chemical toxicity of uranium is a health concern, especially for soluble compounds that can cause kidney damage. Diane D'Arrigo, Ionising Radiation from Nuclear Power and Its Impact on Animals, June 2004, p. 3, available at: http://www.nirs.org/radiation/radstds/radiationandanimals.pdf, accessed

weapons, the severe biological (one-millionth of an ounce can cause cancer if inhaled) and the environmental hazard it poses, and its radioactive decay half-life of 24,000 years.[78] Because it is less radioactive than plutonium, HEU poses less severe health and environmental hazards. However, it has a half-life[79] of more than 700 million years.[80]

Activities relating to the dismantling of nuclear warheads are ongoing at several sites in the US and Russia. There has been repeated criticism of the lack of line management attention to environmental, safety, and health issues at these sites. Though widespread environmental contamination with nuclear materials during dismantling is considered highly unlikely by the governments, an inadvertent nuclear detonation, an accident, or the scatter of nuclear materials from an explosion cannot be ruled out. The dismantling of nuclear warheads generates parts that contain chemical explosives, special nuclear and hazardous materials, and classified components. There is a possibility of exposure to hazardous material during the packaging, storage and transportation of these materials, as the dismantling facilities still employ inefficient processes/technologies and create large amounts of waste.[81]

The clean-up of contaminated sites, disposition of excess fissile material and dismantling of nuclear weapons contaminate the environment and threaten human health. The cleaning up and containment of radioactive products presents the biggest challenge, though there are risks involved in

September 20, 2021.

78 In November 1993, the RAND National Defence Research Institute study, funded by the US Department of Defence for processing and disposition options for plutonium and HEU made their assessment of plutonium's value: "We found that military plutonium is a liability rather than an asset." The RAND analysis predicted that plutonium fuel will not be economical for at least 50-100 years, and advised against storing plutonium in reactor- or weapon-usable forms. Quoted in *Facing Reality: Beyond the Bomb; Dismantling Nuclear Weapons and Disposing of Their Radioactive Wastes*, Peter Gray (ed.), the Council on the Department of Energy's Nuclear Weapons Complex of the Tides Foundation's Project for Participatory Democracy, 1996.

79 The radioactive half-life of the substance is the period of time over which the number of radioactive nuclei decreases by a factor of one-half.

80 Peter Gray (ed.), *Facing Reality: Beyond the Bomb; Dismantling Nuclear Weapons and Disposing of their Radioactive Wastes*, the Council on the Department of Energy's Nuclear Weapons Complex of the Tides Foundation's Project for Participatory Democracy, 1996.

81 US Congress, Office of Technology Assessment, *Dismantling the Bomb and Managing the Nuclear Materials, OTA-O-572*, Washington, DC: US Government Printing Office, September 1993, pp. 45-60.

the dismantling of nuclear weapons too. These include hazards to workers and environmental risks associated with non-nuclear aspects, such as missile destruction. For example, pursuant to the Intermediate-Range Nuclear Forces Treaty, hundreds of Pershing missiles were burned in the open air or exploded on a test stand at the Pueblo Army Depot in Colorado, United States. Such procedures release clouds of toxic hydrochloric acid when the missiles' solid fuel combines with moisture.[82]

Summation

The development of a nuclear weapon requires the use of extremely complex scientific knowledge. Once the scientific hypotheses have been applied to the construction of a nuclear device, it is necessary to validate them by actual testing to ensure the efficacy and safety of the bomb. After the Nagasaki and Hiroshima bombing in 1945, a large number of nuclear weapons tests have been undertaken in the atmosphere, on the Earth's surface, underground, underwater and in space. There are a total of over 65 sites throughout the world that have been used to explode more than 2000 nuclear devices for military or peaceful purposes. All these nuclear explosions have similar physical and biological impacts.

Every stage of nuclear weapons production, development, storage, deployment and use, and dismantling involves health and environmental hazards. Of all the activities connected with nuclear weapons, testing has been the most destructive of human health and the environment. China, France, India, Pakistan, Russia, the US and the UK have collectively conducted over 2,000 nuclear explosions for testing purposes. The largest US and Soviet nuclear tests were, respectively, a 15-megaton test in 1954, and a 50-megaton test in 1961. Radioisotopes, such as carbon-14, caesium-137, strontium-90 and plutonium-239 (half-lives 5,730 years, 30 years, 28 years and 24,400 years respectively), produced by nuclear tests, pose risks to the environment, and to current and future generations through ingestion, inhalation and absorption of external radiation.

The US, France and the UK have used distant locations to conduct their nuclear weapons testing. For more than 50 years beginning in 1945, the islands of the central and south Pacific and the deserts of Australia were used as a 'nuclear laboratory' to conduct more than 315 atmospheric

82 Health and Environmental Effects of the Production and Testing of Nuclear Weapons, available at:http://www.nuclearfiles.org/menu/key-issues/nuclear-weapons/issues/effects/effects-of-nuclear-weapons.htm, accessed September 20, 2021.

and underground nuclear tests. They used deserts and ocean sites because they appeared very vast empty spaces. But the sites were not empty. The Western nuclear powers showed little concern for the health and wellbeing of nearby indigenous communities and the civilian and military personnel who staffed the test sites as well as the natural environment.[83] The people of the Pacific regions have been suffering because nuclear weapons testing were undertaken without their prior knowledge or consent, their lands and seas have been contaminated by the testing of nuclear weapons by distant powers.

The first use and subsequent testing of nuclear weapons by most Nuclear Weapons States (NWS) is associated with lies, denials and betrayal. The US political as well as military leadership was well aware that the target at Hiroshima and Nagasaki were not military. The NWS have conducted nuclear test explosions on rural, minority, disenfranchised and colonised peoples. The US conducted nuclear test explosions in Pacific locations.[84] Soviet nuclear tests were conducted in Kazakhstan and the remote Arctic archipelago of Novaya Zemlya, home to the minority Nenetz people. Chinese nuclear tests were conducted at Lop Nur, in the Xinjiang Uygur Autonomous Region, home to the Uygur minority. The UK undertook its nuclear test explosions in Australia, most in the desert lands of the Maralinga Tjarutja people, and its larger thermonuclear test explosions in its then Pacific territory of the British Gilbert and Ellice Islands Colony. France conducted its nuclear tests in its then colony Algeria until forced by a rising independence struggle to relocate to the home of the Maohi people in its colony of French Polynesia. Attitudes of those conducting the test

83 Macmillan Nic, 2017, *Grappling with the Bomb: Britain's Pacific H-Bomb Tests*, Australian University Press, p.1.

84 The US conducted the "Castle Bravo" test of March 1, 1954 at Bikini, which was 1,000 times as powerful as the Hiroshima bomb. It was the largest US nuclear test ever conducted. The US military had learned many hours before the blast that winds were blowing towards inhabited islands, they chose not to evacuate those in the likely path, nor to delay the explosion. Unlike for other nuclear tests over the previous eight years, there was no warning given to the people on Rongelap and other downwind islands, nor were they moved. Two islands and part of a third were vaporized in the explosion, and fallout rained down on the food crops, water catchments, houses, land and bodies of children, women and men going about their daily activities. Children played with the unknown "snow" and rubbed it in their hair and on their skin. The residents of Rongelap, Ailinginae and Utrik Atolls were finally evacuated 60 hours, after having received near-lethal doses of radiation, the highest following a single test in the history of nuclear test explosions worldwide. For more details see: Ruff Tilman A., The humanitarian impact and implications of nuclear test explosions in the Pacific region, *International Review of the Red Cross*, Vol. 97, No. 899, pp. 775–813.

explosions often differentiated between their own "civilised" personnel and other "primitive" indigenous people. It set a higher maximum radiation dose limit for "primitive" Pacific people exceeding that recommended internationally, and different from that for "civilised."[85] There have been slow and incomplete developments towards accountability, care and compensation programs for those "primitive" harmed people.[86]

Stratospheric fallout results from radioactive particles being thrust into the upper atmosphere, such as by powerful nuclear detonations of more than a megaton. These particles may drift for months or even several years before they return to the earth's surface. Highly radioactive particles with a short half-life decay while remaining in the upper atmosphere. However, strontium-90 and caesium-137, which have long half-lives, are of particular concern, especially as they concentrate through the food chain. Strontium-90, with a half-life of 28 years, deposits in human bones and emits beta radiation over many years, posing a somatic hazard (to the nervous system). Children are especially at risk if their skeletons are in development at the time of exposure. Caesium-137 is both a threat when it falls on a person's skin and also when they eat products in which it has deposited. While it is eliminated from the body faster, caesium-137 emits both beta and gamma radiation and can cause both somatic and genetic damage.[87]

85 The document reveals that the acceptable dosage of radiation was different for British personnel than for the islanders who lived on Christmas Island and on neighbouring inhabited atolls. The British authorities prescribed maximum radiation dose limit for "primitive" Pacific people exceeding that recommended international and different from that of the British personnel. During the nuclear test the radiation dosage was about 15 times higher for "primitive" people that what could have been permitted by the International Commission of radiological Protection. It was further summarized that only "very slight health hazard to people would arise, and that only to primitive people." 'Danger Area', paper from Air Vice Marshall W.E Oulton, November 19,1956, GRA/TS.1008/1/Air. Only 14 copies of the paper, marked 'Top Secret—Guard', were prepared for the British Army and Navy, the Colonial Office, Commonwealth Relations Office and other authorities. CO1036/280. Also see: Macmillan Nic, 2017, *Grappling with the Bomb: Britain's Pacific H-Bomb Tests*, Australian National University Press, p. 113-114.

86 Ruff Tilman A., The humanitarian impact and implications of nuclear test explosions in the Pacific region, *International Review of the Red Cross*, Vol. 97, No. 899, pp. 775–813.

87 Effects of French Nuclear Testing on Radiation Levels in New Zealand, Request for the Indication of Interim Measures of Protection Submitted by the Government of New Zealand. *Nuclear Weapon Tests* (*New Zealand v. France*),p. 82, available at: http://www.icj-cij.org/files/case-related/59/10731.pdf.

Reportedly, the effects and risks of nuclear weapons testing have been underestimated due to the following reasons: (i) Nuclear weapon tests and their results remain state secrets and the information is controlled by a select few in the government and withheld from public view; (ii) Studies of the effects of atmospheric tests have been inadequate; (iii) The risks to future generations from underground testing have not been undertaken seriously; and (iv) The damage to natural environment and flora and fauna due to nuclear weapons tastings has been completely ignored. Many aspects of nuclear weapons testing have been characterised by a disregard, sometimes willful, of public health and the natural environment. Test sites around the world are contaminated. The effects, particularly of atmospheric testing, are global. International Physicians for the Prevention of Nuclear War (IPPNW) estimates that roughly 2.4 million people will eventually die due to cancer-related deaths as a result of the atmospheric nuclear tests conducted in the last 75 years.

Chapter III

Current Nuclear Arsenal and its Modernization Plan

Today, nine states—the US, the UK, Russia, France, China, India, Pakistan, Israel and the Democratic People's Republic of Korea (North Korea)—possess approximately 13,080 nuclear weapons. Out of these, some 3825 are deployed with operational forces and approximately 2000 are kept in a state of high operational alert. The availability of reliable information on the status of nuclear weapons and the capabilities of the nuclear-armed states varies considerably. The US, the UK and France have declared some information. Russia does not publicly disclose the breakdown of its nuclear forces and China releases little information about force numbers or future development plans. The governments of India and Pakistan make statements about some of their missile tests but provide no information about the status or size of their arsenals. North Korea has acknowledged conducting nuclear weapon and missile tests but provides no information about the size of its nuclear arsenal. Israel has been maintaining its policy of not commenting on its nuclear weapons.

Secrecy about the development of nuclear weapons (or for that matter any weapon system), has not been unique to Israel. All nuclear weapons states including India and Pakistan kept their initial development effort secret. Once they acquired nuclear weapons capability, they acknowledged their status while continuing to maintain secrecy concerning technical matters and doctrine.[1] The estimated number of nuclear weapons held by the nine states during the last ten years (2012-2021) is shown in the following table (Table 3.1).[2]

1 Cohen Avner, 1998, *Israel and the Bomb*, New York: Columbia University Press, p. 343.

2 All figures are approximate and are estimates based on assessments by the authors.

Table 3.1: Number of Nuclear Weapons: 2012-2021

	2012	2013	2014	2015	2016	2017	2018	2019	2020	2021
China	240	250	250	260	260	270	280	290	320	350
France	300	300	300	300	300	300	300	300	290	290
India	80-100	90-110	90-110	90-110	100-120	120-130	130-140	130-140	150	156
Israel	80	80	80	80	80	80	80	80-90	90	90
N Korea	?	6-8	6-8	6-8	10	10-20	10-20	20-30	30-40	[40-50][3]
Pakistan	90-110	100-120	100-120	100-120	100-130	130-140	140-150	150-160	160	165
Russia	10,000	8,500	8,000	7,500	7,290	7,000	6,850	6,500	6,375	6,255
UK	225	225	225	215	215	215	215	200	195-215	225
US	8,000	7,700	7,300	7,260	7,000	6,800	6,450	6,185	5,800	5,500
Total	**19,000**	**17,279**	**16,350**	**15,850**	**15,395**	**14,935**	**14,465**	**13,865**	**13,400**	**13,081**

(The estimates presented here are based on publicly available information and contain some uncertainties.)

3 This estimate lists the number of warheads N Korea could potentially build with the amount of fissile material it has produced. There is no publicly available evidence that North Korea has produced an operational nuclear warhead for delivery by an intercontinental-range ballistic missile, but it might have a small number of warheads for medium-range ballistic missiles.

Figure 3.1: Estimated Nuclear Weapons 2012-2021

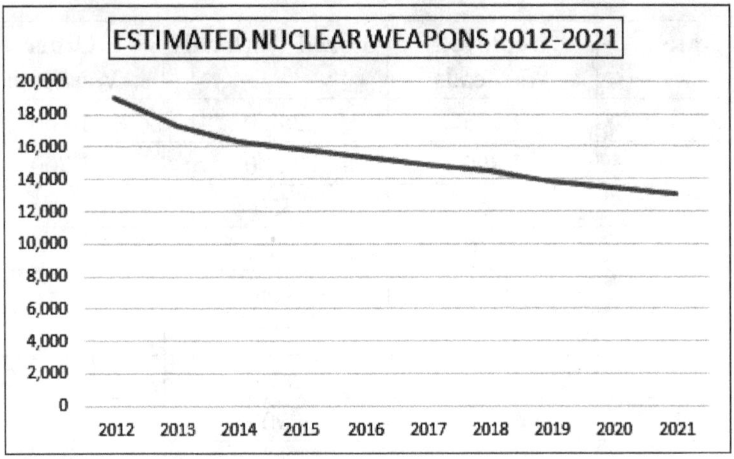

Figure 3.1 indicates a declining trend for nuclear weapons in the last decade. However, this is primarily because of the US and Russia dismantling retired warheads. The SIPRI Yearbook of 2021 provides the following detailed status (Table 3.2 and Figure 3.2) of the nuclear warhead inventory of the nine states.[4]

Figure 3.2: Estimated Current Nuclear Weapon Inventory

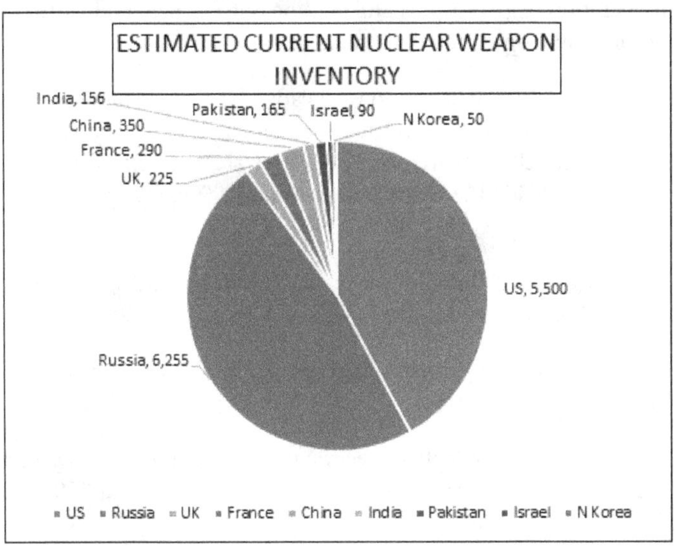

4 *SIPRI Yearbook 2021, Armaments, Disarmament and International Security*, Oxford: Oxford University Press, p. 334.

Table 3.2: Estimated Current Status of Nuclear Warheads Inventory

State	Deployed Warheads	Stored Warheads	Other Warheads
Russia	1,625	2,870	1,760
US	1,800	2,000	1,700
China	-	350	-
France	280	10	-
UK	120	105	-
Pakistan	-	165	-
India	-	156	-
Israel	-	90	-
N Korea	-	-	40-50
Total	3,825	5,746	3,510

Explanation:

- Deployed warheads as shown in the above table are placed on missiles or located on bases with operational forces.
- Stored warheads are in central storage that would require some preparation (e.g. transport and loading onto launchers) before they could become fully operationally available.
- The figures of 1,800 deployed warheads of the US includes approximately 1400 deployed on ballistic missiles and nearly 300 stored at bomber bases in the USA, as well as 100 non-strategic (tactical) nuclear bombs deployed outside the US at North Atlantic Treaty Organization partner bases.
- The figures of 2,000 stored warheads of the US included 130 non-strategic nuclear bombs stored in the USA.
- The figure of 1,750 other warheads of the US is for retired warheads awaiting dismantlement.
- The figure of 1,625 deployed warheads of Russia includes approximately 1425 strategic warheads on ballistic missiles and about 200 deployed at heavy bomber bases.
- The figure of 2,870 stored warheads of Russia includes 960 strategic and 1,910 non-strategic warheads in central storage.

- The British Government declared in 2010 that its nuclear weapon inventory would not exceed 225 warheads. It is estimated that the inventory remained at that number in January 2021. A planned reduction to an inventory of 180 warheads by the mid-2020s was ended by a government review undertaken in 2020 and published in early 2021. The review introduced a new ceiling of 260 warheads.

- The 10 stores warheads assigned to France's carrier-based aircraft are thought to be kept in central storage and are not normally deployed.

- This estimate about N Korea is the number of warheads it could potentially build with the amount of fissile material it has produced. There is no publicly available evidence that N Korea has produced an operational nuclear warhead for delivery by an intercontinental-range ballistic missile, but it might have a small number of warheads for medium-range ballistic missiles.

Modernization Plan of Nuclear Weapons

The world is witnessing a new, dangerous nuclear arms race as the US, Russia and China are rushing to modernize their nuclear arsenals. The term modernization, in this context, consists of three elements of NW capabilities: First, the existing ageing arsenal is replaced with the new but similar weapons to retire or supplement the existing stockpiles; second, the modernization and expansion of the size of existing stockpiles; and third, the development of new types of nuclear weapons, delivery platforms, or integration of new technology into the doctrine to supplement the nuclear arsenal.[5] The modernization applies to all elements of strategic weapons and includes various delivery systems. In the context of nuclear weapons, it may include the followings: (i) the refurbishing of nuclear warhead; (ii) modernization of delivery systems; (iii) revitalization of command & control, and communication systems; (iv) modernization of the production complexes by creating new facilities; (v) implementation of nuclear force improvement to address any setbacks.[6] A modernized nuclear warhead could be able to strike targets more accurately with a smaller explosive yield and reduce radioactive fallout from a nuclear attack and become more military attractive.

5 Warren Aiden and Philip M. Baxter, "Introduction", in Warren Aiden and Philip M. Baxter (ed.), 2020, *Nuclear Modernization in the 21st Century*, London: Rutledge, p. 5.

6 Warren Aiden, "US nuclear weapons modernization and the impact on the nuclear nonproliferation regime," in Warren Aiden and Philip M. Baxter (ed.), 2020, *Nuclear Modernization in the 21st Century*, London: Rutledge, pp. 94-95.

The US and Russia have extensive programmes to replace and modernize their nuclear warheads, missile and aircraft delivery systems, and nuclear weapon production facilities. Both countries have also given new or expanded roles to nuclear weapons in their military plans and doctrines. The nuclear arsenals of the other nuclear-armed states are relatively smaller but all these states are either developing or deploying new weapon systems or have announced their intention to do so. China is in the middle of a significant modernization of its nuclear arsenal. It is developing a nuclear triad [7] for the first time, made up of new land- and sea-based missiles and nuclear-capable aircraft. India and Pakistan are slowly increasing the size and diversity of their nuclear forces, while North Korea continues to prioritize its military nuclear programme as a central element of its national security strategy. However, modernization of the nuclear arsenal is an expensive process. In this chapter, the process of modernization of nuclear weapons and their delivery systems undertaken by the nuclear-weapon states has been covered.[8]

The United States

The United States (US) has the largest deployed nuclear arsenal. Since the 1990s, every US presidential administration has published a Nuclear Posture Review (NPR) that explains the rationales behind its nuclear

7 The nuclear triad consists of land-based intercontinental ballistic missiles (ICBMs), submarine launched ballistic missile (SLBMs), and strategic bomber aircraft. Each leg of the nuclear triad possesses unique strengths that collectively provide a well-balanced capability and greatly improve the security of the state. Removing one leg of the triad would destabilize the effectiveness of the overall nuclear deterrence a state enjoys.

8 The availability of reliable information on the status of the nuclear arsenals and capabilities of the nuclear-armed states varies considerably. The US has disclosed important information about its stockpile and nuclear capabilities but in 2019 the US administration ended the practice of publicly disclosing the size of the US stockpile. The UK and France have also declared some information. Russia does not make publicly available a detailed breakdown of its forces counted under New START, even though it shares this information with the USA. The governments of India and Pakistan make statements about some of their missile tests but provide little information about the status or size of their arsenals. North Korea has acknowledged conducting nuclear weapon and missile tests but provides no information about its nuclear weapon capabilities. Israel has a long-standing policy of not commenting on its nuclear arsenal. Available at:https://www.sipri.org/media/press-release/2020/nuclear-weapon-modernization-continues-outlook-arms-control-bleak-new-sipri-yearbook-out-now.

strategy, doctrine, and requested forces. These reviews have helped inform US government personnel, citizens, allies, and adversaries of the country's intentions and planned capabilities for conducting nuclear deterrence and, if necessary, war. The NPR published by the Trump administration in 2018 states:[9]

> "The United States remains committed to its efforts in support of the ultimate global elimination of nuclear, biological, and chemical weapons. It has reduced the nuclear stockpile by over 85 percent since the height of the Cold War and deployed no new nuclear capabilities for over two decades. Nevertheless, global threat conditions have worsened markedly since the most recent 2010 NPR, including increasingly explicit nuclear threats from potential adversaries. The United States now faces a more diverse and advanced nuclear-threat environment than ever before, with considerable dynamism in potential adversaries' development and deployment programs for nuclear weapons and delivery systems. While the US has continued to reduce the number and salience of nuclear weapons, others, including Russia and China, have moved in the opposite direction. They have added new types of nuclear capabilities to their arsenals, increased the salience of nuclear forces in their strategies and plans, and engaged in increasingly aggressive behaviour, including in outer space and cyberspace. There now exists an unprecedented range and mix of threats, including major conventional, chemical, biological, nuclear, space, and cyber threats, and violent non-state actors. These developments have produced increased uncertainty and risk. Given the diverse threats and profound uncertainties of the current and future threat environment, US nuclear forces play the following critical roles in US national security strategy. They contribute to the: (i) Deterrence of nuclear and non-nuclear attack; (ii) Assurance of allies and partners; (iii) Achievement of US objectives if deterrence fails; and (iv) Capacity to hedge against an uncertain future."

The current US nuclear modernization strategy includes the Ground-Based Strategic Deterrent (GBSD), the B-21 bomber, the Columbia-class submarine, the Long-Range Standoff (LRSO) air-launched cruise missile, the sea-launched nuclear cruise missile, and new nuclear warheads. The

9 Nuclear Posture Review: 2018, Department of Defence, United States of America, p. 74.

US plans to overhaul its nuclear arsenal by rebuilding each leg of the nuclear triad and its accompanying infrastructure. The plans include but are not limited to, a new class of ballistic missile submarines, a new set of silo-based intercontinental ballistic missiles, a new nuclear cruise missile, a modified gravity bomb, a new stealthy long-range strike bomber, and accompanying warheads (with modified or new warhead pits) for each delivery system. The US nuclear weapons were modernized during the presidency of Barack Obama, which comprised the development of new nuclear warheads and weapon delivery systems. It is estimated that this modernization would finally cost more than a trillion US dollars over the next thirty years to maintain its current nuclear arsenal and procure a new generation of nuclear-armed or nuclear-capable bombers, submarines, SLBMs, and ICBMs.[10] In 2017, the Congressional Budget Office (CBO) report estimated that the 30-year cost of nuclear weapons modernization would be $1.2 trillion, which could become $1.7 trillion if inflation is added.[11]The select major nuclear weapons modernization programme of the US is shown in Table 3.3.

10 In January 2014, the James Martin Centre for Nonproliferation Studies (CNS) released its report, "*The Trillion Dollar Nuclear Triad: US Strategic Nuclear Modernization over the Next Thirty Years*." The report concludes that the US will likely spend over $1 trillion during the next three decades to maintain its current nuclear arsenal and purchase their replacement systems. The US plans (from 2024-2029) to build five strategic submarines, 72 strategic bombers, and 240 intercontinental ballistic missiles (ICBMs). This represents more delivery vehicles than the combined nuclear forces of China, the UK and France.

11 Estimating nuclear weapons modernization costs is difficult. To make matters more complicated, nuclear weapons modernization involves long time frames, which makes initial cost estimates unreliable. In addition, nuclear warhead modernization activities are often lumped together with nonnuclear activities like nonproliferation or environmental clean-up. Since budget categories occasionally change year-to-year, it makes assessing their cumulative value over time even more difficult. Since nuclear forces take decades to develop and deploy, some oft-cited estimates tally their costs over a 30-year time frame. The longer the time frame, the more uncertainty estimates they entail. Dodge Michaela, "The Cost of Nuclear Deterrence", in Lowther Adam (ed.), 2020, *Guide to Nuclear Deterrence in the Age of Great-Power Competition*, Bossier City, LA: Louisiana Tech Research Institute, pp. 51-64; The US Nuclear Modernization Programmes: Fact Sheets and Briefs, Arms Control Association, August 2018, available at: https://www.armscontrol.org/factsheets/USNuclearModernization.

Table 3.3: Major Nuclear Weapons Modernization Programme of the US

Triad Leg	Weapon	Plan	Estimated Request	FY21 Request $	Total Cost Estimate US$
Air	B-21 Strategic Bomber	New	175	2.8 billion	97 billion
	Long-Range Standoff Weapon	New	1000	474.4 million	11 billion
	B61-12 Gravity Bomb	Modification	480	45.4 million	10 billion
	W80-4	Life Extension	N.A.	1 billion	12 billion
Sea	Columbia Class Submarine	New	12	4.4 billion	128 billion
	Trident II D5 Missile	Modification	N.A.	1.2 billion	19 billion
	W88	Life Extension	N.A.	257 million	3 billion
	S93	New	N.A.	53 million	14 billion
Ground	Ground-based Strategic Deterrent	New	659	1.5 billion	100 billion
	W87-1	Modification	N.A.	541 million	15 billion

The US military has upgraded and refurbished nearly all of its existing strategic and tactical delivery systems and the warheads they carry to last well beyond their originally planned service life and is now in the early stages of replacing many of these ageing systems with new systems. The overall nuclear modernization plan includes modernized strategic delivery systems, refurbished nuclear warheads, modernized production complex, upgrading command and control systems including communication and early warning, and upgrading command of air force nuclear force to a four-star general rank. The production complex that maintains and produces nuclear weapons and their delivery vehicles is also undergoing significant modernization. Although some modernizations were designed to reduce the size of the stockpile, such as the B61-12 programme, future production of the nuclear SMCM would likely increase for the first time since the post-Cold War period.[12]

The 2018 NPR reaffirmed the US commitment to the nuclear triad and to the modernization programmes for each of the components of that force structure.[13] It noted that "the triad's synergy and overlapping attributes help ensure the enduring survivability of our deterrence capabilities against the attack and our capacity to hold a range of adversary targets at risk throughout a crisis or conflict. Eliminating any leg of the triad would greatly ease adversary attack planning and allow an adversary to concentrate resources and attention on defeating the remaining two legs." [14] The NPR asserts that the total cost of modernization is an affordable priority and a small portion of the overall defence budget.[15] The USAF has started the development of a next-generation ICBM, the Ground-Based Strategic Deterrent (GBSD). It is scheduled to begin replacing the Minuteman III in 2028, with full replacement by 2036. The USAF is also modernizing the nuclear warheads that will be used to arm the GBSD.

Russia

The Soviet Union, at the peak of the Cold War, had stockpiled nearly 45,000 nuclear warheads and had developed a variety of missile systems.[16]

12 Kristensen Hans M., "US modernization efforts and the 2018 Nuclear Posture Review," in Warren Aiden and Philip M. Baxter (ed.), 2020, *Nuclear Modernization in the 21st Century*, London: Rutledge, p. 21.

13 The Trump administration envisaged an increased probability for a nuclear response to a strategic nonnuclear attack, for example, cyber-attacks that might cause large numbers of US or allied casualties; widespread destruction of critical infrastructure, including electric power grids, communications, and digital supervisory control and data acquisition systems; and, especially, cyber-attacks against components of nuclear command, control, and communications (C3) and early warning systems. Cimbala Stephen J., The Trump Nuclear Posture Review: Three Issues, Nine Implications, *Strategic Studies Quarterly*, Summer 2018, pp. 9-16.

14 US Department of State, Bureau of State, Bureau of Arms Control, Verification, and Compliance, New START Treaty Aggregate Numbers of Strategic Offensive Forces, Fact Sheet, Washington, DC, p. 43, available at: https://www.state.gov/newstart-treaty-aggregate-numbers-of-strategic-offensive-arms-15/.

15 Kristensen Hans M., "US modernization efforts and the 2018 Nuclear Posture Review," in Warren Aiden and Philip M. Baxter (ed.), 2020, *Nuclear Modernization in the 21st Century*, London: Rutledge, pp. 12-24.

16 Baxter Philip M., "Russia's nuclear modernization," in Warren Aiden and Philip M.

Since the dissolution of the Soviet Union, there has been a significant reduction in its nuclear arsenal and Russia now holds an inventory of 6,255 nuclear warheads. Russia's "Basic Principles of State Policy of the Russian Federation on Nuclear Deterrence", approved by President Putin in June 2020, states that the Russian Federation considers nuclear weapons exclusively as a means of deterrence. The policy lays out four conditions under which Russia could launch nuclear weapons:

- The arrival of reliable data on a launch of ballistic missiles attacking the territory of the Russian Federation and/or its allies;
- Use of nuclear weapons or other types of weapons of mass destruction by an adversary against the Russian Federation and/ or its allies;
- Attack by an adversary against critical governmental or military sites of the Russian Federation, disruption of which would undermine nuclear forces response actions;
- Aggression against the Russian Federation with the use of conventional weapons when the very existence of the state is in jeopardy.

However, the Russian military planners are pursuing a broad range of upgraded and new versions of nuclear weapons. It suggests that the real doctrine goes beyond basic deterrence and toward regional war-fighting strategies or even weapons aimed at causing terror.[17] Russia has significantly reduced the number of warheads deployed on its ballistic missiles to meet the New START limit of no more than 1,550 deployed strategic warheads. Russia achieved the required reduction by February 5, 2018, when it declared 1,444 strategic warheads attributed to 527 launchers. The most recent data of September 1, 2020, listed Russia with 1,447 deployed warheads attributed to 510 strategic launchers. Russia's nuclear arsenal includes a stockpile of nearly 4,500 warheads. Of these, some 1,600 strategic warheads are deployed on ballistic missiles and at heavy bomber bases, while an additional 985 strategic warheads, along with 1,912 non-strategic warheads, are held in reserve. The Russian arsenal is continuing

---

Baxter (ed.), 2020, *Nuclear Modernization in the 21st Century*, London: Rutledge, pp. 25-39.

17 Hans M. Kristensen Hans M. and Matt Korda, Russian nuclear weapons, *Bulletin of the Atomic Scientists*, Vol. 77:2, 2021, p. 93.

broad modernization intended to replace most Soviet-era weapons by the mid-to-late 2020s.

In two recent conflicts where Russia occupied Crimea in February 2014 and subsequently intervened in the Donbas area of Ukraine, it has demonstrated willingness to use nuclear weapons should conflict escalate.[18] Russia has also made nuclear modernization a major military priority. Russia is in the middle of a decades-long modernization of its strategic and non-strategic nuclear forces to replace Soviet-era weapons with newer systems. Russia's nuclear modernization programmes, combined with an increase in the number and size of military exercises and occasional explicit nuclear threats against other countries, contribute to uncertainty about Russia's long-term intentions and growing international debate about the nature of its nuclear strategy.[19] These concerns, in turn, stimulate increased defence spending, nuclear modernization programmes, and political opposition to further nuclear weapons reductions in Western Europe and the US. Russia's nuclear modernization programme is motivated in part by Moscow's strong desire to maintain overall parity with the US, but also by the Russian leadership's apparent conviction that the US ballistic missile defence system constitutes a real future risk to the credibility of Russia's retaliatory capability.

During the Cold War, the US and Soviet Union both deployed non-strategic nuclear weapons for use in the field during a conflict. In 1991, the US and Soviet Union both withdrew from deployment most and eliminated from their arsenal many of their non-strategic nuclear weapons.[20]

18 Eldridge Colby, *The Role of Nuclear Weapons in the U.S.-Russian Relationship*, white paper, Washington, DC: Carnegie Endowment for International Peace, February 26, 2016.

19 Russia, like the US, could potentially upload several hundreds of extra warheads onto their launchers, but is prevented from doing so by the New START treaty limit, which has been extended for an additional five years to 2026. The treaty provides for important transparency of Russian (and US) strategic nuclear forces: As of December 2020, the US and Russia have completed a combined 328 on-site inspections and exchanged 21,293 notifications. Due to the ongoing Covid-19 pandemic, there have been no on-site Type One or Type Two inspections since April1, 2020. Hans M. Kristensen Hans M. and Matt Korda, Russian nuclear weapons, *Bulletin of the Atomic Scientists*, Vol. 77:2, 2021, p. 90-108

20 The US now has, according to unclassified estimates, approximately 230 nonstrategic nuclear weapons, with around 100 deployed with aircraft in Europe and the remaining stored in the United States. Estimates vary, but experts believe Russia still has between 1,000 and 2,000 warheads for nonstrategic nuclear weapons in its arsenal. Woolf Amy F., Nonstrategic Nuclear Weapons, Congressional Research Service, RL32572, July 15,

China

China became a nuclear weapons state in 1964. Severe financial constraints required China to make several unique decisions regarding the structure and operations of its nuclear forces.[21] Its nuclear arsenal has increased in the last ten years from 240 warheads to 350. The 2018 US *Nuclear Posture Review*, for the first time, described China as a potential adversary of the United States. The *Review* states that China is modernizing and increasing the number, capabilities, and protection of its nuclear forces. China is pursuing entirely new nuclear capabilities tailored to achieve particular national security objectives and its military modernization has resulted in an expanded nuclear force, with little to no transparency into its intentions.[22] China has announced the development of a new nuclear-capable strategic bomber, giving China a nuclear triad. China has also deployed a nuclear-capable precision-guided DF-26 intermediate-range ballistic missile capable of attacking land and naval targets.[23]Like the US, China's declaratory policy and doctrine have not changed, its lack of transparency regarding the scope and scale of its nuclear modernization programme raises questions regarding its future intent.[24] A 2006 RAND

2021, p. 44.

21 Stephen Polk, "China's Nuclear Command and Control," in Goldstein Lyle J., (ed.) *China's Nuclear Force Modernization*, Naval War College Newport, Papers, No. 22, 2005, p. 7.

22 Nuclear Posture Review: 2018, Department of Defence, United States of America, p. 74.

23 China has developed a new road-mobile strategic intercontinental ballistic missile (ICBM), a new multi-warhead version of its DF-5 silo-based ICBM, and its most advanced ballistic missile submarine armed with new submarine-launched ballistic missiles (SLBM). *Ibid*, p. 11.

24 In the summer of 1995, the underground Great Wall project was completed in China, giving the Second Artillery Corps underground facilities for fighting, defending from attacks, maintaining a nuclear stockpile, commanding its nuclear forces, and living. China's land-based strategic nuclear force can retaliate in as few as ten minutes after a nuclear strike, and soldiers from the Second Artillery Corps can live in bunkers for up to a month after a strike. Since 1995, China has had a true, reliable second-strike capability. Hui Zhang, a researcher at Harvard University's Belfer Center for Science and International Affairs, described the infrastructure built by the underground Great Wall project: "These tunnels are hundreds of meters underground, in deep mountainous areas, and are difficult to detect from space. They can withstand nuclear and conventional attacks. The missiles, personnel, and related equipment can be transported by rails and trucks within the network of tunnels to various locations. All the activities for launch preparation can be done in the tunnels without detection. Some of the tunnels could also be used for logistical support or as command and

Corporation study characterized the earliest Chinese nuclear strategy as "existential deterrence," which later evolved into "minimal deterrence" and is currently evolving further into "credible minimal deterrence."[25]

In December 2006, the Chinese government published China's nuclear strategy for the first time in the white paper titled "China's National Defense in 2006." According to the white paper, China is: "Pursuing a self-defensive nuclear strategy. China's nuclear strategy is subject to the state's nuclear policy and military strategy. Its fundamental goal is to deter other countries from using or threatening to use nuclear weapons against China. China remains firmly committed to the policy of no first use of nuclear weapons at any time and under any circumstances. It unconditionally undertakes not to use or threaten to use nuclear weapons against non-nuclear-weapon states or nuclear-weapon-free zones and stands for the comprehensive prohibition and complete elimination of nuclear weapons. China upholds the principles of counterattack in self-defence and limited development of nuclear weapons and aims at building a lean and effective nuclear force capable of meeting national security needs. It endeavours to ensure the security and reliability of its nuclear weapons and maintains a credible nuclear deterrent force. China's nuclear force is under the direct command of the Central Military Commission (CMC). China exercises great restraint in developing its nuclear force. It has never entered into and will never enter into a nuclear arms race with any other country."[26] Similar to the nuclear doctrines of other nuclear-weapon states, China's doctrine has five elements: declaration, nuclear development, nuclear deployment, nuclear employment, and nuclear disarmament. The declared policy element of China's nuclear doctrine is of no first use. China pledges to use nuclear weapons only in self-defence. Since China developed atomic weapons, China has made it very clear that it will not use nuclear weapons first at any time and under any circumstance. Evidence suggests that China seeks to transition from a purely defensive nuclear posture with relatively

control facilities."Hui Zhang, China's Nuclear Weapons Modernization: Intentions, Drivers, and Trends, Belfer Centre for Science and International Affairs, July 15, 2012.Available at: https://www.belfercenter.org/publication/chinas-nuclear-weapons-modernization-intentions-drivers-and-trends.

25 James C. Mulvenon, et al., Chinese Responses to US Military Transformation and Implications for the Department of Defence, Santa Monica, CA: RAND Corporation, 2006, p. 97.

26 China's National Defence in 2006, Information Office of the State Council of the People's Republic of China, December 29, 2006, p. 5, available at; http://fas.org/nuke/guide/china/doctrine/wp2006.html.

minimal options for retaliatory responses (minimum deterrence) to a nuclear posture that is more flexible and able to engage in nuclear war-fighting (limited deterrence).[27]

China has been pushing its nuclear expansion and modernization efforts.[28] As reported, recent improvements to Chinese nuclear forces have been broadly consistent both with a desire to maintain an assured retaliatory capability and with a no-first-use doctrine, although recent developments will provide China with other possible employment strategies. China is enhancing the striking power and survivability of its theatre and strategic missile forces and improving its ability to counter missile defence developments.[29] China is also stepping up its naval and aerial arms of the nuclear triad, including the development of an air-launched ballistic missile possibly with nuclear capability.

China's leaders are planning to strengthen the PLA into a "world-class" military in the next 30 years to rejuvenate it into a "great modern socialist country." However, the People's Republic of China (PRC) has not defined what it means by its ambition to have a "world-class" military by the end of 2049. The PRC is developing new intercontinental ballistic missiles (ICBMs) that will significantly improve its nuclear-capable missile forces. The number of warheads on the PRC's land-based ICBMs capable of threatening the US is expected to grow to roughly 200 in the next

27 Haynes Susan Turner, "Chinese nuclear strategy," in Warren Aiden and Philip M. Baxter (ed.), 2020, *Nuclear Modernization in the 21st Century*, London: Rutledge, pp. 61-85.

28 According to the "Nuclear Notebook" report on *Chinese Nuclear Forces: 2020*, China has continued to deploy the DF-26 intermediate-range ballistic missile (IRBM), and replaced the older road-mobile DF-31A ICBM launchers with "the more maneuverable DF-31AG launcher." The report also noted that China is in the early stage of deploying the new DF-41, a road- and rail-mobile ICBM with multiple independently targetable reentry vehicles (MIRVs). *SIPRI Yearbook 2021*, Armaments, Disarmament and International Security, Oxford: Oxford University Press.

29 For theater nuclear deterrence missions, China currently maintains DF-21 and DF-21A medium-range ballistic missiles (MRBMs) and two classes of intermediate-range ballistic missiles (IRBMs), the aging DF-3 and the newly revealed, and highly accurate, DF-26. China's nuclear ICBM force consists of limited-range DF-4s, silo-based DF-5As and DF-5Bs, and road-mobile DF-31s and DF-31As. Beijing is also moving toward a sea-based nuclear deterrent capability based on the Jin-class (Type 094) SSBN and the JL-2 SLBM. Scholars and analysts estimate that, as of early 2016, China's nuclear stockpile includes roughly 260 nuclear warheads, of which about 134 could be mounted on existing ICBMs and SLBMs. Heginbotham Eric, et al., 2017, *China's Evolving Nuclear Deterrence: Major Drivers and Issues for the United States*, RAND Corporation, p. 37.

five years. The PRC is expanding its inventory of the multi-role DF-26, a mobile, ground-launched intermediate-range ballistic missile system capable of rapidly swapping conventional and nuclear warheads.[30] It has been reported that China's nuclear forces will significantly evolve over the next decade as it modernizes, diversifies, and increases the number of its land-, sea-, and air-based nuclear delivery platforms. Over the next decade, China's nuclear warhead stockpile is projected to at least double in size as China expands and modernizes its nuclear forces. China is pursuing a "nuclear triad" with the development of a nuclear-capable air-launched ballistic missile (ALBM) and improving its ground and sea-based nuclear capabilities. A few developments which took place in 2019 further suggest that China intends to increase the peacetime readiness of its nuclear forces by moving to a launch-on-warning (LOW) posture with an expanded silo-based force.[31]

In light of China's expanding nuclear inventory, authorities in the US and Russia may be reluctant to pursue a follow-on US-Russian agreement (on deep cuts, above and beyond New START) without China's participation in multilateral talks. In contrast to the other recognized nuclear weapons states, Chinese authorities have not made any statement about the production of HEU and plutonium for nuclear weapons. It has also not publicly released information about its total fissile material stocks. Reports indicate that China has sufficient fissile material to continue modernizing its nuclear forces over the next decade, but not enough to challenge US or Russian warhead numbers.[32]

The UK

The UK first tested a nuclear explosive device in October 1952, becoming the third state to develop nuclear weapons after the US and the Soviet Union. Initial capability centred upon the RAF's strategic bomber force. A submarine-launched capability, based upon the Polaris submarine-launched ballistic missile (SLBM), entered service in 1968. The current Trident-based system entered service in the mid-1990s. At present, the UK's nuclear stockpile is 225 warheads. Of these, up to 120 are operationally available for deployment on four ballistic missile submarines. In 2021,

30 Military and Security Developments Involving the People's Republic of China 2020, Annual Report to Congress, Office of the Secretary of Defence, USA, p. 173.

31 Ibid.

32 Heginbotham Eric, et al., 2017, *China's Evolving Nuclear Deterrence: Major Drivers and Issues for the United States*, RAND Corporation, pp. 125-126.

however, the government announced the UK would increase its stockpile ceiling to up to 260 warheads.[33] The U.K. decision reverses decades of progress towards nuclear disarmament. The UK is currently in the process of replacing its SSBN fleet, with a new class of submarines: the Dreadnought. The first submarine is due to enter service in the early 2030s.

The British government in 2006 brought out a White Paper, The Future of the United Kingdom's Nuclear Deterrent, concluding that the international security environment does not justify complete UK nuclear disarmament and that, in terms of both cost and capability, retaining the submarine-based Trident system would provide the most effective deterrent. The decision was therefore taken to maintain the UK's existing nuclear capability by replacing the existing Vanguard-class submarines and have a service life of at least 30 years.[34] The four boats will be named *Dreadnought, Valiant, Warspite,* and *King George VI.*[35] In July 2016, the House of Commons approved the decision to maintain the UK's nuclear deterrent beyond the early 2030s. This has enabled the modernization programme to move into its manufacturing phase, which will see the construction of the four new Dreadnought class ballistic missile submarines over the next 15-20 years, costing nearly US$ 4.5 billion.[36]

The increasing costs and poor management of the UK's nuclear complex have long been sources of frustration. In a bid to resolve some of the issues related to management and oversight, in November 2020, the Ministry of Defence announced a renationalization of the Atomic

33 This decision took nuclear policy experts by surprise and reversed decades of British reductions. The government explained that the decision to increase its nuclear stockpile for the first time in decades was due to a worsening strategic landscape and technological threats, particularly Russian advances in missile defence and hypersonic weapons. William Heather, UK Nuclear Weapons: Beyond the numbers, April 6,2021, available at: https://warontherocks.com/2021/04/u-k-nuclear-weapons-beyond-the-numbers/.

34 Mills Clair, Nuclear Weapons at a Glance: United Kingdom, House of Commons Library Briefing Paper No. 9077, December 9, 2020. Available at: https://commonslibrary.parliament.uk/research-briefings/cbp-9077/.

35 UK Ministry of Defence, Defence Secretary Praises 50 Years of Nuclear Service as New Submarine is Named, Press release, May 3, 2019. Available at: https://www.gov.uk/government/news/defence-secretary-praises-50-years-of-nuclearservice-as-new-submarine-is-named.

36 Mills Clair, The French Nuclear Deterrent, Briefing Paper Number 4079, November 20, 2020, House of Commons Library, p. 43.

Weapons Establishment, which had previously been government-owned but contractor operated via a consortium led by Lockheed Martin.[37]

France

France invested in nuclear weapons for political reasons. The French developed nuclear weapons as the symbol of independence and for defence against any quarter especially the US, and the UK.[38] France considers its nuclear arsenal of 290 warheads as essential both as insurance against future major risks and as support for an independent foreign policy.[39] The French Strategic Nuclear Forces currently consist of two components: an airborne and a seaborne, providing it with both strategic and tactical nuclear capabilities. France had a strategic land-based nuclear weapon component with 18 intermediate-range ballistic missiles holed up in silos in the south of the country; which was dismantled during 1996-1998.[40] The airborne component of the French Strategic Nuclear Forces currently consists of Rafale B twin-seat fighter jets. Unlike previous generations of fighters, Rafale's aircraft were not specially modified for carrying nuclear warheads; instead, the Air Force personnel receive special training to operate them. The bulk of the French deterrent is maritime-based, with the

37 Wallace, B., Defence Update, Daily Hansard, HCWS544, November 2, 2020. Available at: https://hansard.parliament.uk/Commons/2020-11-02/debates/20110250000009/DefenceUpdate.

38 Rotblat Joseph, et. al., 1993, *A Nuclear Weapon-Free World*, Oxford: Westview Press, p. 36.

39 France has been maintaining its policy for several years and was reiterated most recently in a speech on defence and nuclear deterrence by President Macron in February 2020: "Seeking peace, France is committed to a disarmament approach, which furthers global stability and security. France has a unique track record in the world, in keeping with its responsibilities and interests, having dismantled irreversibly its land-based nuclear component, its nuclear test facilities, its fissile material for weapons production facilities, and having reduced the size of its arsenal, which is currently under 300 nuclear weapons. These decisions are in line with our rejecting any type of arms race and our keeping the format for our nuclear deterrent at a level of strict sufficiency." Mills Clair, The French Nuclear Deterrent, Briefing Paper Number 4079, November 20, 2020, House of Commons Library, p. 7.

40 Since 1991, France has scaled back its nuclear arsenal by almost 50 per cent, with a reduction in both its overall holdings but also the withdrawal of several weapons systems. In February 1996 France announced that it had halted the production of fissile material for weapons purposes and that it would dismantle the production facilities dedicated to its weapons programme. Ibid, pp. 10-12.

Navy having responsibility for around 80 per cent of the nuclear arsenal.[41] There is a wide consensus in the country to maintain a nuclear deterrent and a modernization programme is underway to ensure the continued efficacy of the French nuclear force well into the 2030s.

Over the last few years, France has been modernizing its nuclear arsenal, through the deployment of a new Triomphant class of ballistic missile submarines (SSBN), the replacement of its combat aircraft in a nuclear role, the upgrade of both its submarine and air-launched nuclear-armed missile capabilities and the deployment of new nuclear warheads. Research on a next-generation missile to replace the air-launched cruise missile from 2035, has also begun. Historically France's nuclear weapons programme has taken up approximately 10-11 per cent of the total French defence budget annually. In 2020 it is estimated to be 12.5 per cent, which equates to approximately US$ 7.35 billion. In 2018 funding was approved for France's ongoing nuclear modernization programme up to 2025.[42]

France's nuclear forces now comprise a submarine-launched and air-launched component, which provide it with both strategic and tactical nuclear capabilities.[43] France has made clear that it remains important to retain both systems as they have different characteristics and are complementary, providing a "range of necessary and sufficient options". France does not participate in NATO's nuclear planning mechanisms and its forces are not formally assigned to NATO, although it does contribute to the overall deterrent effect of the Alliance. In the longer term, France has

41 The majority of Naval nuclear capability is delivered through its fleet of four Triomphant class SSBN, each of which is capable of deploying up to 16 M-51/ M-51.2 submarine-launched ballistic missiles. The Navy retains a total of 48 SLBM in its inventory. Like the UK, France's SSBN maintain a continuous at-sea deterrent (CASD) posture. The French Navy also operates a single squadron of Rafale MF3 aircraft equipped with nuclear-armed ASMP-A cruise missiles. Those aircraft are deployed aboard its aircraft carrier the Charles de Gaulle.

42 Mills Clair, The French Nuclear Deterrent, Briefing Paper Number 4079, November 20, 2020, House of Commons Library, p. 24.

43 The current French force consists of four strategic submarines (SSBNs) of the Triomphant Class armed with and attack aircraft of the Rafale and Mirage 2000N classes carrying nuclear-armed cruise missiles. France is the only country with a sea-based nuclear air component. In addition to the two land based squadrons, a non-specified number of the naval versions of the Rafale are certified to carry out nuclear missions. These can be deployed on and operate from the aircraft carrier Charles de Gaulle. Granholm Niklas and John Rydqvist, Nuclear Weapons in Europe: British and French deterrence forces, FOI-4587-SE, April 2018, p, 79.

repeatedly outlined its commitment to nuclear disarmament. The French Government supports upholding the NPT, universal ratification of the CTBT, immediate negotiation of a Fissile Material Cut-off Treaty (FMCT) and the continuation of work on nuclear disarmament verification.

France has improved the credibility of its nuclear deterrence in the last 15 years. French have improved the quality of the nuclear arsenal and the armed forces are probably in a position to use more flexible and diverse plans to ensure that the nuclear posture and doctrine can be implemented even while adhering to the policy of a strictly sufficient and minimum arsenal.[44] However, certain modernization programmes are especially important for France and will present challenges from an economic as well as a technical perspective.[45] France is a party to the Protocols to several nuclear-weapons-free zone treaties.[46] As a consequence of its ratification, France has given an undertaking not to test or station nuclear weapons on territories within those zones. In addition, France is a party to the Antarctic Treaty 1959, which bans nuclear tests and weapons in Antarctica.

India

After a successful nuclear test in 1974, India conducted a series of nuclear tests in May 1998, which established its status as a self-declared nuclear-weapon state. In 2003 the Indian government announced that it would not use nuclear weapons against states that do not possess such capability, although it has reserved the right to use nuclear weapons in response to any WMD attack, including a biological or chemical weapons attack. India is not a party to the NPT and has not signed the Comprehensive Test

44 Granholm Niklas and John Rydqvist, Nuclear Weapons in Europe: British and French deterrence forces, FOI-4587-SE, April 2018, p, 79.

45 In the late 2030s the current SSBN fleet will need to be replaced in France. A decision on the acquisition of a next-generation submarine will have to be taken by the mid-2020s at the latest. In the late 2020's a decision on a new missiles and possibly a new aircraft will have to be taken. Thus moving into the 2030s France will have to devote large amounts of money to its next-generation nuclear deterrent. Support for and financial ability to undertake this next modernization effort cannot be taken for granted. Granholm Niklas and John Rydqvist, Nuclear Weapons in Europe: British and French deterrence forces, FOI-4587-SE, April 2018, pp, 79.

46 This includes: (i) The Treaty for the Prohibition of Nuclear Weapons in Latin America and the Caribbean (Treaty of Tlatelolco); (ii) The South Pacific Nuclear Free Zone Treaty (Treaty of Rarotonga); (iii) The African Nuclear-Weapon-Free Zone Treaty (Treaty of Pelindaba); and (iv) The Treaty on a Nuclear-Weapon-Free Zone in Central Asia (Treaty of Semipalatinsk).

Ban Treaty (CTBT). India has consistently declined to join the NPT as a non-nuclear-weapon state, stating that the treaty creates an unfair distinction between the five recognized nuclear-weapon states and the remainder that have to forego such a capability. India also only supports the CTBT within the context of general nuclear disarmament. India has declared a moratorium on nuclear testing in 1998 which it has since maintained.[47]

India is currently estimated to have an arsenal of 156 nuclear weapons. All of India's nuclear weapons are believed to be plutonium-based. These weapons are assigned to a nuclear triad of aircraft, land-based missiles and ballistic missile submarines. The Indian Government does not provide public information about the status of its nuclear forces. There are reports that India is expanding the size of its nuclear weapon inventory as well as its infrastructure for producing nuclear warheads.[48] India's nuclear inventory has been reported as follows:[49]

47 In 2008 the US and India concluded a civil nuclear trade cooperation deal that would allow India to import key nuclear technologies, including reactors and nuclear fuel, from the countries of the Nuclear Suppliers Group (NSG), in return for concluding a Comprehensive Safeguards Agreement with the IAEA which would subject its civilian nuclear facilities to IAEA inspection. It also committed to continuing its moratorium on nuclear testing, instituting effective export control systems consistent with the NSG and refraining from transferring enrichment and reprocessing technologies to states that do not already have them. The agreement ultimately transformed into a parallel agreement of the Nuclear Suppliers Group in September 2008 which exempted India from some of its nuclear export rules. India has since negotiated nuclear cooperation agreements with a number of countries including the UK, Russia, France, South Korea, Canada and Australia. All of these agreements have been reached despite the fact that India is not party to the NPT. For more details see: Kerr Paul K, US Nuclear Cooperation with India: Issues for Congress, June 26, 2012, Congressional Research Service, p. 49.

48 *SIPRI Yearbook 2021, Armaments, Disarmament and International Security*, Oxford: Oxford University Press, p. 378.

49 Stephen Renny, Nuclear-Armed Hypersonic Weapons and Nuclear Deterrence, Appendix A, *Strategic Studies Quarterly*, Winter 2020, p. 12, available at: https://www.airuni versity.af.edu/.

Table 3.4: Estimated Indian Nuclear Inventory

S. No.	Type of Inventory	Total Inventory	Range
1.	ICBM-AGNI V (solid fuel)	Road and rail-mobile launchers	5,000-8,000km
2.	IRBM- AGNI III and IV	4 launchers (road and rail)	3,000-5,000km (III) 3,500-4,000km (IV)
3.	MRBM- AGNI II	8 launchers	2,000-3,500km
4.	SRBM- AGNI I	20 launchers	700-1,200km
5.	SLBM – K-15, K-4 (Solid Fuel)	12 (K-15: *Arihant* submarine with SLBM launchers).	700km (K-15) 3,000-3,500km (K-4)
6	Nuclear capable Fighters: Mirage 2000H, SU-30MKI, Jaguar, Rafale	32 Mirage, 16 Jaguar, 36 Rafale and over 200 Su30MKI	1,850 km-Mirage 1,600 km (Jaguar) 3,500km (Rafale/ Su30MKI)

In the past, the limited ranges of many of India's initial nuclear systems were meant to deter Pakistan. However, with the development of longer-range missiles, India is placing increased emphasis on targeting all of China. India has long adhered to a nuclear no-first-use (NFU) policy; however, this is qualified by a caveat that India could use nuclear forces to retaliate against attacks by non-nuclear weapons of mass destruction. A few analysts think that 'India's NFU policy is unstable or unpredictable and the Indian military and political leadership might use nuclear weapons.[50] There are reports that all India's nuclear weapons are kept unassembled and undeployed as part of India's Credible Minimum Deterrence and NFU policy.[51]

50 The 2003 Indian Nuclear Doctrine includes a significant caveat that in the event of a major attack against India, or Indian forces anywhere, by biological or chemical weapons, India will retain the option of retaliating with nuclear weapons. Thus, there could be contingencies under which India will be the first to use nuclear weapons. See: Sundaram, Kumar and Ramana, M. V., India and the policy of no first use of nuclear weapons, *Journal for Peace and Nuclear Disarmament*, Vol. 1, No. 1, 2018, pp. 152-168.

51 Rajesh Rajagopalan, *India's Nuclear Doctrine Debate*, Washington, D.C.: The Carnegie Endowment for International Peace, June 30, 2016.

India has fighter aircraft which could potentially be used to deliver air-dropped nuclear weapons. India has recently acquired French Rafale aircraft, which is already used in a nuclear role in the French air force. India also has an extensive ballistic missile programme, although to date its nuclear-capable ballistic missile inventory is limited to short and intermediate-range missiles with the ability to strike targets as far as 3,500km. India has been developing a further intermediate-range ballistic missile, the Agni-IV, which has a range of 4,000km. India's first intercontinental ballistic missile (the Agni V), which is reported to be road and rail-mobile and has a reported range of 5,000-8,000 km. The Indian Navy launched its first indigenous Arihant class nuclear-powered ballistic missile submarine in 2014. The submarine is likely to be equipped with SLBM and SSBN with a range of up to 3,500km.

Russia and India worked together on the BrahMos and are currently working on a version of this missile that is hypersonic. This hypersonic variant is usually referred to as BrahMos II. Additionally, India's entry into the Missile Technology Control Regime has removed the 300 km range cap that had limited the BrahMos's further development. India now plans to extend the range of this missile to a minimum of 450 km with the goal of 850 km. This upgraded BrahMos is likely a few years away from deployment. The BrahMos relies on liquid fuel and therefore cannot be stored fully assembled for significant periods.[52]

On June 28, 2021, India launched the Agni-P, a medium-range ballistic missile having a 2000 km range. Agni-P is a two-stage missile, which receives satellite guidance and has a reported circular error probable of 10m. This missile is canisterised and rail-mobile. Cold launches of canisterised missiles, which are enabled by the use of solid fuel propellant, allow the conduct of strikes from any terrain at short notice. The canisterised missiles are stored with their warheads in peacetime. This represents a break from the previous Indian policy of storing warheads separately from missiles and enables a strike posture that leaves an opponent with short warning times.[53] Several of India's nuclear weapons systems also have characteristics

52 The BrahMos cruise missile is stealthy, fast and extremely difficult to shoot down. Its ability to maintain supersonic speeds while skimming at low altitude makes it very difficult to detect and intercept. There are quite a few variants of the BrahMos missile designed to be used by the different platforms of the Indian military against either land or naval targets. Roblin Sebastien, BrahMos: India's Supersonic Mega Missile That China Should Fear, *The National Interest*, August 27, 2017.

53 Kaushal Sidharth, James Byrne, Joe Byrne and Gary Somerville, India's Nuclear Doctrine: The Agni-P and the Stability–Instability Paradox, *RUSI*, July 8, 2021.

that appear tactical, but the Indian government considers them all to be strategic weapons.[54]

Pakistan

Pakistan has had two unique achievements in the last few decades: its nuclear weapons are growing at a fast speed and people associated with acts of terrorism are increasing on its soil daily. Pakistan's nuclear weapons started in response to India's nuclear weapons programme. Pakistan has a checkered nuclear development history with the now infamous AQ Khan providing the know-how and illicit nuclear networks in 1975.[55] In 1985, with Chinese help, Pakistan began building a plutonium reactor. It is believed that Pakistan had a nuclear device as early as 1984 but had not tested a nuclear weapon until May of 1998.[56] Pakistan has declared a nuclear doctrine of "credible minimum deterrence," stating it has a no-first-use policy against non-nuclear states.[57]In brief, there are four policy objectives

54 Kristensen Hans M. and Matt Korda, Tactical nuclear weapons, 2019, Bulletin of the Atomic Scientists, Vol. 75:5, 2019, pp. 252-261.

55 Dr AQ Khan, a metallurgist working in the Dutch subsidiary of the British-based Uranium Enrichment Company (URENCO Group) returned to Pakistan in 1975. Khan brought with him blueprints for various centrifuge designs and a broad array of business contacts. By buying individual components rather than complete gas centrifuges, he was able to evade existing export controls and acquire the necessary equipment. Once in Pakistan, Khan establish an illicit nuclear weapons technology procurement and consulting operation, that played a major role in the transmission of nuclear weapons technology to Iran, Libya and to a lesser extent, North Korea. The Pakistani nuclear effort also received considerable assistance from China. The Pakistani government has denied that it had any knowledge of Khan's illicit side business but under American pressure arrested AQ Khan, sentencing him to house arrest, and dismantled his network. Micallef Joseph V, The Other Bomb: Pakistan's Dangerous Nuclear Strategy, *Huffington Post,* February 7, 2016.

56 Kerr Paul K. and Mary Beth Nikitin, Pakistan's Nuclear Weapons, Washington, DC: Congressional Research Service, 2016.

57 According to authoritative sources Pakistan's nuclear doctrine is based on the following claims: (i) Nuclear weapons are assurance for the territorial integrity of the country as well as national independence and sovereignty; (ii) Pakistani threat perceptions (as narrated above) are only India-centric and sole aim to having these weapons is to deter India from aggression. Such as, (a) Nuclear weapons are essential for India's conventional superiority; and (b) As conventional balance of forces between India and Pakistan, benefitted India so nuclear use is for Balance of Power in conventional force ratios between the two sides; (iii) Deterrence strategy of Pakistan is based on threat of punishment with counter value targets; (iv) Pakistan's strategic stance is that of minimum credible deterrence, it is minimum because as these weapons have no other role but to deter the adversary; (v) As India has advantage in conventional army, so Pakistan cannot commit to a policy of no NFU. As this will enable India to

for Islamabad's nuclear weapons: deter all forms of external aggression; deter through a combination of conventional and strategic forces; deter counterforce strategies by securing strategic assets and threatening nuclear retaliation, and stabilize strategic deterrence in South Asia. This nuclear posture is designed to preserve territorial integrity against Indian attacks, prevent military escalation, and counter India's conventional superiority.[58]

Pakistan currently has nearly 165 nuclear weapons under its control.[59] Despite its minimal deterrent doctrine, Pakistan reportedly has the fastest-growing nuclear arsenal in the world; although its economic situation is gradually deteriorating and cannot support such speculation. Pakistan officials have stated that they are pursuing an inventory of tactical nuclear weapons to offset India's conventional capability and will "enhance" strategic stability. Further, evidence suggests that Pakistan is focused on growing its nuclear force as it pursues submarine-based ballistic missile capability. It is believed that Pakistan has produced and stockpiled around 3,000 kg of weapons-grade HEU and about 200 kg of plutonium. Pakistan's HEU based warheads utilize an implosion design that requires between 15 and 20 kg of HEU. The current stockpile is enough for an additional 150 to 200 weapons, depending on the warhead's desired yield.[60] According to experts, Pakistan may have the 5th largest nuclear arsenal by 2025 with 220-250 warheads.[61]

Pakistan's nuclear missile arsenal consists primarily of short to medium-range ballistic missiles but is making significant progress in its cruise missile capabilities. The ground arsenal consists of approximately

fight conventional war with impunity; (vi) The National Command Authority (NCA), comprising the Employment Control Committee, Development Control Committee and Strategic Plans Division, is the center point of all decision-making regarding nuclear issue; and (vii) Nuclear assets are considered to be safe, secure and almost free from risks of improper or accidental use. Latif Amir, A Comparative Study of Nuclear Doctrines of India and Pakistan, *Journal of Global Peace and Conflict*, Vol. 2, No. 1, June 2014, pp. 129-146.

58 Mahmud Ali Durrani, Pakistan's Strategic Thinking and the Role of Nuclear Weapons, Cooperative Monitoring Centre Occasional Paper 37, July 2004.

59 *SIPRI Yearbook 2021, Armaments, Disarmament and International Security*, Oxford: Oxford University Press.

60 Micallef Joseph V, The Other Bomb: Pakistan's Dangerous Nuclear Strategy, *Huffington Post*, February 7, 2016.

61 Pakistan's Nuclear Inventory, Centre for Arms Control and Non-Proliferation, Federation of American Scientists, Congressional Research Service, available at: armscontrolcenter.org.

102 land-based missiles with yields of 5-40 kt. The F-16 combat aircraft, along with some Mirage III and V aircraft, are believed to be dual-capable (capable of both conventional and nuclear strikes) and constitute the air component of Pakistan's nuclear force. Pakistan has approximately 36 warheads for the nuclear air branch. The F-16 A/B has about 24 launchers and a range of 1,600 km while the Mirage III/V has approximately 12 launchers and a range of 2,100 km. A new, highly accurate air-launched cruise missile, the Ra'ad, has a range of 350+ km. In January of 2017, Pakistan tested for the first time the Babur-3, the sea-launched version of the ground-launched nuclear-capable Babur-2. Because the test launch took place on a submerged platform and not from a submarine, Pakistan is not yet considered to have a sea-based deterrent. Pakistan reportedly keeps its nuclear weapons disassembled and separate from its delivery vehicles. All of Pakistan's ground-launched missiles are road-mobile and rely on this mobility to ensure at least some of them survive a potential first strike. In the event of nuclear use, nuclear warheads could be delivered by a multiplicity of delivery vehicles.

Over the past decade, Pakistan has been focusing on the development of tactical nuclear weapons (TNW).[62] Pakistan fears that India has a doctrine for rapid ground attacks into Pakistan, known as 'Cold Start' and that India's capability to conduct such an operation is increasing. In reality, the Indian military has a wide range of options for military action against Pakistan, which probably include numerous options for 'surgical strikes' of varying degrees of military ambition and risk. Pakistan's response to this perceived threat has been the development of low-yield, nuclear-capable ballistic missile Haft-IX (Nasr), with a range of up to 60 km.[63] The Pakistani Inter-Services Public Relations (ISPR) described the missile as

62 Unlike other types of nuclear weapons and associated delivery systems, there is no universally accepted definition for a "tactical," "nonstrategic," or "theater" nuclear weapon. During the Cold War, such weapons were also referred to as "battlefield" nuclear weapons. According to Russian Federation, Tactical Nuclear Weapons are designed to engage objects in the tactical depth of enemy deployment (up to 300 km) to accomplish a tactical mission. Under certain conditions, TNWs may be involved in operational and strategic missions. According to the US Defence Department's publication Nuclear Matters Handbook, "Non-strategic or tactical nuclear weapons refer to nuclear weapons designed to be used on a battlefield in military situations. This is opposed to strategic nuclear weapons, which are designed to be used against enemy cities, factories, and other larger-area targets to damage the enemy's ability to wage war."

63 Barry Ben, Pakistan's Tactical Nuclear Weapons: Practical Drawbacks and Opportunity Costs, *Survival: Global Politics and Strategy*, Vol. 60, No. 1, Feb-March 2018, pp. 75-81.

a 'Short Range Surface to Surface Ballistic Missile'.[64]Pakistan military has acknowledged that the missile has been developed to add deterrence with shoot and scoot attributes.[65]

Some observers believe that Pakistan's expansion of its nuclear arsenal, development of new types of nuclear weapons, and adoption of a doctrine called "full-spectrum deterrence" indicate "the growing nuclearization of Pakistan's national security policy." These developments have sparked international concerns about the safety and security of the country's nuclear weapons, as well as raised "concerns that these weapons might be used through intentional, inadvertent, or accidental launch in a crisis or limited warfare with India."[66] Together with growing fundamentalism, ethnic violence, weak political leadership, and a fragile economy; Pakistan makes an ideal state for the proliferation of nuclear weapons and related technologies to rogue states and non-state actors. Dr Khan, father of Pakistan's nuclear weapon was rightly accused of transferring uranium-enriched equipment and know-how to Korea, Iran and Libya as well as Iraq. There is strong evidence that Khan acted on behalf of the government. In the eye's of US Former President Barack Obama, Pakistan's nuclear weapons worried him the most and according to US arms-control expert Joseph Cirincione, Pakistan is the most dangerous country on Earth.[67]

Israel

Israeli nuclear weapons programme has remained shrouded in secrecy, officially unacknowledged and insulated from domestic politics.[68]

64 The main characteristics of Pakistan's nuclear doctrine and weapons are the following. Firstly, they are primarily directed towards India; second, it espouses a policy of nuclear first-use; thirdly, it views its nuclear weapons as deterring all forms of external aggression including any conventional military offensive by India. Nagappa Rajaram et. al., Hatf-IX NASR - Pakistan's Tactical Nuclear Weapons: Implications for India, International Strategic and Security Studies Programme, Bangalore: National Institute of Advanced Studies, July 2013, p. 34.

65 Joshi Shashank, Pakistan's tactical Nuclear Nightmare: Déjà vu? *The Washington Quarterly*, Vol. 36, No. 3, Summary 2013, pp. 159-172.

66 Toby Dalton and Michael Krepon, A Normal Nuclear Pakistan, Stimson Center and Carnegie Endowment for International Peace, 2015.

67 Fitzpatric Mark, 2014, *Overcoming Pakistan's Nuclear Dangers*, International Institute for Strategic Studies, London: International Institute for Strategic Studies, p. 10. Also see: *Nuclear Black Markets: Pakistan, A.Q. Khan and the rise of proliferation networks—a net assessment*, 2007, London: International Institute for Strategic Studies, pp. 65-105.

68 Mordechai Vanunu, an Israeli former nuclear technician (b. 1954), has been serving an 18-year sentence of imprisonment in solitary confinement in Israel since October

Apparently, in 1966-67, Israel completed the development of its first rudimentary nuclear weapon and on the eve of the Six-Day War, it had operational nuclear weapon capability.[69] By 1970 Israel's became the sixth state in the world to develop a nuclear weapon and the first one in the West Asia. However, to this date, Israel has not acknowledged conducting a nuclear test or possessing a nuclear weapon.[70] Along with India and Pakistan, Israel has therefore considered a de facto nuclear-weapon state. Israel is not a State Party to the NPT. Israel signed the CTBT in 1996 but has not ratified the treaty. Israel opposes a fissile material cut-off treaty on the basis that it would undermine Israel's official position of ambiguity on nuclear weapons.[71]

According to the SIPRI Yearbook of 2021, Israel has 90 nuclear weapons warheads in its inventory, though it has a long-standing policy of not commenting on its nuclear arsenal.[72] The Israeli Government has been

---

1986. Vanunu was abducted by agents of the Israeli Government, apparently in Italy on September 30, 1986, and secretly moved to Israel after providing a British newspaper with classified information about the Atomic Research Reactor at Dimona, where he had worked from 1977 to 1985. The information, indicating that Israel was running a major nuclear military programme, was published on October 5, 1986. Vanunu maintained that he disclosed such information for reasons of conscience in order to promote a public debate on Israel's nuclear programme, a subject surrounded by strict secrecy in Israel. His trial, including the appeal before the Supreme Court, was held entirely in camera. He was convicted on charges of treason and aggravated espionage. Amnesty International, AI Index: MDE 15/05/94 May 1994.

69 Israel's pursuit of a nuclear option was partly the result of an inability to secure an extended deterrent from the US, and partly the traumatic experience of the Holocaust, which caused the Israelis to put a strong emphasis on self-reliance. France's diplomatic defeat in the subsequent 1956 Suez War led it to agree to collaborate with Israel and thereby facilitate an Israeli nuclear weapons programme. France's motivation was initially commercial — to sell Israel a reactor — but their shared experience with Nazism during the Second World War and of confronting Arab nationalists, of both being defeated during the 1956 Suez crisis, and of both being frozen out of Anglo-American nuclear efforts predisposed them to a joint nuclear effort. However, the actual French decision to build a nuclear weapons infrastructure for Israel was the consequence of determined Israeli lobbying in an extremely fragmentary French executive political structure. Schofield Julian, 2014, *Strategic Nuclear Sharing*, New York: Palgrave Macmillan, pp. 50-58.

70 Cohen Avner, 1998, *Israel and the Bomb*, New York: Columbia University Press, p. 470.

71 Mills Claire, Nuclear Weapons at a glance: Israel, House of Commons, Briefing Paper No. 9075, December 9, 2020, p. 6.

72 Due to Israel's unique lack of transparency, there is significant uncertainty about the size of its nuclear arsenal and associated warhead capabilities. The estimates are largely based on calculations of Israel's inventory of weapon-grade plutonium and the number

maintaining that Israel will not be the first to introduce nuclear weapons into the West Asia. An interpretation of the term 'introducing' nuclear weapons suggests that Israel in reality possesses a significant nuclear stockpile.[73] The International Panel on Fissile Materials (IPFM) currently estimates that Israel has 0.3 tons of HEU and 0.9 tons of plutonium stockpiled for weapons production. Further, Israel has enough stockpiled fissile material for the production of up to 200-second generation warheads.[74]

Unconfirmed reports suggest that Israel could own the nuclear triad, i.e. capable of delivering a nuclear capability via land, air and sea. Air-launched capability Over the last few decades Israel has acquired several aircraft types capable of delivering a nuclear weapon, including US-sourced F-16 and F-15 fast jet aircraft. It is thought that approximately 30, of its 90 nuclear warheads, are gravity bombs assigned to the F-16.[75] Ground-launched ballistic missiles Israel has also pursued the indigenous development of the Jericho family of ground-launched ballistic missiles. The Jericho 1, with a range of 1,200km was first deployed in the 1970s, although it is now believed to have retired from service. The Jericho 2, first deployed in 1990, is understood, after a series of improvements, to have a range of 1,500- 1,800km. In 2013 Israel tested a Jericho III missile, possibly designated the Jericho IIIA, with a new motor that some sources believe may give the missile an intercontinental range—that is, a range exceeding 5500 km.[76] On December 6, 2019, the Israeli Ministry of Defense (MOD) announced that it had conducted a test launch of an unspecified rocket propulsion system from a military base in central Israel. It did not identify which missile or military base was used for the test.

---

of operational nuclear-capable delivery systems. The locations of the storage sites for the warheads, which are thought to be stored partially unassembled, are unknown. *SIPRI Yearbook 2021, Armaments, Disarmament and International Security*, Oxford: Oxford University Press, p. 391.

73 It is unclear what circumstances would prompt Israel to 'introduce' nuclear weapons into the region under its own narrow definition. It is believed that one such scenario would involve a crisis that poses an existential threat to the State of Israel. Ibid.

74 According to the International Panel on Fissile Materials (July 2020), a first-generation warhead would require15-18kg of HEU or 5-6kg of plutonium. The amount of fissile material in a warhead can be reduced, and their yield increased, by using tritium to 'boost' the fission process. A second generation boosted warhead would require 12kg of HEU or 4-5kg of plutonium.

75 *SIPRI Yearbook 2021, Armaments, Disarmament and International Security*, Oxford: Oxford University Press, p. 392.

76 Ben David, A., Israel tests Jericho III missile, *Aviation Week & Space Technology*, July 22, 2013.

Since 1999 Israel has procured five diesel-powered Dolphin 2-class submarines from Germany. In 2002 former Pentagon officials suggested that they were being armed with indigenously modified Harpoon cruise missiles capable of carrying nuclear warheads. That development would provide Israel with a sea-based second-strike capability.[77] There have been numerous unconfirmed reports that Israel has modified some or all of the submarines to carry indigenously produced nuclear-armed sea-launched cruise missiles (SLCMs), giving it a sea-based nuclear strike capability. In line with Israel's policy of nuclear opacity, Israeli officials have declined to comment publicly on the reports. Israeli naval arsenal may include 10 cruise missile warheads (two per submarine).

Israel's doctrine of nuclear ambiguity not only fosters deterrence but also allows the government to minimize the adverse political, military, and diplomatic ramifications of Israel's regional nuclear monopoly. It is believed that Israel's nuclear policy has provided an effective deterrent against an all-out attack by an Arab coalition.[78]

North Korea

North Korea signed the Nuclear Non-Proliferation Treaty (NPT) in 1985 and later withdrew from it in 2003. Within four years of exit from the NPT, it detonated its first nuclear device, creating a course of instability in North-East Asia that persists even today. Since then N Korea has conducted five nuclear tests in 2009, and 2013, twice in 2016, and once again in 2017. N Korea's has a history of belligerent threats and its arsenal of weapons of mass destruction reportedly includes chemical, biological, and nuclear weapons. North Korea has stated repeatedly that it will use its nuclear weapons to strike Western targets, specifically the US, if it is attacked or threatened. In 2016, North Korea successfully tested a solid-fueled submarine-launched ballistic missile with a range of 1,200 km. In 2017, the North successfully conducted three ICBM tests and detonated a device with a yield reported to be more than 100 kilotons of TNT, which N Korea claimed was a hydrogen bomb.

77 Mills Claire, Nuclear Weapons at a glance: Israel, House of Commons, Briefing Paper No. 9075, December 9, 2020, pp. 8-9.

78 Maoz Xeev, The Mixed Blessing of Israel's Nuclear Policy, *International Security*, Vol. 28, No. 2, Fall 2003, pp. 44–77.

By an estimate, N Korea's nuclear inventory includes 40-50 warheads, an increase of 10 from the previous year's estimate.[79]An assessment by the US in 2018 concluded that N Korea probably had more than one covert uranium enrichment plant and that the country was seeking to conceal the types and numbers of production facilities in its nuclear weapon programme.[80] There are no confirmed reports that how many nuclear weapons N Korea has produced with its fissile material, how many have been deployed on missiles, and what the military characteristics of the weapons are. According to SIPRI estimates, N Korea could potentially produce 40–50 nuclear weapons with its current inventory of fissile materials. It is also unclear which of N Korean missiles would carry nuclear weapons.[81] N Korea is developing a new two-stage ICBM, the Hwasong-15 (KN22), which has a larger second stage and powerful booster engines. In 2020, the US Air Force's National Air and Space Intelligence Centre (NASIC) assessed that the range of the Hwasong-15 could exceed 12 000 km, putting it in range of Washington, DC, and other targets on the east coast of the USA. Four Hwasong-15 ICBMs were displayed during North Korea's October 2020 military parade.[82]

The Pakistan-Turkey clandestine collaboration in the nuclear and missile field has been reportedly growing very fast. While earlier Turkish companies were importing material for Pakistan, now Pakistan is illegally importing nuclear weapon-related material from China to Turkey.[83] In September 2019, Turkish President Erdogan, complaining that nuclear-armed nations retain an unacceptable monopoly on nuclear weapons, suggested that his nation acquire its nuclear arsenal.[84] Turkey signed the NPT as a non-nuclear-weapon state in 1980, meaning that Ankara agreed to forgo developing or acquiring nuclear weapons. Turkey has also signed the 1996 Comprehensive Test Ban Treaty, which bans all nuclear test

79 The numbers and types of North Korean warheads and delivery vehicles is fraught with uncertainty due to limited official public data. SIPRI yearbook 2021, p. 395.

80 Kube, C., Dilanian, K. and Lee, C. E, 'North Korea has increased nuclear production at secret sites, say US officials', NBC News, 1 July 2018; and Nakashima, E. and Warrick, J., 'North Korea working to conceal key aspects of its nuclear program, US officials say', *Washington Post*, July 1, 2018.

81 *SIPRI Yearbook 2021, Armaments, Disarmament and International Security*, Oxford: Oxford University Press, p. 399.

82 Ibid p. 402.

83 Pradhan S.D., Sino-Pak Nuclear Proliferation activities and Turkey, *Nuclear Security*, Vol. 14, No. 3, March 1, 2020, p. 9.

84 Lynch Colum, Turkey has long had nuclear dreams, *Foreign Policy*, November 1, 2019.

explosions. Additionally, since 1952, Turkey has been a part of NATO and under NATO's nuclear sharing arrangements, five European countries—Belgium, Germany, Italy, the Netherlands, and Turkey—host US tactical nuclear weapons.[85] The officials from the US State and Energy are reviewing contingency plans for the possible evacuation of tactical nuclear weapons stored at Turkey's Incirlik Air Base under American control.[86] Nuclear weapons might be seen as a source of national prestige and attempts by Turkey to acquire them in future cannot be ruled out altogether.

Nuclear modification, weapons as well as delivery systems, will strengthen capabilities and bring out new agile tools in the nuclear arsenal. Upgrading systems, introducing new nuclear capabilities, intermingling new technologies and advancing new strategic models all are indicative of the elevated importance of nuclear weapons.[87] Nuclear modernization by the United States, Russia, China or N-Korea poses a serious threat to international security the stability. Modification efforts and the emergence of new nuclear technologies will introduce challenges for the existing framework of strategic stability. In response to an adversary's development of new technologies or nuclear arsenal, nuclear modernization will introduce a new arms race. Integration of new classes of low-yield nuclear weapons[88] with autonomous weapons delivery systems may create a

85 Turkey hosts US tactical nuclear weapons on its territory in smaller numbers. They are limited to one location, the Incirlik base near Adana on the eastern Mediterranean coast of Turkey. Mustafa Kibaroglu, Reassessing the Role of US Nuclear Weapons in Turkey, *Arms Control Today*, June 2010, pp. 8-13. According to unofficial reports, the US stores approximately 50 B61 nuclear bombs at Incirlik Air Force Base. After the failed coup in Turkey in mid-July 2016, the government arrested several high-ranking officers from the base and cut power for nearly a week. In late July, Turkish citizens protested outside the base, calling for its closure, though Turkish officials have assured US officials that the US will retain access to Incirlik and other bases in Turkey. These events have sparked debate about the weapons' security and plans to continue storing them at Incirlik. Woolf Amy F., US Nuclear Weapons in Turkey, August 2, 2016, CRS Insight, available at: https://fas.org/sgp/crs/nuke/IN10542.pdf.

86 Trump followed His Gut on Syria. Calamity Came Fast, *The New York Times*, October 14, 2019.

87 Baxter Philip M. and Warren Aiden, "Afterword," in Warren Aiden and Philip M. Baxter (ed.), 2020, *Nuclear Modernization in the 21st Century*, London: Rutledge, pp. 191-197.

88 Russia believes that limited nuclear first use, potentially including low-yield weapons, can provide an advantage. This belief is based on Moscow's perception that its greater number and variety of non-strategic nuclear systems provide a coercive advantage in crises and at lower levels of conflict. Recent Russian statements on this evolving

dangerous scenario for international security. The US, Russia (Project 4202) and China (DZ-ZF) are developing a new class of hypersonic ballistic glider weapons which within a decade, may render most of the world's nuclear arsenals vulnerable to lightning-fast penetration and attack.[89]Russia has reportedly deployed Avangard hypersonic missile system in the Urals recently. Mounted on top of an intercontinental ballistic missile, the Avangard can carry a nuclear weapon of up to two megatons. The nuclear-capable missiles can travel more than 20 times the speed of sound and could penetrate current and future missile defence systems.[90]The US, however, claims that in continuing support of nuclear non-proliferation, it will work to increase transparency and predictability, where appropriate, to avoid potential miscalculation among nuclear weapons states and other possessor states through strategic dialogues, risk-reduction communications channels, and the sharing of best practices related to nuclear weapons safety and security.[91] Pakistan is the only one of the nine nuclear-armed states where nuclear weapons were developed by the military, is essentially under military control, and the decision to use them will be made by the military rather than civilian leadership.[92] Pakistan military's association with no state actors is well exposed and this increases the risks of theft and acquisition of nuclear warheads by the militant groups.

---

nuclear weapons doctrine appear to lower the threshold for Moscow's first-use of nuclear weapons. Nuclear Posture Review: 2018, Department of Defence, United States of America, p. XII.

89 Hyperglide vehicles (HGVs) weapons would be launched by ballistic missiles and reach hypersonic speeds of at least Mach 5 or more, they would remain maneouverable and largely untrackable after the initial boost phase of their flight. Unlike an intercontinental ballistic missile (ICBM), an HGV's aerodynamics enables it to generate enough lift to potentially glide over distances approaching 10,000 kms; before hitting their targets with accuracies down to a few meters. The US is focusing on the estimated $2.4 billion Advanced Hypersonic Weapon (AHW), which would have a range of about 8,000 kilometers. Dorminey Bruce, Russian Hypersonic Glider Weapons Would Easily Penetrate US Defences: Says Expert, *Forbes*, June 14, 2016.

90 Russia deploys Avangard hypersonic missile system, December 27, 2019, available at: https://www.bbc.com/news/world-europe-50927648.

91 Nuclear Posture Review: 2018, Department of Defence, United States of America, p. XVI.

92 Thakur Ramesh and Gareth Evans (eds.), 2013, *Nuclear Weapons: The State of Play*, Canberra: Centre for Nuclear Non-Proliferation and Disarmament, p. 44.

Conclusion

According to the SIPRI Yearbook 2021, there has been a marginal reduction in the total number of nuclear warheads in the world.[93] At the same time, there has been an appreciable effort at modernizing nuclear inventories among several nuclear-weapon states. The total number of nuclear weapons in the world, which grew to approximately 70,000 at the peak of the Cold War era, has been reduced significantly since the late 1980s. As of close 2020, the nine nuclear powers in the world possess 13,080 nuclear weapons. Out of this, 3,825 are deployed, with around 2,000 of them in a state of high operational alert.[94] With the US and Russia engaged in dismantling old retired nuclear warheads, there has been a small decline in the overall size of the nuclear inventories. Nevertheless, there are continuing efforts by the US, Russia and China to upgrade their nuclear capabilities by improving warheads, delivery vehicles (missiles and aircraft), and nuclear production facilities. Other nuclear weapon states are also not lagging in their efforts. North Korea's recent nuclear test and Iran's refusal to stop its programme to enrich uranium to weapons-grade highlight the fact that the world is now heading towards a new kind of dangerous nuclear arms race.[95] Pakistan now has the world's fastest-growing nuclear stockpile. Today, with nine nations possessing nuclear weapons and three others that may soon develop their own, the situation is becoming more volatile. This also leads to a possibility that non-state actors will sooner or later get their hands on nuclear weaponry—the ultimate means of mass destruction.

93 *SIPRI Yearbook 2021, Armaments, Disarmament and International Security*, Oxford: Oxford University Press.

94 *SIPRI Yearbook 2021, Armaments, Disarmament and International Security*, Oxford: Oxford University Press, p. 334.

95 Israel has recently claimed that Iran is five years away from developing a nuclear weapon. William Dan, Israel sees Iranian atomic bomb in five years, deal or no deal, *Reuters*, November 23, 2021.

Chapter IV

Nuclear Weapons in International Law

The president of the International Committee of the Red Cross, Jakob Kellenberger, while delivering a speech in April 2010 said, "Nuclear weapons are unique in their destructive power, in the unspeakable human suffering they cause, in the impossibility of controlling their effects in space and time, in the risks of escalation they create, and in the threat, they pose to the environment, to future generations, and indeed to the survival of humanity."[1]Despite this abominable destructive power, nuclear weapons are not subject to any specific prohibition under international law. The 1968 Nuclear Non-Proliferation Treaty (NPT) bans the possession and production of nuclear weapons by all non-nuclear-weapon states that are party to the NPT, but it does not prohibit the use of nuclear weapons. In contrast, the other two weapons of mass destruction, i.e., biological and chemical weapons are banned under the respective weapons ban treaties which prohibit the possession, production and transfer of such weapons and oblige states parties to destroy all stockpiles within a specific time. However, several customary and conventional international legal rules have an impact on the use, possession, testing, transfer or production of nuclear weapons.

This chapter covers discussions related to the 1996 Advisory Opinion by the International Court of Justice (ICJ) on the legality of the threat or use of nuclear weapons; the effectiveness of the Nuclear Non-Proliferation Treaty; legality of the use of nuclear weapons under international humanitarian law and customary law; the impact of nuclear weapons on human rights and the natural environment. In the backdrop of these

1 "Brining the Era of Nuclear Weapons to an End," Statement by Jakob Kellenberger, President of the ICRC, to the Geneva Diplomatic Corps, Geneva, April 20, 2010. Available at: https://www.icrc.org/en/doc/resources/documents/statement/nuclear-weapons-statement-200410.htm.

international treaties and rules, the chapter will also analyse whether the dropping of nuclear weapons over Hiroshima and Nagasaki would be lawful today? At present, over 100 countries worldwide are parties to an NWFZ treaty system, representing over 50 per cent of the Earth's surface. The treaty regimes on NWFZ explicitly or implicitly generally prohibit the production, receipt, storage, testing or use of nuclear weapons, and several also contain a prohibition on dumping radioactive matter at sea or elsewhere. The effectiveness of the NWFZ treaties will be discussed in Chapter IV. The recently adopted Nuclear Weapon Ban Treaty has been analysed in Chapter V.

The United Nations Charter

The United Nations Charter had as its primary objective to 'save succeeding generations from the scourge of war'. The Charter forbids the use of military force in general, with very few exceptions. These rules in the Charter apply equally to all use of force against states irrespective of weapon type, and no particular restrictions are imposed on nuclear weapons as such. The extent, however, to which the use of nuclear weapons could be lawful under the UN Charter is extremely limited.

In response to a request from the UN General Assembly for an advisory opinion on the legality of the threat or use of nuclear weapons, the International Court of Justice (ICJ), in July 1996, stated unanimously that "a threat or use of force by means of nuclear weapons that is contrary to Article 2, paragraph 4, of the UN Charter and that fails to meet all the requirements of Article 51, is unlawful", and that "a threat or use of nuclear weapons should also be compatible with the requirements of the international law applicable in armed conflict, particularly those of the principles and rules of international humanitarian law, as well as with specific obligations under treaties and other undertakings which expressly deal with nuclear weapons".[2]

Nuclear Weapons under International Humanitarian Law

After World War II, a new set of treaties concerning the laws of war and governing the restriction or illegality of weapons and the methods of warfare established the standards of international humanitarian law (IHL). IHL applies only to armed conflict and focuses on two issues: the protection

2 The International Court of Justice (ICJ) Advisory Opinion, *Legality of the Threat or Use of Nuclear Weapons*, July 8, 1996, General List No. 95, p. 36.

of persons who are not, or are no longer, taking part in the hostilities; and restrictions on the means and methods of warfare, including weapons and military tactics. A single nuclear weapon that can kill indiscriminately and cause massive destruction is unfortunately not banned under IHL. But, there has been no explicit rule of international that universally prohibits the use of nuclear weapons, except the Treaty on the Prohibition of Nuclear Weapons (TPNW), which has entered into force on January 22, 2021. The International Court of Justice (ICJ) did condemn the use of nuclear weapons in a 1996 advisory opinion, stating, "the threat or use of nuclear weapons would generally be contrary to the rules of international law applicable in armed conflict, and in particular the principles and rules of humanitarian law."[3] The ICJ, however, declined to determine the legality of using nuclear weapons in an extreme situation, such as self-defence.

Nuclear weapons, as compared to conventional weapons, have three distinct characteristics: (i) they are indiscriminate in nature—they cannot discriminate between civilians and military targets; (ii) when used, they would cause mass destruction, triggering catastrophic consequences that may even be more devastating than any other weapon known today; and (iii) they have long-lasting effects; people in Nagasaki and Hiroshima still live in the shadow of nuclear weapons.[4]

Legal scholars are divided on the issue of whether using nuclear weapons in an armed conflict is illegal under international law. One view is that the health and physical effects of nuclear weapons make their use incompatible and illegal under the humanitarian principles of customary international law. They argue that the military advantage can never outweigh the vast humanitarian concerns because radiation will spread indiscriminately and uncontrollably. This indiscriminate aspect, by itself, precludes nuclear weapons from ever being used. Even if nuclear weapons could be used strategically, it is believed that the use of nuclear weapons in an armed conflict can have the adverse effect of causing a total war in which indiscriminate attacks would likely occur. According to another view, customary international law does not completely prohibit using nuclear weapons, and therefore they could be used in self-defence. In situations

3 Legality of the Threat or Use of Nuclear Weapons (1996), International Court of Justice, para. 266, 266–67.

4 Beri SHI, Protecting the Right to Life From Nuclear Weapons, FICHL Policy Brief Series No. 22, 2014, pp. 4.

where the distinction between civilians and combatants is possible, the use of nuclear weapons is not prohibited.[5]

The Treaty on the Prohibition of Nuclear Weapons (TPNW) has entered into force on January 22, 2021. However, it has not been signed or ratified by a large number of states, having stakes in nuclear weapons. The provisions of TPNW have been discussed separately in Chapter VI.

IHL seeks to minimise unnecessary suffering and destruction by controlling and mitigating the harmful effects of hostilities through standards of protection to be accorded to combatants, non-combatants, civilians, and civilian property.[6] IHL does contain several general rules regulating the conduct of hostilities which are customary in nature and would also apply to the use of nuclear weapons in an armed conflict. These are (i) the rule of distinction; (ii) the prohibition on indiscriminate attacks; (iii) the rule of proportionality; (iv) the obligation to take precautions in attack; (v) the prohibition on using weapons of a nature to cause superfluous injury or unnecessary suffering; and (vi) the rules on the protection of the natural environment.[7] These rules must be considered collectively as they impact and interrelate with each other. The ICRC study Customary IHL offers a comprehensive overview of customary IHL rules, including rules on the conduct of hostilities.[8] These rules will also apply to the use of nuclear weapons in international or non-international armed conflict.

A. The Rule of Distinction: The rule of distinction obliges parties to a conflict to distinguish between combatants and the civilian population and to distinguish between military objectives and protected property and places. The rule of distinction is a fundamental tenet of IHL and is derivative of both military necessity and humanity. Distinction requires parties to a conflict to recognise and respect a framework of legal categories for persons and objects, each category with different rights, duties, and liabilities. Principally, distinction separates those taking part in hostilities

5 Vail Christopher, The Legality of Nuclear Weapons for Use and Deterrence, *Georgetown Journal of International Law*, Vol. 48, 2017, pp. 839-872.

6 The Commander's Handbook on the Law of Naval Operation, US Nay, US Marine Corps and US Coast Guard, NWP 1-14M/MCTP 11-10B/COMDTPUB P5800.7A, August 2017, Para 5.3, page 5-3.

7 Maresca Louis and Eleanor Mitchell, The human costs and legal consequences of nuclear weapons under international humanitarian law, *International Review of the Red Cross*, Vol. 97, No. 899, 2015, pp. 621-645.

8 Jean-Marie Henckaerts and Louise Doswald-Beck, 2005, *Customary International Humanitarian Law, Vol. 1: Rules*, Cambridge: Cambridge University Press, p. 621.

such as the armed forces, and those taking no active part in hostilities such as the civilian population. By requiring parties to recognise and respect different legal categories that derive from military necessity and humanity, distinction seeks to confine the fighting between opposing armed forces and thereby spare the civilian population as much as possible.[9] Attacks may only be directed against combatants or military objectives. It follows from this rule that the use of a nuclear weapon in an armed conflict that cannot be directed at a specific military objective would contravene the rule of distinction.

B. The Prohibition on Indiscriminate Attacks: Customary rules of IHL identify various kinds of attacks as indiscriminate. Those are (i) which cannot be directed at a specific military objective; (ii) which employ a method or means of combat which cannot be directed at a specific military objective; or (iii) which employ methods or means of combat the effects of which cannot be limited as required by IHL.[10] Accordingly, the US Naval Commanders Handbook states, "It is a fundamental tenet of IHL that the right of nations engaged in armed conflict to choose methods or means of warfare is not unlimited. Weapons, which bytheir nature are incapable of being directed specifically against military objectives, and thereforeput civilians and noncombatants at equivalent risk, are forbidden due to their indiscriminate effect."[11] Today, as claimed by a few nuclear weapon states, nuclear weapons incorporating precision guidance features can be directed at the intended military target. However, in such situations, it will be nearly impossible to limit the spread of radiation beyond international borders, which would impact neighbouring areas/states and affect many more people than those in the area initially affected by the blast.[12] The impact

9 The Commander's Handbook on the Law of Land Warfare, August 2019, Headquarters, Department of the Army, US Marine Corps, FM 6-27, page 1-9.

10 Jean-Marie Henckaerts and Louise Doswald-Beck, 2005, *Customary International Humanitarian Law, Vol. 1: Rules*, Cambridge: Cambridge University Press, Rule 12, p. 40.

11 The Commander's Handbook on the Law of Naval Operation, US Navy, US Marine Corps and US Coast Guard, NWP 1-14M/MCTP 11-10B/COMDTPUB P5800.7A, August 2017, para 9.1, page 9-1.

12 The severity and spread of radioactive particles will depend on the yield of the weapon and where it is detonated (ground burst, air burst or underwater), as well as a range of geographic, climatic and meteorological factors. These latter elements are generally beyond the control of the parties to the conflict, making the spread of radiation nearly impossible to constrain. Maresca Louis and Eleanor Mitchell, The human costs and legal consequences of nuclear weapons under international humanitarian law, *International Review of the Red Cross*, Vol. 97, No. 899, 2015, p. 632.

of radiation on human health can be long-term, with illness and cancers occurring years or even decades after the exposure. If a nuclear weapon is used in populated areas, the blast, thermal and radiation effects would impact over much larger population thus violating this rule.

C. The Rule of Proportionality: Proportionality rule (disproportionate attacks), requires combatants to refrain from attacks in which the expected loss or injury to civilians and damage to civilian objects incidental to such attacks would be excessive concerning the concrete and direct military advantage expected to be gained. The relevant advantage must be military, concrete and direct, and must not be remote, long-term or hypothetical.[13] The rule also underlies the requirement to take feasible precautions to reduce the risk of harm to civilians, other protected persons and civilian objects. The use of a nuclear weapon will have extensive immediate and long-term consequences, especially if used against military objectives located in or near populated areas, thus violating a rule of proportionality.[14]

In war, incidental harm to the civilian population and civilian objects is unfortunate, but rules of proportionality demand that excessive harm to civilians incidental to attacks must be avoided or minimised. In case the nuclear weapon is used for gaining the concrete and direct military advantage in war; such military advantage would have to be of paramount value and importance to justify such a high and foreseeable level of death, injury to civilians and destruction of their properties. In reality, such justification may never be possible to achieve. Therefore, the use of nuclear weapons against a military objective located in or near a populated area would contravene the prohibition on disproportionate attacks.

D. Precautions in Attack: In an armed conflict, parties to an armed conflict are required to take constant care and precautions in the conduct

---

13 Sandoz Yves, Christophe Swinarski and Bruno Zimmerman (eds), 1987, *Commentary on the Additional Protocols*, Geneva: ICRC, para 2209.

14 A study by Enger Elin and Thomas Vik (2013), "Scenario of a Nuclear Detonation" at Norwegian Defence Research Establishment, examined the impact of the air-burst detonation of a 20-kiloton nuclear weapon over a European capital city. While the effects can be influenced by a number of factors, it was estimated that the blast radius of a weapon would extend more than 5 km from the epicentre of the explosion and that thermal heat would be distributed across some 4.5 km, with tens of thousands of people swiftly killed or injured in the moments following the detonation. Massive destruction of civilian buildings and infrastructure would also be expected. In Hiroshima it is estimated that buildings and infrastructure across some 12 sq km of the city were destroyed. Study report available at<https://www.regjeringen.no/globalassets/upload/ud/vedlegg/hum/hum_enge.pdf>

of military operations to spare the civilian population and civilian objects.[15] The specific precautions required by IHL during an attack include doing everything feasible to verify that targets are military objectives and taking all feasible precautions in the choice of means and methods of warfare to avoid, or in any event minimising, incidental civilian casualties and damage to civilian objects.[16] IHL does not dictate the kinds of weapons that are to be used in attacking particular targets. However, with the use of a nuclear weapon in an armed conflict, the possibility of achieving this rule is very remote. The application of the rule on precautions in attack would likely preclude the use of nuclear weapons in or near a populated area and would require the employment of a less destructive and harmful means of warfare.[17]

E. Prohibition on Weapons Causing Superfluous injuries or Unnecessary Suffering: The terms "unnecessary suffering" and "superfluous injury" are regarded as synonymous and are used interchangeably. In determining whether a means or method of warfare causes unnecessary suffering or superfluous injury, the suffering or injury incurred by the combatant must not be manifestly disproportionate to the military advantage to be gained by the weapon's use. IHL prohibits the use of means and methods of warfare that are of a nature to cause superfluous injury or unnecessary suffering.[18] The US Commander's Handbook,states, "The employment of weapons, materiel, and methods of warfare that are designed to cause superfluous injury or unnecessary suffering is prohibited."[19] This rule is primarily intended to protect combatants from injury and suffering that has little or no military purpose. The ICJ in the Nuclear Weapons Advisory Opinion has mentioned this rule as one of the cardinal principles of IHL

15 ICRC Customary Law Study, Rule 15, p. 51.

16 ICRC Customary Law Study, Rule 16, p. 55.

17 Maresca Louis and Eleanor Mitchell, The human costs and legal consequences of nuclear weapons under international humanitarian law, *International Review of the Red Cross*, Vol. 97, No. 899, 2015, p.. 636.

18 This rule was included in the Preamble of the 1868 St. Petersburg Declaration Renouncing the Use, in Time of War, of Explosive Projectiles under 400 Grammes Weight. It later found expression in the 1899 and 1907 Hague Conventions with respect to the Laws and Customs of War on Land. Applications of the rule to specific weapons are found in the 1899 Hague Declarations on asphyxiating gases and expanding bullets and the 1925 Geneva Gas Protocol.

19 The Commander's Handbook on the Law of Naval Operation, US Navy, US Marine Corps and US Coast Guard, NWP 1-14M/MCTP 11-10B/COMDTPUB P5800.7A, August 2017, para 9.1.1.

and identified it as having direct regulatory relevance for the use of nuclear weapons.[20] Radiation exposure from a detonated nuclear weapon will cause horrific short- and long-term illnesses, permanent disability and suffering to soldiers as well as civilians. Article 35(2) of the 1977 Additional Protocol I also prohibits the use of "weapons, projectiles and material and methods of warfare of a nature to cause superfluous injury or unnecessary suffering."[21]

F. Protection of Natural Environment: IHL treaties contain several provisions intended to protect the natural environment from the effects of armed conflict.[22] The natural environment is understood in a broad sense and includes air, water, agriculture, livestock, forests, flora, fauna and other biological and climatic elements. Customary Rules 43 to 45 deal with the protection of the environment during armed conflict. The parts of the environment may be lawfully attacked only if they constitute a military

20 Nuclear Weapons Advisory Opinion, above note 4, para. 78.

21 This rule applies not only to instances where a weapon is designed or intentionally altered to increase the suffering of combatants, but also to situations where the suffering is not intentional but is foreseeable as a result of the weapon's design and intended use. Thus, the impact of radiation and the injury and suffering it will cause must be weighed against the military objective being sought. Maresca Louis and Eleanor Mitchell, The human costs and legal consequences of nuclear weapons under international humanitarian law, *International Review of the Red Cross*, Vol. 97, No. 899, 2015, p. 639.

22 Articles 35(3) and 55 of the 1977 Additional Protocol I to the Geneva Convention explicitly addressed environmental harm. Article 35 concerns basic rules regarding the means and methods of warfare. Paragraph 3 stipulates that "it is prohibited to employ methods or means of warfare which are intended, or may be expected, to cause widespread, long-term and severe damage to the natural environment." The Article thus protects the natural environment from not only to intentional damage, but also to expected collateral damage. Importantly, specific intent is not necessary. Article 55 provides specific protection for the environment within the context of the protection granted to civilian objects. It also explicitly prohibits attacks on the environment by way of reprisals. The common core of these two Articles is the prohibition of warfare that may cause "widespread, long-term and severe damage to the natural environment." this triple standard is a cumulative requirement, meaning that to qualify as prohibited "damage," the impact must be widespread and long-term and severe. In addition, Article (1) of the UN Convention on the Prohibition of Military or Any Other Use of Environmental Modification Techniques (ENMOD) requires that "each State Party to this Convention undertakes not to engage in military or any other hostile use of environmental modification techniques having widespread, long-lasting or severe effects as the means of destruction, damage or injury to any other State Party." David Jensen and Silja Halle (ed.), Protecting the environment during armed conflict: An inventory and analysis of international law, The United Nations Environment Programme (UNEP), 2009, p. 88.

objective. In addition, the destruction of any part of the environment is prohibited, unless it is required by imperative military necessity.[23] IHL also has a specific rule that prohibits the use of means and methods of warfare that are or may be expected to cause "widespread, long-term and severe"damage to the natural environment.[24]Nuclear weapons detonation will have catastrophic consequences on the natural environment. These include the destruction of flora and fauna by the detonation's release of blast forces and thermal radiation; contamination of land and water supplies by radioactive particles; and the dispersal of dirt and soot affecting the atmosphere and climate, with potentially serious consequences for humans, plants and wildlife. However, the scale and level of such consequences will vary with the yield of the particular nuclear weapon.

Rome Statute of the International Criminal Court (ICC)

According to Article 7(1) of the Rome Statute of the International Criminal Court (ICC), crimes against humanity means any of the listed acts [25] when committed as part of a widespread or systematic attack directed against a civilian population, with knowledge of the attack. The use as well threat of use of nuclear weapons satisfies several of the listed acts, and it may in itself amount to an attack against the civilian population.[26] In addition, Article 6(c) of the Nuremberg Charter states that the extermination of a

23 ICRC Customary Law Study, Rules 43, 44, pp. 143–151.

24 ICRC Customary Law Study, Rules 43, 44, pp. 143–151. However, the customary status of this rule has been disputed, with France, the United Kingdom and the United States asserting that the rule has not achieved customary status with regard to nuclear weapons.

25 Article 7 of the Rome Statute of ICC defines the "Crimes Against Humanity", which includes any of the following acts when committed as part of a widespread or systematic attack directed against any civilian population, with knowledge of the attack: (i) Murder; (ii) Extermination; (iii) Enslavement; (iv) Deportation or forcible transfer of population; (v) Imprisonment or other severe deprivation of physical liberty in violation of fundamental rules of international law; (vi) Torture; (vii) Rape, sexual slavery, enforced prostitution, forced pregnancy, enforced sterilization, or any other form of sexual violence of comparable gravity; (viii) Persecution against any identifiable group or collectivity on political, racial, national, ethnic, cultural, religious, gender, or other grounds; (ix) Enforced disappearance of persons; (x) The crime of apartheid; and (xi) Other inhumane acts of a similar character intentionally causing great suffering, or serious injury to body or to mental or physical health.

26 The use or threat of use of use of nuclear weapons in such attacks must meet the criteria of "widespread" and "systematic". Wolf Willem-Jan van der, 2011, *Crimes Against Humanity and International Criminal Law*, The Hague, The Netherlands: International Courts Association, pp. 438, at p. 215.

population, in whole or in part, is a crime against humanity.[27] Therefore, a nuclear strike against any area inhabited by civilians would contravene the dictates of the Charter. In reality, the atomic bombing of Hiroshima and Nagasaki had no moral or military justification; it was a crime against humanity.[28]

The State leaders who order the use or threat of use of nuclear weapons can be held accountable under international law regardless of their official position. By Article 8.2(b)(iv) of the ICC, the following acts committed during international armed conflict constitute war crimes:

> Intentionally launching an attack in the knowledge that such an attack will cause incidental loss of life or injury to civilians or damage to civilian objects or widespread, long-term and severe damage to the natural environment which would be clearly excessive in relation to the concrete and direct military advantage anticipated.

This provision is interesting for several reasons. There are two significant modifications as regards the protection of the environment. First, the Rome Statute requires both intention and knowledge of the outcome rather than either intention or expectation as outlined in the Protocol. Second, for the act to qualify as a war crime, the damage to the natural environment must be excessive concerning the military advantage anticipated.

Criminal responsibility will therefore extend to those who order operations with the knowledge that widespread, long term, and severe damage will occur. According to Article 28 of the Rome Statute, a commander or superior who "knew, or owing to the circumstances, should have known" that those under his or her command and/or control were committing environmental crimes and "failed to take all necessary and reasonable measures within his or her power to prevent or repress their commission" is subject to prosecution. Indeed, commanders or superiors

27 The Charter of the International Military Tribunal (The Nuremberg Charter) 1945, Article 6(c) defines "Crimes against humanity" as: namely, murder, extermination, enslavement, deportation, and other inhumane acts committed against any civilian population, before or during the war, or persecutions on political, racial or religious grounds in execution of or in connection with any crime within the jurisdiction of the Tribunal, whether or not in violation of the domestic law of the country where perpetrated.

28 Eamonn McCann, Hiroshima was a crime against humanity, *The Irish Times*, August 6, 2015, available at: https://www.irishtimes.com/opinion/eamonn-mccann-hiroshima-was-a-crime-against-humanity-1.2307837.

will be criminally responsible even if they merely fail to "submit the matter to the competent authorities for investigation and prosecution."

Nuclear Weapons and Human Rights

The detonation of a nuclear weapon will produce incinerating heat, powerful shock waves, overpressures, ionising radiation, and a massive amount of smoke and soot that can seriously impact the Earth's climate. Unlike conventional weapons, a single nuclear weapon will kill most people in a city, destroy infrastructure and devastate the environment. Acute radiation sickness can cause death within hours, days or weeks; those who recover may remain ill for months of the entire duration of their remaining life. Lower doses of ionising radiation can cause leukaemia, thyroid cancer, and many other cancers, and other chronic diseases like cardiovascular disease, even many years after radiation exposure. Radiation exposure can also cause birth and genetic defects affecting future generations. A nuclear war with weapons in the existing arsenal could kill many more people in a single day than were killed during the entire Second World War. It will produce radioactive contamination and toxicity that remains active for hundreds of years, causing cancers and genetic diseases that can persist across generations.

In the aftermath of nuclear detonation doctors and health care workers would also be killed or severely injured along with the general population. Hospitals, clinics, and other medical facilities would be destroyed or rendered unusable. Medicines, blood for transfusion, diagnostic equipment, and other essential medical supplies would be unavailable. In Hiroshima, 90 percent of physicians and nurses were killed or injured and 42 out of 45 hospitals became non-functional. Even in the recent Covid-19 pandemic, such shortage of healthcare workers, medicines and life support systems were evident the world over. Electric supplies may be destroyed for longer durations thus causing an extreme shortage of water. Surviving doctors and healthcare workers would be unable to treat other survivors. Dangerous levels of radiation may make it impossible for the healthcare workers to move to the affected area in search of survivors. Therefore, the complete collapse of medical response is possible after the detonation of a nuclear bomb.[29] An electromagnetic pulse would disrupt electricity

29 The health and humanitarian case for banning and eliminating nuclear weapons; IPPNW and World Medical Association Working paper submitted to the Open-Ended Working Groups taking forward multilateral Nuclear Disarmament Negotiations (OEWG), May 2016, pp. 8.

supply and grid, damaging electronic equipment including computers and satellite communications.

The detonation of a nuclear warhead would cause a significant threat to local biodiversity as, unlike conventional weapons, the energy released is partitioned into three distinct categories including thermal, kinetic, and radioactive energies. Thermal emissions from nuclear blasts will incinerate every form of life in the vicinity of the epicentre. Due to extreme heat, local vegetation will be burnt and may impact adjacent forests resulting in a spread of wildfires. Animal species occupying "sheltered" habitats may survive. Animals caught within the blast wave can be impacted in a variety of ways. Terrestrial species are likely to experience damage resulting from overpressure injury. Marine mammals, given the presence of large gas-filled lungs, would also be expected to suffer high rates of mortality under a nuclear blast. Radioactive exposure may also lend itself to more chronic impacts on animal populations. It would be expected to significantly reduce life expectancies and survival in wild animals.[30] Moreover, the environmental consequences of a nuclear war will have extreme and long-lasting environmental consequences, including disruption of the Earth's climate and agricultural productivity leading to famine. No meaningful disaster relief or environmental restoration programme will be possible in response to the nuclear detonation.

Nuclear weapons are the worst weapons of mass destruction ever created. International human rights law (IHRL) and international environmental law (IEL) both potentially apply to and control weapons and in particular their testing, transfer and use. IHRL's regulation of the use of force encompasses two core rules: first, any force used must be only the minimum necessary (the principle of necessity); and second, the force used must be proportionate to the threat (the principle of proportionality). These rules are cumulative, and violation of either means that human rights (in particular the right to life, the right to freedom from inhumane treatment, and the right to health) have been violated.[31]Since nuclear weapons are indiscriminate and disproportionate in their effects, they violate IHRL as well as IEL. The enormous destructive effect of a nuclear detonation, as well as the long-term radioactive effects, is likely to result

30 Lawrence Michael J. Holly L.J. et.al., The effects of modern war and military activities on biodiversity and the environment, *Environmental Review*, Vol. 23, 2015, pp. 443-460.

31 Casey-Maslen Stuart, The use of nuclear weapons and human rights, *International Review of the Red Cross*, Vol. 97, No. 899, 2015, pp. 663-680.

in the violation of almost every human right: the rights to life, to humane treatment, to a healthy environment and the highest attainable standard of health.[32]

The Right to Life. World War II and the establishment of the United Nations (UN) are the two important events in the evolution of the modern corpus of international human rights law and the existing international human rights system. The UN embraced the recognition and protection of human rights as a core strategy for world peace. A substantial body of international law has developed recognising basic human rights and their promotion and protection. The right to life is one of a few peremptory norms of international law. Article 3 of the 1948 Universal Declaration of Human Rights (UDHR) stipulated that "everyone has the right to life, liberty and security of the person", embedded in an instrument that is now considered customary international law. Correspondingly, Article 6(1) of the 1966 International Covenant on Civil and Political Rights (ICCPR) says that "every human being has the inherent right to life. This right shall be protected by law. No one shall be arbitrarily deprived of his life". Under Article 4(2) of the ICCPR, there can be no derogations from Article 6(1). The peremptory nature of the right to life has been confirmed by the UN Human Rights Committee's General Comment No. 14, 15 based on the practice of States Parties. Moreover, several national constitutions and judicial bodies have acknowledged the peremptory naturc of the right to life in their decisions.

The International Court of Justice (ICJ) in the nuclear weapon case (1996) clarified the interrelationship between human rights law and IHL about the conduct of hostilities. The ICJ held:

> The test of what is an arbitrary deprivation of life ... falls to be determined by the applicable *lex specialis*, namely, the law applicable in armed conflict which is designed to regulate the conduct of hostilities. Thus whether a particular loss of life, through the use of a certain weapon in warfare, is to be considered an arbitrary deprivation of life contrary to Article 6 of the Covenant, can only be decided by reference to the law applicable in armed conflict and not deduced from the terms of the Covenant itself.[33]

32 Doswald-Beck Louise, "Human Rights Law and Nuclear Weapons," Gro Nystuen Gro, Stuart Casey-Maslen and Annie Golden Bersagel (eds), 2014, *Nuclear Weapons under International Law*, Cambridge: Cambridge University Press, p. 435-460.

33 International Court of Justice, Nuclear Weapons Advisory Opinion (1996), para. 25.

Thus, the use of a nuclear weapon in the conduct of hostilities during the international armed conflict will violate e human rights law if that use also constitutes a violation of the rules of IHL. If the user does not violate IHL, it will not violate human rights law. We have seen in the preceding discussions, how the use of a nuclear weapon will violate IHL. The protection under ICCPR does not cease in times of war, except by operation of Article 4 of the Covenant whereby certain provisions may be derogated from in a time of national emergency. Respect for the right to life is not, however, such a provision. In principle, the right not arbitrarily to be deprived of one's life also applies in hostilities.

The Right to Health. Article 25 of the UDHR affirms: "Everyone has the right to a standard of living adequate for the health of himself and of his family, including food, clothing, housing and medical care and necessary social services". The International Covenant on Economic, Social and Cultural Rights (ICESCR) is the most important in terms of the right to health. Article 12 of ICESCR provides that the right to health includes the enjoyment of the highest attainable standard of physical and mental health.[34] A human right to health is also recognised in numerous other international human rights authorities that establish prohibitions against government conduct that is detrimental to health. Such treaties include the 1965 International Convention on the Elimination of All Forms of Racial Discrimination, the 1979 Convention on the Elimination of All Forms of Discrimination against Women, and the 1989 Convention on the Rights of

34 Article 12 of the ICESCR: "1. The States Parties to the present Covenant recognize the right of everyone to the enjoyment of the highest attainable standard of physical and mental health. 2. The steps to be taken by the States Parties to the present Covenant to achieve the full realization of this right shall include those necessary for: (a) The provision for the reduction of the stillbirth-rate and of infant mortality and for the healthy development of the child; (b) The improvement of all aspects of environmental and industrial hygiene; (c) The prevention, treatment and control of epidemic, endemic, occupational and other diseases; (d) The creation of conditions which would assure to all medical service and medical attention in the event of sickness." The Committee on Economic, Social and Cultural Rights, a body composed of independent experts in charge of monitoring the implementation of the Covenant, provided a broad interpretation of Article 12 of the Covenant (General Comments No. 14, adopted at the Twenty-second Session of the Committee on Economic, Social and Cultural Rights, on August 11, 2000): "The right to health is an inclusive right, extending not only to timely and appropriate health care, but also to the underlying determinants of health, such as access to safe and potable water and adequate sanitation, healthy occupational and environmental conditions, and access to health-related education and information, including on sexual and reproductive health (Paragraph 11).

the Child.[35] The UN also has established several international agencies to promote economic and social development worldwide. The World Health Organization (WHO) has a legislative capacity to make international health regulations in addition to its health promotion functions. The WHO constitution states a right to the "highest attainable standard of health" and defines health broadly as "a state of complete physical, mental and social well-being and not merely the absence of disease or infirmity." The right to health could be understood on a continuum. At a minimum, it could mean a right to conditions that protect health in the population. It might also include civil and political rights concerning access to population-based and personal health care services. At most, it could also include the provision of medical care for the diagnosis and treatment of disease and injury for those unable to pay.

Right to Clean Environment. Human rights law provides additional guidance about state conduct affecting the environment and natural resources of the use of a nuclear weapon in an armed conflict. Both treaty law and customary international law contain rules that ensure that the basic social and political rights of individuals are respected, including several that have been linked to environmental protection. "Environment" and "environmental protection" are not mentioned explicitly in the UDHR. However, a contemporary reading of the UDHR could make several provisions relevant to environmental protection. These include, for example, Article 3 on the "right to life," Article 25 on adequate standards of living and Article 30 reflecting the "do no harm" principle. Two articles of the ICCPR could help protect the environment during armed conflict. Article 17 has frequently been interpreted as prohibiting environmental damage that negatively affects family and home life. Article 27, providing minority groups with protection for their culture and their traditional practices, has a long history of case law behind it.

In *Temeharo v. France Case* (1995-1996), which concerned nuclear tests in the South-Pacific, was dismissed by the Human Rights Committee because the applicants were unable to adequately demonstrate that they were victims of the environmental damage. However, the Committee implicitly conceded that if the claim for environmental damage was supported by clear scientific data and there were clear victims of this damage, it could be considered a violation of Article 17.

35 Convention on the Rights of the Child, Article 24(1) states: "States Parties recognize the right of the child to the enjoyment of the highest attainable standard of health."

The current literature indicates that when IHL treaties, as *lex specialis,* do not provide clear guidance, human rights law may mandate more stringent protections of the environment and natural resources. Furthermore, if significant damage were done to the environment or natural resources during an internal conflict, human rights law would suggest that an affected person or community could seek relief with the UN and regional human rights organs, rather than rely only on grave breaches of IHL and war crimes proceedings.[36] To conclude, while human rights law does not outlaw the use of nuclear weapons altogether, but it offers a reasonable chance of accountability in case these weapons are used again.[37]

Opinion of the International Court of Justice

As the principal judicial organ of the United Nations (UN), the role of the International Court of Justice (ICJ) is to settle legal disputes submitted to it by states and to give advisory opinions on legal questions referred to it by the UN organs and specialised agencies. In this latter regard, on December 15, 1994, the General Assembly decided to request the ICJ urgently to render its advisory opinion on the following question: Is the threat or use of nuclear weapons in any circumstance permitted under international law?[38] On July 8, 1996 the ICJ replied to the question put by the General Assembly, as follows:

- There is in neither customary nor conventional international law any specific authorisation of the threat or use of nuclear weapons (unanimously);
- There is in neither customary nor conventional international law any comprehensive and universal prohibition of the threat or use of nuclear weapons as such (by eleven votes to three);
- A threat or use of force by means of nuclear weapons that is contrary to Article 2, paragraph 4, of the UN Charter and that fails to meet all the requirements of Article 51, is unlawful (unanimously);
- A threat or use of nuclear weapons should also be compatible

36 David Jensen and Silja Halle (ed.), Protecting the environment during armed conflict: An inventory and analysis of international law, The United Nations Environment Programme (UNEP), 2009, pp. 48-50.

37 Casey-Maslen Stuart, The use of nuclear weapons and human rights, *International Review of the Red Cross*, Vol. 97, No. 899, 2015, p. 679-680.

38 UN General Assembly doc. A/RES/49/75K dated December 15, 1994.

with the requirements of the international law applicable in armed conflict particularly those of the principles and rules of international humanitarian law, as well as with specific obligations under treaties and other undertakings which expressly deal with nuclear weapons (unanimously);

- It follows from the above-mentioned requirements that the threat or use of nuclear weapons would generally be contrary to the rules of international law applicable in armed conflict, and in particular the principles and rules of humanitarian law. However, in view of the current state of international law, and of the elements of fact at its disposal, the Court cannot conclude definitively whether the threat or use of nuclear weapons would be lawful or unlawful in an extreme circumstance of self-defence, in which the very survival of a State would be at stake (by seven votes to seven, by the President's casting vote);
- There exists an obligation to pursue in good faith and bring to a conclusion negotiations leading to nuclear disarmament in all its aspects under strict and effective international control (unanimously).

An advisory opinion of the ICJ derives its status and authority from the fact that it is the official pronouncement of the principal judicial organ of the UN, but as the word "advisory" implies, such opinions, although authoritative, are non-binding on states. The ICJ acknowledged the unique characteristics of nuclear weapons and in particular their destructive capacity:

> The Court also notes that nuclear weapons are explosive devices whose energy results from the fusion or fission of the atom. By its very nature, that process, in nuclear weapons as they exist today, releases not only immense quantities of heat and energy, but also powerful and prolonged radiation. According to the material before the Court, the first two causes of damage are vastly more powerful than the damage caused by other weapons, while the phenomenon of radiation is said to be peculiar to nuclear weapons. These characteristics render the nuclear weapon potentially catastrophic. The destructive power of nuclear weapons cannot be contained in either space or time. They

have the potential to destroy all civilisation and the entire ecosystem of the planet."[39]

The ICJ stated that the survivors of the initial blast and heat would be exposed to the resulting effects of nuclear winter. Nuclear winter would be an ecological disaster of the same … magnitude as the [one that occurred] … 65 million years ago. The initial blast and the scourging fires thereafter would emit huge amounts of dust and smoke into the air. The dust and smoke would circle the northern hemisphere quickly and the temperature at the surface would be low [while] the temperature of the upper part of the troposphere would rise because the sunlight would be absorbed by the smoke. This drastic temperature change would destroy crops and bring about global starvation.

The ICJ provided a broad framework for the application of the rules of IHL to nuclear weapons but left certain questions open. The court said that the use of nuclear weapons is subject to IHL and would be generally unlawful under such law. It emphasised the wide scope of humanitarian law:

> The cardinal principles contained in the texts constituting the fabric of humanitarian law are the following. The first is aimed at the protection of the civilian population and civilian objects and establishes the distinction between combatants and non-combatants; States must never make civilians the object of attack and must consequently never use weapons that are incapable of distinguishing between civilian and military targets. According to the second principle, it is prohibited to cause unnecessary suffering to combatants: it is accordingly prohibited to use weapons causing them such harm or uselessly aggravating their suffering. In application of that second principle, States do not have unlimited freedom of choice of means in the weapons they use.
>
> The Court would likewise refer, in relation to these principles, to the Martens Clause, which was first included in The Hague Convention II with Respect to the Laws and Customs of War on Land of 1899 and which has proved to be an effective means of addressing the rapid evolution of military technology. A modern version of that clause is to be found in Article 1, paragraph 2, of Additional Protocol I of 1977, which reads as follows: "In cases not covered by this Protocol or

39 International Court of Justice, *Legality of the Threat or Use of Nuclear Weapons*, Advisory Opinion, July 8, 1996, I.C.J. Reports 1996 (hereafter ICJ Advisory Opinion), para. 35.

> by other international agreements, civilians and combatants remain under the protection and authority of the principles of international law derived from established custom, from the principles of humanity and from the dictates of public conscience."
>
> In conformity with the aforementioned principles, humanitarian law, at a very early stage, prohibited certain types of weapons either because of their indiscriminate effect on combatants and civilians or because of the unnecessary suffering caused to combatants, that is to say, a harm greater than that unavoidable to achieve legitimate military objectives. If an envisaged use of weapons would not meet the requirements of humanitarian law, a threat to engage in such use would also be contrary to that law.[40]

The ICJ went on to find the use of nuclear weapons "scarcely reconcilable" with IHL:

> The principles and rules of law applicable in armed conflict—at the heart of which is the overriding consideration of humanity—make the conduct of armed hostilities subject to a number of strict requirements. Thus, methods and means of warfare, which would preclude any distinction between civilian and military targets, or which would result in unnecessary suffering to combatants, are prohibited. In view of the unique characteristics of nuclear weapons, to which the Court has referred above, the use of such weapons, in fact, seems scarcely reconcilable with respect for such requirements.[41]

The ICJ further stated:

> A threat or use of nuclear weapons should ... be compatible with the requirements of the international law applicable in armed conflict, particularly those of the principles and rules of international humanitarian law, as well as with specific obligations under treaties and other undertakings which expressly deal with nuclear weapons.[42]

The Court then summarised the diametrically opposite contentions of certain other States:

> Recourse to nuclear weapons could never be compatible with the principles and rules of humanitarian law and is therefore prohibited.

40 ICJ Advisory Opinion, para 78.

41 Ibid., para 95.

42 Ibid., para 105 (2) D.

> In the event of their use, nuclear weapons would in all circumstances be unable to draw any distinction between the civilian population and combatants, or between civilian objects and military objectives, and their effects, largely uncontrollable, could not be restricted, either in time or in space, to lawful military targets. Such weapons would kill and destroy in a necessarily indiscriminate manner, on account of the blast, heat and radiation occasioned by the nuclear explosion and the effects induced; and the number of casualties which would ensue would be enormous. The use of nuclear weapons would therefore be prohibited in any circumstance, notwithstanding the absence of any explicit conventional prohibition.[43]

The argument has been made by some States and commentators that low-yield nuclear weapons could be compatible with IHL. However, after examining the issue, the ICJ stated that none of the States claiming the legality of nuclear weapons under such circumstances had presented precise scenarios in which these weapons would be used or had addressed the associated risk of escalation to a more devastating nuclear war. In addition, while the use of low-yield nuclear weapons in a remote area might not have immediate effects on civilians, there would remain significant concerns about radiological contamination of the environment and the impact of radiation on combatants. This being so, the Court does not consider that it has a sufficient basis for a determination of the validity of this view.[44]

Similarly, in discussing proportionality, the court stated that it did "not find it necessary to embark upon the quantification" of risk factors surrounding the use of nuclear weapons and did not "need to enquire into the question whether tactical nuclear weapons exist which are sufficiently precise to limit those risks."[45] As to the limits on a State's right of self-defence, the court, after noting that a State's exercise of the right of self-defence must comply, inter alia, with the principle of proportionality, specifically stated that a "use of force that is proportionate under the law of self-defence, must, to be lawful, also meet the requirements of the law applicable in armed conflict which comprise in particular the principles and rules of humanitarian law."[46] The court also referred to the contentions of the UK: "Assuming that a State's use of nuclear weapons meets the requirements

43 ICJ Advisory Opinion, para 92.

44 Ibid., para 94.

45 Ibid., para 43.

46 Ibid., para 42.

of self-defence, it must then be considered whether it conforms to the fundamental principles of the law of armed conflict regulating the conduct of hostilities."[47]

The ICJ noted that under the UN Charter, the threat or use of force is prohibited except in individual or collective self-defence in response to an armed attack or instances of military enforcement measures undertaken by the Security Council,[48] and stated that under customary international law the right of self-defence is subject to the conditions of necessity and proportionality. The court quoted its decision in *Military and Paramilitary Activities in and against Nicaragua*: "There is a 'specific rule whereby self-defence would warrant only measures which are proportional to the armed attack and necessary to respond to it, a rule well established in customary international law.'"[49] It observed, "The destructive power of nuclear weapons cannot be contained in either space or time."[50] Because their effects are uncontrollable, nuclear weapons cannot be used in such a way as to limit their effects to those permitted under the rules of distinction, proportionality, and necessity.

The ICJ opined those certain fundamental principles of the Stockholm and Rio Declaration are now a part of customary international law, specifically, "the existence of the general obligation of the States to ensure that activities within their jurisdiction and control respect the environment of the other States or of areas beyond national control is now a part of the corpus of international law relating to the environment." The ICJ also held that the natural environment enjoys the protection given by IHL to civilian objects. In other words, the elements of the natural environment cannot be made the object of attack, unless their destruction would give direct military advantage in the particular circumstances in question; and an attack cannot be made if the risk of collateral damage to the environment is disproportionate to the direct military advantage of the attack. These principles apply to both nuclear and conventional attacks that may cause environmental damage.[51] In conclusion, the ICJ gave a strong presumption

47 ICJ Advisory Opinion, (quoting Written Statement of the Government of the UK), para. 91.

48 ICJ Advisory Opinion, (citing UN Charter Article 51), para 38.

49 ICJ Advisory Opinion, (quoting Military and Paramilitary Activities in and against Nicaragua [*Nicaragua v. US* of 1986], para 41.

50 ICJ Advisory Opinion, para 35.

51 Michael J. Matheson, The Environmental Effects of Nuclear Weapons and the 1996 World Court Opinion, Vol. 25 (3), *Vermont Law Review*, 2000-2001), p. 776.

of illegality. Of the fourteen Judges sitting, ten determined that the use of nuclear weapons would generally be unlawful. Further, six judges were of the view that all uses of nuclear weapons would be unlawful *per se*.

ICJ: Dissenting Opinion of Judge Weeramantry

According to Justice Weeramantry:[52]

> Humanitarian law and custom have a very ancient lineage. They reach back thousands of years. They were worked out in many civilisations—Chinese, Indian, Greek, Roman, Japanese, Islamic, modern European, among others. Through the ages many religious and philosophical ideas have been poured into the mould in which modern humanitarian law has been formed. They represented the effort of the human conscience to mitigate in some measure the brutalities and dreadful sufferings of war. In the language of a notable declaration in this regard (the St. Petersburg Declaration of 1868) international humanitarian law is designed to "conciliate the necessities of war with the laws of humanity." In recent times, with the increasing slaughter and devastation made possible by modern weaponry, the dictates of conscience have prompted ever more comprehensive formulations.
>
> My considered opinion is that the use or threat of use of nuclear weapons is illegal *in any circumstances whatsoever*. It violates the fundamental principles of international law, and represents the very negation of the humanitarian concerns which underlie the structure of humanitarian law. It offends conventional law and, in particular, the Geneva Gas Protocol of 1925, and Article 23*(a)* of the Hague Regulations of 1907. It contradicts the fundamental principle of the dignity and worth of the human person on which all law depends. It endangers the human environment in a manner which threatens the entirety of life on the planet.
>
> The extent of damage to the environment, which no other weapon is capable of causing, has been summarised in 1987 by the World Commission on the Environment and Development in the following terms: "The likely consequences of nuclear war make other threats to the environment pale into insignificance. Nuclear weapons represent a qualitatively new step in the development of warfare. One

52 Available at: http://www.icj-cij.org/icjwww/icases/iunan/iunan_judgment_advisory%20opinion_199607, accessed September 20, 2021.

thermonuclear bomb can have an explosive power greater than all the explosives used in wars since the invention of gunpowder. In addition to the destructive effects of blast and heat, immensely magnified by these weapons, they introduce a new lethal agent—ionising radiation—that extends lethal effects over both space and time."[53]

Nuclear weapons have the potential to destroy the entire ecosystem of the planet. Those already in the world's arsenals have the potential of destroying life on the planet several times over. Nuclear weapons: (i) cause death and destruction; (ii) induce cancers, leukaemia, keloids and related afflictions; (iii) cause gastro-intestinal, cardiovascular and related afflictions; (iv) continue for decades after their use to induce the health-related problems mentioned above; (v) damage the environmental rights of future generations; (vi) cause congenital deformities, mental retardation and genetic damage; (vii) carry the potential to cause a nuclear winter; (viii) contaminate and destroy the food chain; (ix) imperil the eco-system; (x) produce lethal levels of heat and blast; (xi) produce radiation and radioactive fallout; (xi) produce a disruptive electromagnetic pulse; (xiii) produce social disintegration; (xiv) imperil all civilisation; (xv) threaten human survival; (xvi) wreak cultural devastation; (xvii) span a time range of thousands of years; (xviii) threaten all life on the planet; (xix) irreversibly damage the rights of future generations; (xx) exterminate civilian populations; (xxi) damage neighbouring States; (xxii) produce psychological stress and fear syndromes, *as no other weapons do.*

There is now a consensus that the climatic effects of a nuclear winter and the resulting lack of food aggravated by the destroyed infrastructure could have a greater overall impact on the global population than the immediate effects of the nuclear explosions. The evidence is growing that in a post-war nuclear world *Homo sapiens* will not have an ecological niche to which he could flee. It is apparent that life everywhere on this planet would be threatened.[54]

Justice Weeramantry commented that nuclear war has the potential to destroy all civilisation. Such a result could be achieved through the use of a minute fraction of the weapons already in existence in the arsenals of the nuclear powers.

53 World Commission on Environment and Development (the Brundtland Commission), *Our Common Future*, 1987, p. 295.

54 Legality of the Threat or Use of Nuclear Weapons (separate opinion by Justice Weeramantry), 1996 ICJ 25, July 8, 1966, para 21.

Judge Koroma noted, with respect to the atomic attacks on Hiroshima and Nagasaki, "Over 320,000 people who survived but were affected by radiation still suffer from various diseases caused by radiation, including leukaemia, thyroid cancer, breast cancer, lung cancer, gastric cancer and cataracts. More than half a century after the disaster, they are still said to be undergoing medical examinations and treatment."[55]

In its Advisory Opinion, the ICJ seems to have contributed to confusion about the rules governing the justification for and/or legality of the use of military force on the one hand, and the rules governing the actual conduct of hostilities (and thus, the use of weaponry) on the other. These regimes are distinct, and they apply independently of each other, also simultaneously. IHL rules must apply irrespective of the justness or legality of the use of force; otherwise, they cannot reasonably have any effect.[56]The ICJ's Advisory Opinion[57] makes it quite clear that nuclear weapons would generally breach all of the following:

- The Declaration of St. Petersburg, 1868, because unnecessary suffering would be caused;[58]
- The Martens Clause, 1899, because humanity would not remain under the protection and authority of the principles of international law derived from established custom, the principles of humanity and the dictates of public conscience;
- The Hague Conventions, 1907, because unnecessary suffering would be caused and there would be no guarantee of the inviolability of neutral nations;[59]

55 *Legality of the Threat or Use of Nuclear Weapons*, 1996 I.C.J. 226, at 567 (J. Koroma, dissenting).

56 Nystuen Gro, Legal aspects of nuclear weapons: a 'birds-eye view' of international law and nuclear weapons, *ILPI-UNIDIR*, Paper 6, 2014, pp. 7.

57 There are views that the ICJ's Nuclear Weapons Opinions highlight the shortcomings of judicial intervention into a politically-charged domain. In terms of substance, the ICJ pitched its tent in the middle ground of international opinion, formulating a compromise that affords no viewpoint, neither absolute victory nor absolute defeat. Liz Heffernan, The Nuclear Weapons Opinion: Reflections on the Advisory Procedure on the International Court of Justice, *Stetson Law Review*, Vol. XXVIII, 1998, p. 169.

58 For example, the Declaration of St. Petersburg of 1868 proclaimed "that the only legitimate object which States should endeavour to accomplish during war is to weaken the military force of the enemy."

59 The Hague Convention IV of 1907 reminds belligerents that their right to adopt means of injuring the enemy is not unlimited. The Convention also proclaimed occupying

- The UN Charter;[60]
- The Universal Declaration of Human Rights, 1948, because long-lasting radioactive contamination would interfere with innocent people's inherent right to life and health;
- The Geneva Conventions, 1949, because the protection of the wounded, the sick, the infirm, expectant mothers, civilian hospitals and health workers would not be ensured; and
- The Protocols Additional to the Geneva Conventions, 1977, because there would be massive incidental loss of civilian lives and widespread, long-term and severe damage to the environment.[61]

The Nuclear Non-proliferation Treaty

From the beginning of the use of nuclear weapons in Hiroshima and Nagasaki in 1945, it has been apparent that the development of nuclear capabilities by states could enable them to divert technology and materials for weapons purposes. Due to serious political differences between the major Powers, the initial efforts to create an international system enabling all states to have access to nuclear technology under appropriate safeguards were terminated in 1949. China's initial nuclear test of October 15, 1964 prompted US President Johnson to seek a comprehensive review of nuclear proliferation that involved a higher-level look at the problem of

forces to be no more than "administrators and usufructuaries of public buildings, real estate, forest, and agricultural estates belonging to the hostile State, and situated in the occupied country." Johan D. van der Vyver,The Environment: State Sovereignty, Human Rights and Armed Conflict, *Emory International Law Review*,Vol. 23, No. 1,2009, p. 98.

60 The UN Charter had as its primary objective to 'save succeeding generations from the scourge of war'.The Charter forbids the use of military force in general, with very few exceptions. These rules in the Charter (Article 2.4) apply equally to all the *use of force* and the *threat of use of force* against states irrespective of weapon type, and no particular restrictions are imposed on nuclear weapons as such. The extent, however, to which the use of nuclear weapons could be lawful under the Charter, is extremely limited. Hence, if possession (and thus deterrence) of nuclear weapons is deemed to constitute *threat of use*, one could conclude that the mere possession of nuclear weapons constitutes a breach of the UN Charter.

61 Since the use of nuclear weapons would violate IHL, especially because their destructive power cannot be contained in either space or time, their threatened use is likewise illegal. Under Article 51(2) of AP I acts or threats of violence, the primary purpose of which is to spread terror among the civilian population, are prohibited.

nuclear spread.[62] With this, international fears grew, especially among non-nuclear states about nuclear weapons proliferation. However, there were fundamental differences in the approach of nuclear and non-nuclear states towards limiting the spread of nuclear weapons.

Within the framework of the United Nations, the principle of nuclear non-proliferation were negotiated as early as 1957 and gained significant momentum in the early 1960s. The structure of a treaty to uphold nuclear non-proliferation as a norm of international behaviour had become clear by the mid-1960s, and by 1968 final agreement had been reached on a Treaty that would prevent the proliferation of nuclear weapons, enable cooperation for the peaceful use of nuclear energy and further the goal of achieving nuclear disarmament. The Treaty represents the only binding commitment in a multilateral treaty to the goal of disarmament by the nuclear-weapon States. Opened for signature in 1968, the Nuclear Non-proliferation Treaty (NPT) entered into force in 1970. On May 11, 1995, the Treaty was extended indefinitely.[63] A total of 191 States have joined the Treaty, including the five nuclear-weapon States (the US, Russia, France, China, the UK).[64]

The objective of NPT is to prevent the spread of nuclear weapons and weapons technology, to promote cooperation in the peaceful uses of nuclear

62 The US President created the Committee on Nuclear Proliferation— known as the Gilpatric Committee, after chairman Roswell Gilpatric—that studied possible options between November 1964 and January 1965. The state department wanted to continue pursuing the Multilateral Nuclear Force (MLF) to prevent European proliferation, but Gilpatric preferred the Arms Control and Disarmament Agency's effort to develop a global strategy. The US and the Soviet Union each exchanged draft treaties on non-proliferation in 1965. Siracusa Joseph M., The Eight Pillars of the Nuclear Nonproliferation Regime and the Search for Global Security, Global Policy Essay, September 2012, pp. 17.

63 The Treaty provided, in article X, for a conference to be convened 25 years after its entry into force to decide whether the Treaty should continue in force indefinitely, or be extended for an additional fixed period or periods. Accordingly, at the NPT Review and Extension Conference in May 1995, States parties to the Treaty agreed—without a vote—on the Treaty's indefinite extension, and decided that review conferences should continue to be held every five years.

64 The five Nuclear Weapon States (NWS) as defined by the Treaty on the Nonproliferation of Nuclear Weapons (NPT), 1968 - the United States, Russia, the United Kingdom, France, and China - are compelled under Article VI to "undertake to pursue negotiations in good faith on effective measures relating to cessation of the nuclear arms race at an early date and to nuclear disarmament, and on a treaty on general and complete disarmament under strict and effective international control." Non signatories to NPT include India, Israel, Pakistan, North Korea and South Sudan.

energy and to achieve complete nuclear disarmament. The disarmament obligation under the NPT is contained in Article VI. It provides: "Each of the Parties to the Treaty undertakes to pursue negotiations in good faith on effective measures relating to cessation of the nuclear arms race at an early date and nuclear disarmament, and on a treaty on general and complete disarmament under strict and effective international control."

The obligations of the state parties under Article VI of the Treaty are three-fold: (i) ending the nuclear arms race at an early date; (ii) achieving nuclear disarmament; and (iii) achieving a treaty on general and complete disarmament.[65] NPT's preamble also covers the issue of complete disarmament. The preamble states that the states party to the NPT to declare their intention to achieve at the earliest possible date the cessation of the nuclear arms race and to undertake effective measures in the direction of nuclear disarmament.[66] Unfortunately, the five nuclear weapons states have failed measurably in their nuclear weapons disarmament.

The five nuclear-weapon states were the only nuclear-armed states at the time the NPT was signed. The basis for this exclusivity was extremely arbitrary: These five states declared themselves to be "responsible" world powers but said that any other nation that developed nuclear weapons could not be trusted to deal with them responsibly. They also decided that sanctions would be imposed on any other country that attempted to develop nuclear capability. They have been blind to the hypocrisy of the entire agreement, which has not prevented the five nuclear-weapon states from conducting additional nuclear tests as it suits them, or developing new nuclear-weapon capacity and delivery vehicles.[67]

Nuclear weapons states appear unwilling to implement their disarmament undertaking under the NPT's Articles VI. At the same time, they insist that non-nuclear-weapon states meticulously observe Article II

---

65 Ford Christopher A., Debating Disarmament: Interpreting Article VI of the Treaty on the Non-Proliferation of Nuclear Weapons, *Nonproliferation Review*, Vol. 14, No. 3, November 2007, pp. 401-428.

66 The correct meaning of a treaty should be identified with the pieces of information conveyed by that treaty with regard to its norm content, according to the intentions of the treaty parties – all those states, for which the treaty is in force – insofar as these intentions can be considered mutually held. Linderfalk Ulf, 2007, *On the Interpretation of Treaties: The Modern International Law as Expressed in the 1969 Vienna Convention on the Law of Treaties*, The Netherlands: Springer, p. 33.

67 Nayar Ranvir, 50 years of failure: Anniversary of NPT is nothing to celebrate, *Arab News*, March 13, 2020, available at: https://www.arabnews.com/node/1641106.

(renunciation of nuclear weapons) and III (nuclear safeguards), and they even adhere to new requirements every now and then (such as renouncing fuel cycle activities).[68] The stance adopted by the nuclear-weapon states enhances the discomfort of an increasing number of non-nuclear-weapon states with the treaty. The interest of non-nuclear-weapon states is in reducing the number of nuclear weapons, leading eventually to their elimination, and in enjoying the peaceful uses of nuclear energy.[69]

The NPT succeeded in its initial task of preventing the proliferation of nuclear weapons and helped to prevent the spread of nuclear weapons to numerous countries.[70] Its effectiveness started eroding very soon. India and Pakistan never signed the treaty. They have been building their nuclear weapons and North Korea (claimed to have withdrawn from the treaty) has also declared itself a state possessing nuclear weapons.[71] India while refusing to sign NPT gave three strong reasons: (i) The NPT defines "nuclear weapons states" as those that tested devices before 1967, which means India cannot ever be one; (ii) No fixed timelines have been mentioned for disarmament; and (iii) NPT is an unfair treaty as nuclear-weapon states have no obligation to give them up while non-nuclear states are not allowed to have them.

Clandestine nuclear weapons programmes had been proceeding in Iran, Libya, and South Africa. Some of these have been forcible whereas some were voluntarily abandoned. Iraq, though falsely claimed by the US; never had any nuclear weapons programme. In case Saddam Hussein had nuclear weapons he might have used them as an act of last resort since the regime and his own life were at stake. The NPT is in jeopardy because

68 Muller Harald, Farewell to Arms: What's Blocking Nuclear Disarmament, IAEA Bulletin 46/2, March 2005, pp. 4.

69 Rauf Tariq, The NPT at 50: Perish or Survive. Arms Control Association, March 2020, available at: https://www.armscontrol.org/act/2020-03/features/npt-50-perish-survive.

70 Nobuyasu Abe, The NPT at Fifty: Successes and Failures, *Journal for Peace and Nuclear Disarmament*, Vol. 3 (2), 2020, pp. 224-233.

71 The Democratic People's Republic of Korea (DPRK) became a state party to the NPT in 1985, but announced in 2003 that it would no longer be bound by the treaty. Since that time, negotiations over the North Korean nuclear program have not resolved the dispute between the DPRK and the international community. North Korea tested a nuclear weapon in 2006 and again in 2009. Subsequently the Security Council adopted two Chapter VII resolutions condemning the tests and imposing sanctions. Both the DPRK's withdrawal from the NPT and its nuclear-weapon tests constitute significant challenges to the efficacy to the NPT regime.

the nuclear-weapon states have paid little attention to their disarmament commitments. The US and others have treated Article VI much like Article V (as if it did not exist).[72] The treaty is suffering from a growing legitimacy deficit. Article VI has failed in specifying the measures which should be pursued. Despite seven decades of living with the bomb and constructing an international non-proliferation regime, the basic question remains: Whether five nuclear weapons states will ever complete elimination of nuclear weapons as envisaged under Article VI of the Treaty? Article VI is too vague to provide benchmarks for legal assessments of compliance the way, for example, safeguards agreements do.[73] To sum up, NPT is one of the most discriminatory multilateral agreements. The nuclear-weapon states and their followers need to shoulder the greater share of responsibility to build common ground for advancing disarmament.

Today, several challenges threaten the effectiveness of the NPT. These include continuing proliferation efforts, nationalism, great power competition, the spread of nuclear technology, the increasing burden on the International Atomic Energy Agency, and polarisation among NPT member states. This polarisation is partly the result of many non-nuclear-weapon states' frustration with the lack of progress toward nuclear disarmament as set out in Article VI of the NPT. [74] The probability of use increases as the number of nuclear-weapon States rises, and the probability of proliferation increases if the commitments of the NPT are not honoured.

With Israel as an exception, whose nuclear arsenal is integral to the security problems of the West Asia; all states having nuclear weapons are looking at each other, justifying their acquisitions about stronger adversaries: Pakistan to India, India to China, China to the US, France and the UK to Russia, and Russia to the US.[75]If the US and the other nuclear-weapon states do not demonstrate a genuine commitment to nuclear disarmament, NPT may even collapse. [76]

72 Lodgaard Sverre, 2011, *Nuclear Disarmament and Non-Proliferation: Towards a nuclear-weapon-free world*? London: Routledge, pp. 263, at p. 78.

73 Ibid, p. 85.

74 Lee Manseok and Natch Michael, Challenges to the Nuclear Non-Proliferation Treaty, *Strategic Studies Quarterly*, Fall 2020, pp. 95-120.

75 Lodgaard Sverre, 2011, *Nuclear Disarmament and Non-Proliferation: Towards a nuclear-weapon-free world*? London: Routledge, p. 95.

76 In order to salvage and strengthen this important treaty regime, steps will need to be taken in the near future to maintain the high level of commitment of states parties to the noble goal of nonproliferation. Some are small, some are enormous, but one of

Conclusion

There is a growing interest worldwide to ensure that nuclear weapons are subject to the rule of law, the limitations of IHL, and the fundamental norms of human rights. Since the adoption of 1977 Additional Protocol I and the Nuclear Weapons Advisory Opinion, the practice of nuclear-armed States has confirmed that general IHL principles and rules on the conduct of hostilities are relevant to the use of nuclear weapons. The 2013 Secretary of Defence's report on the nuclear employment strategy of the US specifies, "The new guidance makes clear that all plans must also be consistent with the fundamental principles of the Law of Armed Conflict (IHL). Accordingly, plans will, for example, apply the principles of distinction and proportionality and seek to minimise collateral damage to civilian populations and civilian objects. The US will not intentionally target civilian populations or civilian objects."[77]

Since its inception in 1968, the NPT has proven less effective concerning nuclear disarmament by its five nuclear-weapon states (China, France, Russia, the UK and the US). Four other states (India, Israel, Pakistan and the Democratic People's Republic of Korea) have also obtained nuclear weapons. Comparing the NPT with the two other weapons of mass destruction, biological and chemical weapons, the nuclear weapons have the potential for the most devastating impact from a humanitarian point of view.

The ICJ in the *Nuclear Weapons* Case identified the principles of distinction and unnecessary suffering as cardinal principles of the law of armed conflict. The former protects civilians from direct attack, while the latter prohibits weapons that cause unnecessary suffering to combatants.[78] The International Court of Justice did not express a view on the use of a nuclear weapon as a reprisal in response to the first use of a nuclear weapon by another State. The Court only noted that any reprisal must

---

the keys will be a convincing commitment by the nuclear-weapon states that they are determined to fulfil their commitment to Article VI sooner rather than later. Riggle Sharon, Could the Non-Proliferation Treaty Collapse? The Uncertain Road Ahead, *Disarmament Forum*, 2000, pp. 29-38.

77 US Secretary of Defence, Nuclear Employment Strategy of the United States specified in Section 491 of 10 USC, June 2013, pp. 4–5. Available at: https://uploads.fas.org/2013/06/NukeEmploymentGuidance_DODbrief061213.pdf.

78 Stephens Dale, Human Rights and Armed Conflict—The Advisory Opinion of the International Court of Justice in the Nuclear Weapons Case, *Yale Human Rights and Development L. J.*, Vol. 4, 2001, pp. 1-24.

be proportionate to the violation it aims to stop. It is, therefore, difficult to see how the use of nuclear weapons—the ultimate weapon of mass destruction—could ever be consistent with the customary principles of IHL. The indiscriminate nature of nuclear weapon render the protection of civilians' virtually impossible thus violating customary international law reiterated in the 1949 Geneva Conventions and hosts of other treaties related to the protection of victims of war. It will also be extremely difficult to confine the effects of a nuclear explosion, particularly radioactive contamination, to the territories of the states at war. The 1968 St Petersburg declaration was quite specific as to what was allowed in a war and what is prohibited. It proclaimed that the only legitimate objective which states may endeavour to accomplish during war is to weaken the military forces of the enemy, and that, the employment of arms that uselessly aggravate the suffering of disabled men, or render their death inevitable, is contrary to the laws of humanity.

Chapter V

Nuclear-Weapons Free Zones

The US nuclear attack on Hiroshima and Nagasaki shapes the perspective on nuclear weapons even today. One of the important strategies to eliminate nuclear weapons is the negotiation by groups or individual states on regional nuclear-weapon-free zones (NWFZ). These zones ban the manufacture, use, deployment and transit of nuclear weapons in a specific geographical region and assurance from the nuclear-weapon states not to threaten or use nuclear weapons against such zones or states therein. NWFZs today cover 56% of the Earth's surface, 60% of the United Nations membership and 39% of the world's population. The establishment of NWFZ is a regional approach to strengthen global nuclear non-proliferation and disarmament norms and consolidate international efforts towards peace and security. An NWFZ denotes an area established by a group of states by a treaty that defines the status of the absence of nuclear weapons from the zone and sets up a system of verification and control to guarantee compliance. United Nations agencies and processes have generally supported the establishment of NWFZs.[1]

NWFZs cover populated areas and emanate from the sovereign states within the prospective zones. The concept of a nuclear-free zone rests on four main pillars: (i) The participatory countries must undertake a legal obligation under international law not to produce or deploy nuclear weapons in their territories, nor to permit other countries within their zone to carry out such deployment. This obligation must be equally valid in times of war and in times of peace. (ii) The nuclear states, for their part, must undertake to respect the status of the NWFZ and to refrain from using or threatening to use nuclear weapons against states within such a

1 Mendenhall Elizabeth, Nuclear-Weapon-Free Zones and Contemporary Arms Control, *Strategic Studies Quarterly*, Vol. 14, No. 4, Winter 2020, pp. 122-151.

zone. (iii) An international control apparatus or system must be set up to ascertain that the parties to an NWFZ, as well as the nuclear states, comply with their commitments. (iv) NWFZs must be so established and administered that they enhance international peace and security.

Concept and Germination

The idea of nuclear-weapon-free zones was first introduced by the Soviet Union in 1956; just 11 years after the first nuclear weapons were dropped on Hiroshima and Nagasaki. It had its historical precedent in the concept of demilitarized zones in conventional warfare, in which a partial or total ban on the deployment, production or use of particular weapons or troops was established.[2] Most demilitarized zones were temporary and limited in scope, in most cases encompassing only parts of the territory of member states. The nuclear environment leading to the formulation of the first denuclearization proposals created the need for an explicit renunciation and the complete banning of nuclear weapons by signatory nations. In principle, therefore, NWFZs were understood as geographical areas with the complete absence of nuclear weapons thus minimizing the danger of nuclear war. During the late 1950s and early 1960s, as the cold war nuclear arms race intensified, further NWFZ proposals were advanced for several regions, including Africa, East Asia and Europe. In 1959 Romania reiterated its 1957 proposal for a Balkan NWFZ. In the same year, Soviet Union Chairman Khruschev advanced proposals for NWFZs on the Korean Peninsula and in the Asian Pacific. All of the proposals were rejected by the Western NWSs which considered regional deployment of nuclear weapons a necessity to counter the numerically superior conventional forces of their adversaries.[3] Despite the opposition by the Western powers to these proposals for NWFZ, the first nuclear weapon free geographical region---the Antarctic--- was established through a treaty in 1959 on an initiative by the US. The treaty established a nuclear-weapon-free and demilitarized

2 In March 1956, a proposal was presented to a United Nations Committee on Disarmament which sought to obtain partial arms restrictions, the establishment of regions under constant inspection, as well as a prohibition of the stationing of nuclear equipped forces, nuclear weapons and hydrogen weapons, on German soil and in neighbouring states. This proposal, which had been presented by the Soviet Union, was adopted and rephrased in a more sophisticated form by the Foreign Minister of Poland, Adam Rapacki, and presented during a session of the United Nations General Assembly in October 1957.

3 Hamel-Green Michael, 'Peeling the orange: regional paths to a nuclear-weapon-free world', Nuclear Weapon Free Zones, *Disarmament Forum*, Vol. 2, 2011, United Nations Institute for Disarmament Research, p. 5.

zone by prohibiting military bases, manoeuvres and weapons testing, and banning nuclear explosions and disposing of radioactive waste.[4]

During this period, there was increasing regional and international concern over the health impacts of radioactive fallout from atmospheric nuclear testing in several regions of the world (Central Asia, Oceania and the Sahara). In 1962 the Cuban Missile Crisis greatly heightened international and regional awareness of the risks of a major nuclear conflict. This led to the negotiation of the Partial Test Ban Treaty and renewed interest in NWFZs. Six months after the Cuban Missile Crisis, five Latin American states (Bolivia, Brazil, Chile, Ecuador and Mexico) called for a multilateral agreement to denuclearize Latin America.[5] This resulted in the Treaty of Tlatelolco, the first NWFZ treaty, followed by other regional agreements.

Nuclear Weapons Free Areas

Current areas that are nuclear-weapon-free can be divided into three categories: (1) nuclear-weapon-free zones (NWFZ) established by treaties; (2) nuclear-weapon-free geographical regions established by treaties; and (3) nuclear-weapon-free status states. There exist five NWFZs in the world today; the Latin and Caribbean NWFZ, the South Pacific NWFZ, the Southeast Asia NWFZ, the African NWFZ, and the Central Asian NWFZ. Each zone is legitimized by specific treaties, namely, the Treaty for Prohibition of Nuclear Weapons in Latin America and the Caribbean (Treaty of Tlatelolco, 1967), the South Pacific Nuclear Free Zone Treaty (Rarotonga Treaty, 1986), the Treaty on the Southeast Asia Nuclear Weapons Free Zone (Bangkok Treaty, 1997), the Treaty on the Nuclear Weapons Free Zone in Africa (Pelindaba Treaty, 2009), and the Central Asia Nuclear Weapons Free Zone Treaty (Semipalatinsk Treaty, 2009). In addition, Mongolia has been accorded Nuclear Weapons Free Zone Status by the UN General Assembly resolution 53/77.

There are three nuclear-weapon-free geographical regions: (i) The Antarctic as established by the 1959 Antarctic Treaty; (ii) Outer space as established by the 1967 Treaty on Principles Governing the Activities of States in the Exploration and Use of Outer Space, including the Moon and

4 Articles I and V of the 1959 Antarctic Treaty.

5 Hamel-Green Michael, 'Peeling the orange: regional paths to a nuclear-weapon-free world', Nuclear Weapon Free Zones, *Disarmament Forum*, Vol. 2, 2011, United Nations Institute for Disarmament Research (UNIDIR), p. 5.

Other Celestial Bodies;[6] and (iii) The Seabed as established by the 1971 Treaty on the Prohibition of the Emplacement of Nuclear Weapons and Other Weapons of Mass Destruction on the Sea-Bed and the Ocean Floor and in the Subsoil Thereof. Antarctica, outer space and the international seabed are our global commons. In each of these cases, the nuclear power states agreed to restrain themselves to avoid the expansion of the Cold War arms race into new parts of the planet, which could lead to dangerous and expensive new forms of competition.[7]

In addition, there are two demilitarized zones, sometimes referred to as a "zone of peace". A demilitarized zone can be defined as "a world region in which there are no military weapons of any kind, nuclear or conventional; no military personnel, equipment or bases." The Antarctic Treaty of 1959 established the Antarctic as a demilitarized zone, with the exception that scientific research can be conducted in the territory by military personnel using military equipment. The Svalbard Treaty of 1920 recognizes the sovereignty of Norway over the Arctic Archipelago of Svalbard. Norway's exercise of sovereignty over the islands is, however, constrained by some of the treaty's provisions. Most of these constraining provisions have to do with economic activity and resources extraction. Article IX of the treaty, however, prohibits Norway from the development of any military infrastructure or fortifications on the islands, making Svalbard a demilitarized zone.

6 The Outer Space Treaty constitutes the cornerstone of the international legal framework for the peaceful application of outer space. Its four core principles are that the exploration and use of outer space shall be carried out "for the benefit and interest of all countries", that outer space will be "the province of all mankind", that outer space shall be "free for exploration and use by all countries", and that the States Parties of the Treaty undertake not to place in orbit "any object carrying nuclear weapons or any other weapons of mass destruction" in the orbit of the earth, moon or any other celestial body. It further enjoins the States Parties to use these bodies exclusively for peaceful purposes, not to subject these to weapons testing or military manoeuvring, and prohibits the establishment of military bases, installations and fortifications thereon. However, the use of military personnel for scientific research or for any other peaceful purposes is not prohibited, nor is the use of any equipment or facility necessary for peaceful exploration of the Moon and other celestial bodies. The Treaty on Principles Governing the Activities of States in the Exploration and Use of Outer Space, Including the Moon and Other Celestial Bodies, January 27, 1967, entered into force on October 10, 1967.

7 Fujita Edmundo, Prevention of Geographical Proliferation of Nuclear Weapons: Nuclear-Free Zones and Zones of Peace in the Southern Hemisphere, UNIDIR Paper No. 4, April 1, 1989, p. 52.

Definition of NWFZ

UN General Assembly Resolution of 1975 defines an NWFZ as: "any zone, recognized as such by the General Assembly, which any group of States, in the free exercises of their sovereignty, has established by virtue of a treaty or convention whereby: (a) The statute of total absence of nuclear weapons to which the zone shall be subject, including the procedure for the delimitation of the zone, is defined; and (b) An international system of verification and control is established to guarantee compliance with the obligations deriving from that statute.[8] The Resolution also defines the "principal obligations of the nuclear-weapon States towards nuclear-weapon-free zones and towards the States included therein" as follows:

> In every case of a nuclear-weapon-free zone that has been recognized as such by the General Assembly, all nuclear-weapon States shall undertake or reaffirm, in a solemn international instrument having full legally binding force, such as a treaty, a convention or a protocol, the following obligations:
>
> (a) To respect in all its parts the statute of total absence of nuclear weapons defined in the treaty or convention which serves as the constitutive instrument of the zone;
>
> (b) To refrain from contributing in any way to the performance in the territories forming part of the zone of acts which involve a violation of the aforesaid treaty or convention;
>
> (c) To refrain from using or threatening to use nuclear weapons against the States included in the zone.

In other words, the nuclear-weapon states are technically obligated by the Resolution to provide formal negative security assurances to the members of an NWFZ. Most NWFZs contain protocols for this purpose.[9]

The Relation between the NPT and Nuclear Weapons Free Zones

The objective of the Nuclear Non-Proliferation Treaty (NPT) is to prevent

8 UN General Assembly Resolution A/RES/3472(XXX) dates December 11, 1975. Para 3 of the Resolution further provides that the above definitions in no way impair the resolutions which the General Assembly has adopted or may adopt with regard to specific cases of nuclear-weapon-free zones nor the rights emanating for the Member States from such resolutions.

9 Mendenhall Elizabeth, Nuclear-Weapon-Free Zones and Contemporary Arms Control, *Strategic Studies Quarterly*, Vol. 14, No. 4, Winter 2020, p. 124.

the spread of nuclear weapons and weapons technology, to promote cooperation in the peaceful uses of nuclear energy and to further the goal of achieving complete disarmament (Article VI). The Treaty represents the only binding commitment in a multilateral treaty to the goal of disarmament by the nuclear-weapon States. A total of 191 States have joined the Treaty, including the five nuclear-weapon States. The NPT prohibits transfer to, acceptance of, as well as the manufacture of any nuclear weapons or other military explosive nuclear devices whatsoever by non-nuclear-weapon states. However, as is clear from Article 2 of the Treaty, the stationing of nuclear weapons is not prohibited; in other words, a loophole to the regime exists.

The establishment of NWFZ is a regional approach for the abolishment of nuclear weapons in certain geographical areas to eliminate the danger of being involved in a nuclear war. Article VII of the NPT states: "Nothing in this Treaty affects the right of any group of States to conclude regional treaties to assure the total absence of nuclear weapons in their respective territories". The NWFZ treaties, in addition to all the matters that the NPT prohibits, do not allow for the stationing of nuclear weapons or other nuclear explosive devices within the territories of state parties. Therefore, NWFZ treaties are more rigorous than the NPT in terms of proliferation. To sign and ratify NWFZ treaties (and certain additional protocols) along with the NPT, therefore, promotes a healthy path towards nuclear disarmament and non-proliferation. The establishment of an NWFZ should be seen not just as a measure for non-proliferation, but also as one for complete nuclear disarmament.[10]

Guidelines and Principles for the Nuclear-Weapon-Free Zones

The UN Disarmament Commission in its report of April 30, 1999 recommended a set of principles and guidelines for the establishment of an NWFZ, which included the following:

- NWFZ should be established based on arrangements freely arrived at among the States of the region concerned.
- The initiative to establish an NWFZ should emanate exclusively from states within the region concerned and be pursued by all States of that region.

10 Mukai Wakana, The importance of Nuclear Weapons Free Zones, *ISYP Journal on Science and World Affairs*, Vol. 1, No. 2, 2005, pp. 79-86.

- In cases where consensus exists on the goal to establish an NWFZ in a given region, efforts exerted by the states of the region for the establishment of such a zone should be encouraged and supported by the international community.
- All the states of the region concerned should participate in the negotiations on and the establishment of such a zone based on arrangements freely arrived at among the states of the region concerned.
- The status of an NWFZ should be respected by all states parties to the treaty establishing the zone as well as by states outside the region, including the nuclear-weapon states (NWS) and other states whose cooperation and support are essential for the maximum effectiveness of such a zone.
- The NWS should be consulted during the negotiations of each treaty and its relevant protocol(s) establishing an NWFZ to facilitate their signature to and ratification of the relevant protocol(s) to the treaty containing legally binding commitments of not to use or threaten to use nuclear weapons against states parties to the treaty.
- Every treaty through which an NWFZ is established should provide for the effective prohibition of the development, manufacturing, control, possession, testing, stationing or transporting by the states parties to the treaty of any type of nuclear explosive device for any purpose, and should stipulate that states parties to the treaty do not permit the stationing of any nuclear explosive devices by any other State within the zone.
- Every treaty through which an NWFZ is established should provide for the effective verification of compliance with the commitments made by the parties to the treaty, inter alia, through the application of full-scope IAEA safeguards to all nuclear activities in the zone.
- An NWFZ should not prevent the use of nuclear science and technology for peaceful purposes and could also promote, if provided for in the treaties establishing such zones, bilateral, regional, and international cooperation for the peaceful use of nuclear energy in the zone, in support of socio-economic, scientific, and technological development of the states parties.

Nuclear-Weapon-Free Zones

Five NWFZs cover territory in most of the Southern Hemisphere and Central Asia. Mongolia and Antarctica are also nuclear-weapon-free. As of 2021, five NWFZ treaties cover highly populated geographic regions and 108 states belong to such treaties. The details of five NWFZ treaties and their ratification state is shown in the table below, followed by a brief discussion on each of the treaty.

Table 5.1: State of Existing Nuclear Weapon Free Zones

Zone	Opened for signature	Entry into Force	Number of State Parties
Latin America (Treaty of Tlatelolco)	14 Feb 1967	22 Apr 1968	33
South Pacific (Treaty of Rarotonga)	06 Aug 1985	11 Dec 1986	13
Southeast Asia (Treaty of Bangkok)	15 Dec 1996	27 Mar 1997	10
Africa (Treaty of Pelindaba)	11 Apr 1996	15 Jul 2009	47
Central Asia	08 Sep 2006	21 Mar 2009	5

I. Treaty for the Prohibition of Nuclear Weapons in Latin America and the Caribbean

Latin America has not been directly exposed to the problem of nuclear deterrence; however, the impact of the Cuban missile crisis of 1962 made regional states aware of the risks involved in a nuclear crisis.[11] The creation of the Latin American NWFZ involved intense bargaining and several compromises among the Latin American states leading to the signature of

11 The Cuban Missile Crisis of October 1962 was a direct and dangerous confrontation between the US and the Soviet Union during the Cold War. During crisis, leaders of the US and the Soviet Union engaged in a tense, 13-day political and military standoff over the installation of nuclear-armed Soviet missiles on Cuba, just 90 miles from US shores and came closest to nuclear conflict. The crisis was unique in a number of ways, featuring calculations and miscalculations as well as direct and secret communications and miscommunications between the two sides. After this, both superpowers began to reconsider the nuclear arms race and took the first steps in agreeing to a nuclear Test Ban Treaty.

the Treaty of Tlatelolco in 1967.[12] The first draft treaty was prepared in a meeting held in November 1964, attended by 14 Latin American delegates in Mexico City. The issues discussed during this meeting included: the advantages and viability of an NWFZ in the region; the benefits of setting up a commission; the geographical definition of the envisaged NWFZ; and the impact of China's nuclear explosion and the terms of expected nuclear powers' guarantees. The negotiations of the treaty and its subsequent implementation helped Latin American states to assess the benefits and costs of non-proliferation commitments. The Treaty for the Prohibition of NuclearWeapons in Latin America and the Caribbean (Treaty of Tlatelolco) was opened for signature on February 14, 1967 in Mexico City. The Latin American NWFZ became the first denuclearized region embracing a significant number of states.

Obligations contained under Article 1 of the treaty provide that the contracting parties are to use the nuclear material and facilities which are under their jurisdiction exclusively for peaceful purposes. The states parties are to prohibit and prevent in their respective territories:

(a) The testing, use, manufacture, production or acquisition by any means whatsoever of any nuclear weapons, by the Parties themselves, directly or indirectly, on behalf of anyone else or in any other way, and

(b) The receipt, storage, installation, deployment and any form of possession of any nuclear weapons, directly or indirectly, by the Parties themselves, by anyone on their behalf or in any other way.

The term "Nuclear weapon", has been defined under Article 5 of the treaty as, "any device which is capable of releasing nuclear energy in an uncontrolled manner and which has a group of characteristics that are appropriate for use for warlike purposes. An instrument that may be used for the transport or propulsion of the device is not included in this definition if it is separable from the device and not an indivisible part thereof."

12 The negotiations of the Treaty of Tlatelolco were facilitated by setting up COPREDAL (*ComisionPreparatoria para la Denuclearizacion de America Latina*), an international organization responsible for the negotiations. Although the negotiations was a long and complicated process, COPREDAL provided an umbrella under which negotiations took place and preliminary consensus was built up as the basis for subsequent and more specific regulation. Serrano Monica, "Latin America—The Treaty of Tlatelolco," in Thakur Ramesh (ed.), 1998, *Nuclear Weapons-Free Zones*, New York: Macmillan Press Ltd, p. 37.

Article 4 of the Treaty of Tlatelolco delineates its Zone of Application as the whole of the territories for which the Treaty is in force. The Zone of Application-defined by the Treaty encompasses a surface of more than 20 million square kilometres. It includes areas of the high seas, defined by the UN Convention of the Law of the Sea, and the national territories of the 33 countries of Latin America and the Caribbean,[13] home to more than 600 million people. The Treaty of Tlatelolco does not extend nor does claim sovereignty of the aforementioned high seas regions for the States Parties; it establishes them as nuclear-weapon-free in accordance with Additional Protocol II of the Treaty.

The parties are also required to conclude agreements individually with the IAEA for the application of safeguards to their nuclear activities. The IAEA has the exclusive power to carry out special inspections.[14]To verify compliance with the obligations entered into by the Contracting Parties under Article 1, a control system has been established under Article 12, which shall be used in particular to verify: (a) That devices, services and facilities intended for peaceful uses of nuclear energy are not used in the testing or manufacture of nuclear weapons; (b) That none of the activities prohibited in Article 1 of this Treaty is carried out in the territory of the Contracting Parties with nuclear materials or weapons introduced from abroad; and (c) That explosions for peaceful purposes are compatible with article 18 of this Treaty.

To ensure compliance with the obligations of the Treaty, the Agency for the Prohibition of Nuclear Weapons in Latin American and the Caribbean (OPANAL) was established in 1969. The Agency is responsible for holding meetings among the Member States related to the purposes, provisions and procedures established by the Treaty. The Treaty establishes the General Conference, the Council and the Secretariat as principal organs of OPANAL. The Secretary-General is the highest officer of the Secretariat. Under Article 7 of the Treaty, OPANAL headquarters is located in Mexico City. The General Conference is the supreme organ of OPANAL, is composed of all the Contracting Parties, namely, all the 33 Latin America and the Caribbean countries; it holds regular meetings every two years and

13 The current States Parties to the Treaty are: Antigua and Barbuda, Argentina, Bahamas, Barbados, Belize, Bolivia, Brazil, Chile, Colombia, Costa Rica, Cuba, Dominica, Dominican Republic, Ecuador, El Salvador, Grenada, Guatemala, Guyana, Haiti, Honduras, Jamaica, Mexico, Nicaragua, Panama, Paraguay, Peru, St. Kitts and Nevis, St. Lucia, St. Vincent and the Grenadines, Suriname, Trinidad and Tobago, Uruguay, and Venezuela.

14 Article 13, the Treaty of Tlatelolco.

may also hold special sessions whenever the Treaty so provides or, in the opinion of the Council, the circumstances so require.

The treaty includes two protocols. The first, by which parties agree to apply key provisions of the treaty to their territories within the zone, has been signed and ratified by France, the UK and the US. All NWS have signed and ratified Protocol II, which promises respect for the treaty's aims and provisions, and provides negative security assurances (NSAs: pledges not to attack non-NWS with nuclear weapons) to states parties. The US, however, did so with two significant reservations. First, it sought to preserve its interpretation of "the relevant rules of international law" under which contracting parties retained "exclusive power and legal competence… to grant or deny non-Contracting Parties transit and transport privileges." Second, it qualified its NSA by making clear that an armed attack by a contracting party in which it was assisted by an NWS would be incompatible with the contracting party's obligations under the treaty. There has been no recorded violation of the treaty by states parties.[15]

The Treaty of Tlatelolco was conceived as one contribution to a global strategy in the matter of disarmament. A few countries such as Mexico and Venezuela have maintained that the Treaty should be linked with a future regime for limiting conventional armaments, believing that it could provide a good basis for an analogous experiment aimed at controlling and limiting conventional weapons in Latin America.[16]

II. The South Pacific Nuclear Free Zone Treaty

The availability of largely unpopulated areas in the South Pacific made this region suitable for testing nuclear devices. From 1946-1958, the US conducted some 66 atmospheric and underwater tests in the Marshall Islands in the northern Pacific region, which lies outside the South Pacific Nuclear-Free Zone (SPNFZ). The UK conducted atmospheric tests between 1952-1957 on Australian territory at Maralinga, Emu Field, and Monte Bello Island. Both the UK and the US conducted atmospheric nuclear tests on Christmas Island until the signing of the Partial Test Ban Treaty (PTBT) in 1963, which banned further atmospheric nuclear detonations.

15 In February 2012, Argentina accused the UK of violating its commitment under Protocol I by sending a nuclear-capable submarine to the South Atlantic. The incident was dismissed by the British Deputy Prime Minister as baseless. 'Argentina submarine claim baseless,' says Nick Clegg, BBC News, March 27, 2012.

16 Cobo Jose R. Martin, The Tlatelolco: An Update, *IAEA Bulletin*, Vol. 26, No. 3, 1984, pp. 25-30.

The South Pacific States, besides being concerned with nuclear testing in their region and its vicinity, were also worried about the dumping of nuclear wastes at sea, fearing radioactive contamination of the marine environment. The South Pacific Forum (SPF) took up the issue in 1975 in response to a proposal by New Zealand calling for the setting up of an NWFZ in the region. This proposal was endorsed by the UN General Assembly that same year. In 1979, in response to reports of nuclear dumping in the region, the SPF strongly condemned the use of the Pacific as a dumping ground for nuclear wastes. Japan also opposed nuclear dumping in the Pacific.

On August 6, 1985, eight leaders of the South Pacific Forum (SPF) formally signed the South Pacific Nuclear Free Zone Treaty (SPNFZ). This included Australia, New Zealand (two states having significant nuclear capabilities and military establishments), Cook Islands, Kiribati, Fiji, Tuvalu, Western Samoa and Niue. The Treaty required that eight members ratify it for it to become registered with the United Nations.[17] The treaty is open for signature by members of the Pacific Islands Forum. Three eligible states (the Marshall Islands, Federated States of Micronesia, and Palau - which, as former members of a UN trusteeship administered by the United States, are now in "free association" with the United States) have not signed the treaty.

The Treaty contains 16 articles, three protocols and four annexures. Annexure 1 defines the area of the South Pacific Nuclear Free Zone, Annexure 2 provides the IAEA safeguards, Annexure 3 establishes a consultative committee in pursuant to Article 10 of the Treaty, and Annexure 4 provides details for the complaint procedure. The Preamble of the Treaty reaffirms the importance of the NTP in preventing the proliferation of nuclear weapons and in contributing to world security; in particular, Article VII of the NPT recognizes the right of any group of States to conclude regional treaties to assure the total absence of nuclear weapons in their respective territories. It refers to the decision of the Fifteenth South Pacific Forum at Tuvalu that a nuclear-free zone should be established in the region at the earliest possible opportunity.

The issue of whether an NWFZ treaty should allow a 'peaceful nuclear explosion' has been a contentious one. The Western nuclear states have been of opinion that there is no effective way to distinguish and control

17 The Treaty entered into force on December 11, 1986. There are 13 States parties to the Treaty of Rarotonga: Australia, Cook Islands, Fiji, Kiribati, Nauru, New Zealand, Niue, Papua New Guinea, Samoa, Solomon Islands, Tonga, Tuvalu, and Vanuatu.

such explosions and NWFZ treaties should specifically outlaw them.[18] The Rarotonga Treaty, under Article 1(c) has adopted an all-embracing definition of a nuclear weapon, which is as follows:

> "... any nuclear weapon or other explosive devices capable of releasing nuclear energy, irrespective of the purpose for which it could be used. The term includes such a weapon or device in unassembled and partly assembled forms, but does not include the means of transport or delivery of such a weapon or device if separable from and not an indivisible part of it."

States Parties to the Rarotonga Treaty are obliged not to manufacture or otherwise acquire, possess, or have control over any nuclear explosive device anywhere inside or outside the Treaty zone; not to seek or receive any assistance in this; not to take any action to assist or encourage the manufacture or acquisition of any nuclear explosive device by any State, and not to provide sources or special fissionable materials or equipment to any non-nuclear-weapon State (NNWS), or any nuclear-weapon State (NWS) unless it is subject to safeguards agreements with the IAEA.[19] States Parties are also obligated to prevent in the territory of States Parties the stationing of any nuclear explosive device; to prevent the testing of any nuclear explosive device; not to dump radioactive wastes and other radioactive matter at sea, anywhere within the SPNFZ, and to prevent the dumping of radioactive wastes and other radioactive matter by anyone in the territorial sea of the States Parties.[20] Each party remains free to allow visits, as well as transit, by foreign ships and aircraft regardless of whether they are conventionally or nuclear powered and whether they may or may not be carrying nuclear weapons. The Treaty does not explicitly prohibit the transport of nuclear weapons through the zone on foreign vessels or aircraft. The testing of nuclear explosive devices is prevented under Article 6, whereas dumping of radioactive waste and other radioactive matter at sea anywhere within the SPNFZ is prohibited under Article 7 of the Treaty.

Article 8 of the Treaty of Rarotonga establishes a control system for reports and exchange of information as detailed in Article 9; consultations as specified in Article 10 and Annexure 4(1) The treaty also includes an

---

18 Hamel-Green Michael, "The South Pacific – The Treaty of Rarotonga," in Thakur Ramesh (ed.), 1998, *Nuclear Weapons-Free Zones*, New York: Macmillan Press Ltd, pp. 59-80.

19 Article 3 and 4, the Treaty of Rarotonga.

20 Article 5, the Treaty of Rarotonga.

amendment provision (Article 11) under which proposals for amendment would be considered by the Consultative Committee and would require consensus support to be adopted. However, there is one shortcoming in the Treaty of Rarotonga that its control system under Article 8 applies only to the treaty parties and not to the protocol parties; as a result, there is no mechanism for verifying and ensuring compliance by NWS signatories to the Protocols. The treaty establishes a Consultative Committee (Annexure 3) to hear complaints by parties over breaches of obligations to the treaty (Annexure 4).

There are two main differences in the Treaties of Tlatelolco and Rarotonga. First, the Treaty of Tlatelolco permitted nuclear explosions for peaceful purposes (Article 18); the Treaty of Rarotonga however, bans such explosions (Article 4). To the drafters of the Rarotonga Treaty, no distinction could be drawn between tests for peaceful purposes and tests for warlike purposes. Second, the Treaty of Tlatelolco placed no ban on the dumping of radioactive wastes and other radioactive materials at sea. The Treaty of Rarotonga bans this under Article 7. This is perhaps the more innovative provision of the Treaty of Rarotonga. The Treaty of Rarotonga is considered an improvement upon the Tlatelolco Treaty in preventing the dumping of nuclear wastes and banning nuclear explosions even for peaceful purposes.[21]

The treaty includes three additional protocols.[22] Of the initial five nuclear-weapon states, France and the United Kingdom have ratified all three protocols while Russia and China have only ratified Protocols II and III and the US has not ratified any protocol.[23]

---

21 South Pacific Nuclear-free Zone (SPNFZ), Treaty of Rarotonga, Nuclear Threat Initiative, available at: https://www.nti.org/learn/treaties-and-regimes/south-pacific-nuclear-free-zone-spnfz-treaty-rarotonga/.

22 Protocol I calls on each Party with respect to the territories situated within the SPNFZ for which it is internationally responsible, to apply the prohibitions of the Treaty. Protocol II calls on the NWS not to use or threaten to use nuclear explosive devices against any Party to the Treaty or against each other's territories located within the zone. Protocol III calls on the NWS not to test nuclear explosive devices within the zone established by the Treaty.

23 According to the US Department of State, the Treaty of Rarotonga meets all seven of the criteria that the United States has established for supporting any proposed nuclear weapon free zone. The criteria are as follows: (i) the initiative for the creation of the zone should come from the States in the region concerned; (ii) all States whose participation is deemed important should participate; (iii) the zone arrangement should provide for adequate verification of compliance with its provisions; (iv) the establishment of the zone should not disturb existing security arrangements to the

It is more than 36 years since the South Pacific Nuclear Weapons Free Zone was adopted. There have been few developments in the last few years. However, the treaty remains a priority with the Pacific Island Forum (PI). The PIF supports states parties in observing and implementing the treaty. The Treaty has been successful in putting diplomatic pressure on France to cease nuclear testing in the region.[24] The SPNFZ dialogue partners are Canada, China, the European Union, Japan, South Korea, the UK and the US. France was one of the dialogue partners; however, its dialogue partner status was suspended in 1995 in protest of its nuclear tests in Mururoa but restored in 1996.

III. Treaty on the Southeast Asia Nuclear-Weapon-Free Zone

All the 10 member-states of ASEAN have signed the NPT;[25] however, the peaceful use of nuclear power for generating electricity has never been rejected by any one of them. Since ASEAN's formation in 1967, the Southeast Asian states have had concerns about nuclear weapons. In January 1968 the former Malaysian minister of the interior proposed the neutralization of Southeast Asia. The notion of a Southeast Asia Nuclear-

---

detriment of regional and international security or otherwise abridge the inherent right of individual or collective self-defense guaranteed in the Charter of the United Nations; (v) the zone arrangement should effectively prohibit its Parties from developing or otherwise possessing any nuclear device for whatever purpose; (vi) the establishment of the zone should not affect the existing rights of its Parties under international law to grant or deny other States transit privileges within their respective land territory, internal waters, and airspace to nuclear powered and nuclear capable ships and aircraft of non-party nations, including port calls and overflights; and (vii) the zone arrangement should not seek to impose restrictions on the exercise of rights recognized under international law, particularly the high seas freedoms of navigation and overfl ight, the right of innocent passage of territorial and archipelagic seas, the right of transit passage of international straits, and the right of archipelagic sea lanes passage of archipelagic waters. South Pacific Nuclear Free Zone Treaty, Bureau of International Security and Nonproliferation, available at: https://2009-2017.state.gov/t/isn/5189.htm. US Secretary of State Hillary Clinton informed the 2010 NPT Review Conference on May 3, 2010 that the administration was preparing to submit the treaty protocols to the US Senate for approval. President Obama submitted all three protocols to the Senate in May 2011 with a view to securing the Senate's consent to ratification. The Senate has so far taken no action on the matter.

24 Hamel-Green Michael, "The South Pacific – The Treaty of Rarotonga," in Thakur Ramesh (ed.), 1998, *Nuclear Weapons-Free Zones*, New York: Macmillan Press Ltd, p. 68.

25 Malaysia and Laos became parties to the NPT in 1970, the Philippines and Cambodia in 1972, Thailand and Singapore in 1976, Indonesia in 1979, Brunei in 1984, Vietnam in 1985 and Myanmar in 1992.

Weapon-Free Zone (SEANWFZ) was realized on November 27,1971, when the original five members of the ASEAN signed a Declaration on a Zone of Peace, Freedom, and Neutrality (ZOPFAN).[26] During that time, ASEAN took note of the nuclear-weapons-free zone elsewhere, in particular the Treaty of Tlatelolco and the Lusaka Declaration on the proposed African nuclear-weapon-free zone. The first major component of the ZOPFAN pursued by ASEAN was the establishment of a SEANWFZ. However, owing to the political environment in the region, the formal proposal for the establishment of such a zone was tabled only in the mid-1980s. After a decade of negotiating and drafting efforts by the ASEAN Working Group on a ZOPFAN, the SEANWFZ Treaty was signed by the heads of states/ governments of all 10 regional states in Bangkok on December 15, 1995.[27] The Treaty came into force on March 27, 1997, when Vietnam, as the seventh signatory, deposited its instrument of ratification and accession.

The Southeast Asia Nuclear-Weapon-Free Zone Treaty (Bangkok Treaty) consists of 22 Articles and a Protocol. The Treaty and its Protocol applies to the territories, continental selves, and EEZ of the States Parties within the Zone in which the Treaty is in force.[28] The Treaty essentially declares that Southeast Asia, including its waters and airspace, would be free from nuclear weapons. The term "Nuclear Weapon" as defined under Article 1(c) of the Treaty means "any explosive device capable of releasing nuclear energy in an uncontrolled manner but does not include the means of transport or delivery of such device if separable from and not

26 The spread of nuclear facilities in southeast Asia arose from three factors: the inclination of the united States to station more nuclear facilities or weapons in countries allied to it; the fear of facing the existent and fast-growing Chinese nuclear threat with conventional forces or relying on Western guarantees; and the desire of neutral and expansive countries such as Indonesia to avoid the diplomatic paralysis which comes from facing a nuclear power, such as Britain. Singh Bilveeer, ASEAN: The Southeast Asia Nuclear-Weapon-Free Zone and the Challenge of Denuclearization in Southeast Asia, Problems and Prospects, Canberra Papers on Strategy and Defence No. 138, The Australian National University, 2000, p. 26.

27 Member States: Brunei Darussalam, Cambodia, Indonesia, Laos, Malaysia, Myanmar, Philippines, Singapore, Thailand, and Vietnam.

28 Article 19 (a), of the Treaty of Bangkok provides: Southeast Asia Nuclear-weapon-Free Zone, means the area comprising the territories of all States in southeast Asia, namely, Brunei Darussalam, Cambodia, Indonesia, Laos, Malaysia, Myanmar, Philippines, Singapore, Thailand and Vietnam, and their respective continental shelves and Exclusive Economic Zones (EEZ).

an indivisible part thereof." The treaty also defines the term, "radio-active material", "radioactive wastes", and "dumping."[29]

The Treaty of Bangkok prohibits the development, manufacture, acquisition or testing of nuclear weapons by the parties anywhere inside or outside the zone, as well as the stationing and transport of nuclear weapons in or through the zone. Each state party may decide for itself whether to allow visits and transit by foreign ships and aircraft. The parties undertake not to dump at sea, or discharge into the atmosphere anywhere within the zone, any radioactive material or waste, or to dispose of radioactive material on land.[30] The zone includes not only the territories but also the continental shelves and exclusive economic zones (EEZs) of the states parties. The use of nuclear energy for peaceful purposes is permitted under Article 4 of the Treaty. The parties are also required to conclude agreements individually with the IAEA for the application of full-scope safeguards to their peaceful nuclear activities.[31]

Verification is to be achieved through reports by members and the exchange of information, and the application of IAEA safeguards. Under Article 7 of the Treaty, the States Parties have discretion over visits by foreign ships and aircraft to ports and airfields, transit of airspace by foreign aircraft, and navigation by foreign ships carrying nuclear weapons. The treaty provides for a Commission for the Southeast Asia Nuclear-weapons-free Zone (Article 8) to oversee the implementation of this treaty and ensure compliance with its provisions. An executive committee, a subsidiary organ of the Commission, is composed of all States Parties to the Treaty. Each State Party shall be represented by one senior official as its representative, who may be accompanied by alternates and advisers.

The Treaty also gives each State Party the right to ask another State Party for clarification or a fact-finding mission (Article 12) to resolve an ambiguous situation or one which may give rise to doubts about compliance. If there is a breach by a State Party, that State Party shall, within a reasonable time, take all steps necessary to bring itself into full compliance with this treaty. If this fails, the commission shall decide on any measure it deems appropriate to cope with the situation, including the submission of the matter to the IAEA and, where the situation might endanger international peace and security, the Security Council and the

29 See Article 1(e), (f) and (g) of the Treaty of Bangkok.

30 Article 3, the Treaty of Bangkok.

31 Article 4, the Treaty of Bangkok.

General Assembly of the United Nations. The procedure for a fact-finding mission, as established under Article 13, has been provided in Annexure to the Treaty.

The one protocol to the treaty is open for signature by the five NWS and commits the parties to "respect the Treaty and not to contribute to any act which constitutes a violation of the Treaty or its Protocol."[32] The Protocol (Article 2) also commits the parties not to use or threaten to use nuclear weapons against any state party to the treaty or within the zone itself. None of the NWS has ratified the protocol. Prominent among their concerns is the geographical scope of the treaty (which includes states parties' continental shelves and EEZs) and its implications for freedom of navigation in international waters.[33]

There are a few limitations of the Treaty of Bangkok: (i) It does not prohibit the transit of nuclear weapons or devices through the territorial seas of its members. For instance, Article 7 allows states parties to determine for themselves whether to grant transit rights through their territories to foreign ships and aircraft. (ii) While the Treaty bans the dumping of radioactive wastes in the zone, there is no prohibition on nuclear activities which could produce such wastes. (iii) The Treaty does not ban the production of nuclear power plants. These plants could pose dangers to nuclear proliferation because nuclear wastes from reactors contain weapons-usable plutonium which could be used in nuclear weapon production by the rogue states. (iv) The treaty also runs the risk of being weakened by its full recognition of the rights of innocent passage or transit passage of international straits, archipelagic sea lanes and high seas that attracts the provisions of the UN Convention on the Law of Sea (UNCLOS). This means ships carrying nuclear weapons can continue to enjoy these rights in various UNCLOS regimes. (v) The Treaty does not

32 Article 1, Protocol to the Bangkok Treaty.

33 By signing the Protocol to the Bangkok Treaty, all NWS countries will be essentially offering negative security assurances to one another and even to those de facto nuclear---armed countries outside of the NPT framework. There might even be concern that some nuclear---armed countries might therefore deliberately hide their SSBNs within the vast maritime area of the zone and use it as a sanctuary to protect their nuclear forces from being threatened. As a result, some NWS countries do not want their signature on the protocol to restrict their military options against other nuclear---armed countries. Zhao Tong, Nuclear Weapon States and the Southeast Asia Nuclear---Weapon---Free Zone, Asia Pacific Leadership Network for Nuclear Non---Proliferation and Disarmament & Centre for Nuclear Non--Proliferation and Disarmament, Policy Brief No. 28, February 2017, pp. 8.

have any additional protocol binding the NWS to desist from nuclear testing within the zone application.[34]

The Bangkok Treaty does not have any designated Secretariat, given the informal style of ASEAN, but the Commission at the level of Foreign Ministers and the working group of Senior Officials works to promote the full implementation of the zone. During the 36th ASEAN Summit on June 26, 2020 (via teleconference from Hanoi, Vietnam) the Chairman's reiterated the ASEAN member states' commitment to preserving Southeast Asia as a region free of nuclear and other weapons of mass destruction.

IV. African Nuclear-Weapon-Free Zone Treaty

The African continent, except for a brief South African adventure, has never posed any threat to global peace on the possession of nuclear weapons. Since political independence in the 1960s, the region remained extremely vulnerable to external domination and exploitation. However, the African states have pursued denuclearization energetically.[35] Africa's security concerns changed after France carried out nuclear tests in the Sahara desert in 1960. These tests had the direct implication of severe contamination of the region and were opposed by a few African states. This led to a few African leaders approaching the UN General Assembly which adopted the following resolution in November 1961 declaring Africa a denuclearized zone:[36]

> Concerned about the present rate of nuclear armament and the possible spread of nuclear weapons, as well as the resumption of nuclear tests in the continent of Africa which is being emancipated,
>
> Recognizing the need to prevent Africa from becoming involved in any competition associated with the ideological struggles between the Powers engaged in the arms race and, particularly, with nuclear weapons,
>
> Recognizing further that the task of economic and social development in the African States requires the uninterrupted attention of those States in order to allow them to fulfil their goals and to contribute

34 Hernandez Carolina G., "Southeast Asia – The Treaty of Bangkok,' in Thakur Ramesh (ed.), 1998, *Nuclear Weapons-Free Zones*, New York: Macmillan Press Ltd, pp. 81-92.

35 Ihonvbere Julius O., "Africa—The Treaty of Pelindaba," in Thakur Ramesh (ed.), 1998, *Nuclear Weapons-Free Zones*, New York: Macmillan Press Ltd, pp. 93-120.

36 UN General Assembly Resolution 1652(XVI) November 24, 1961.

fully to the maintenance of international peace and security,

Calls upon the Member States:

(a) To refrain from carrying out or continuing to carry out in Africa nuclear tests in any form;

(b) To refrain from using the territory, territorial waters or air space of Africa for testing, storing or transporting nuclear weapons;

(c) To consider and respect the continent of Africa as a denuclearized zone.

The Organization of African Unity (OAU) was established in 1963 and at Cairo inaugural conference; African leaders reaffirmed their commitment to keep the continent as NWFZ. The OAU called for the peaceful use of nuclear technology in the interest of development. The OAU leaders also called on the UN to convene an international conference aimed at concluding an international treaty for the denuclearization of Africa. Though the General Assembly approved the OAU resolution on Africa's anti-nuclear agenda, nothing was done internationally to ensure the denuclearization of the continent. Finally, at the sixty-second session of the OAU Council of Ministers in June 1995, a resolution was adopted in favour of the implementation of a treaty declaring Africa an NWFZ.[37] This resolution adopted the draft treaty prepared by a group of experts. The Treaty was finally signed in Cairo on April 11, 1996, and entered into force on July 15, 2009.

The African Nuclear-Weapons-Free Zone Treaty, also known as the Treaty of Pelindaba, has been signed by 47 of the continent's 53 states.[38] It is permanent and shall remain in force indefinitely. The Treaty's Protocols were signed at the same time by the NWS except for Russia, which sought clarification on the status of the Indian Ocean island of Diego Garcia

37 For more details on the negotiations for the Treaty, refer: AdenijiOluyemi, 2002, *The Treaty of Pelindaba on the African Nuclear-Weapon-Free Zone*, Geneva: United Nations Institute for Disarmament Research, UNIDIR/2002/16, pp. 353.

38 Ratified by the following states: Algeria, Angola, Benin, Botswana, Burkina Faso, Burundi, Cabo Verde, Cameroon, Chad, Comoros, Congo, Cote d'Ivoire, Equatorial Guinea, Ethiopia, Gabon, Gambia, Ghana, Guinea-Bissau, Guinea, Kenya, Lesotho, Libya, Madagascar, Malawi, Mali, Mauritania, Mauritius, Mozambique, Namibia, Niger, Nigeria, Rwanda, Sahrawi Arab Democratic Republic (not a UN member state), Senegal, South Africa, Swaziland, Togo, Tunisia, Tanzania, Zambia, Zimbabwe.

(controlled by the UK formerly used as a base for nuclear weapons by the US).

Under the terms of the treaty, African states pledge not to conduct research on, develop, manufacture, stockpile or otherwise acquire, possess, or have control over any nuclear explosive device by any means anywhere; not to seek or receive any assistance in the research on, development, manufacture, stockpiling or acquisition, or possession of any nuclear explosive device; and not to take any action to assist or encourage the research on, development, manufacture, stockpiling or acquisition, or possession of any nuclear explosive device. The Parties also undertake to prohibit, in their territory, the stationing of any nuclear explosive device. However, they are allowed to decide whether to allow visits by foreign ships and aircraft to their ports and airfields, transit of their airspace by foreign aircraft, and navigation by foreign ships in their territorial seas or archipelago waters. The terms "nuclear explosive device", "nuclear installation", and "nuclear material" have been defined under Article 1(3), (5) and (6) of the Treaty of Pelindaba respectively.

The Treaty further prohibits the state parties from testing or allowing testing in their territory or assisting or encouraging the testing of any nuclear explosive device; as well as the dumping of radioactive waste. The Parties undertake to declare any capability for the manufacture of nuclear explosive devices; dismantle and destroy any nuclear explosive device that they have manufactured prior to the coming into force of this Treaty; destroy facilities for the manufacture of nuclear explosive devices or, where possible, to convert them to peaceful uses; and to permit the IAEA to verify the processes of dismantling and destruction of the nuclear explosive devices, as well as the destruction or conversion of the facilities for their production.[39] The Treaty under Article 8 allows the Parties to engage in peaceful nuclear activities and obligates them to conclude full-scope safeguard agreements with the IAEA to verify the peaceful character of such activities. The Parties also undertake not to take, or assist, or encourage any action aimed at an armed attack by conventional or other means against nuclear installations in the Treaty's zone of application.[40]

The Treaty provides for maintaining the highest standards of security and effective physical protection of nuclear materials, facilities and equipment to prevent theft or unauthorized use and handling. The

39 Article 5 and 6, the Treaty of Pelindaba.

40 Article 9, the Treaty of Pelindaba.

states must apply measures of physical protection as recommended and developed by IAEA.[41] Under the Treaty, the states have an obligation not to take, or assist, or encourage any action aimed at an armed attack by conventional or other means against nuclear installations in the African nuclear-weapon-free zone.[42] However, the transport of nuclear weapons through ports, airfields and territorial waters within the zone is the independent decision of each state party.[43]

Upon entry into force, the Treaty provides for the establishment of the African Commission on Nuclear Energy (AFCONE) to ensure compliance with the obligations under the Treaty.[44] AFCONE shall have a Bureau consisting of the Chairman, the Vice-Chairman, and the Executive Secretary. The Commission is to meet once a year although an extraordinary session may be required to settle disputes. The headquarters and membership of AFCONE were decided at the first Treaty conference in November 2010. South Africa was selected to host the commission headquarters.

A Party with grounds for a complaint that another Party to the Treaty or Protocol II is in breach of its obligations shall bring the subject matter of the complaint to the attention of the offending Party and shall allow the latter 30 days to provide the former with an explanation to resolve the matter. If the matter is not resolved, the complaining Party may bring its concerns before AFCONE, which may request that the IAEA conduct an inspection as soon as possible. AFCONE may also designate its representatives to accompany the Agency's inspection team. If AFCONE

41 Article 10, the Treaty of Pelindaba.

42 Article 11, the Treaty of Pelindaba: Article 11, which prohibits armed attacks on nuclear installations, is distinct in that few of the other NWFZ treaties include such a provision and thus "reassures parties that other parties will neither launch such an attack nor assist others in doing so". This is important given that a number of African states have operational nuclear research reactors. While South Africa is the only state at present to have nuclear power reactors, a number of African states are in the process of investigating the feasibility of developing nuclear power plants for generating electricity. Stott Noel, The Treaty of Pelindaba: towards the full implementation of the African NWFZ Treaty, *Disarmament Forum*, Vol. 2, 2011, p. 17.

43 Article 3 and 4, the Treaty of Pelindaba.

44 Article 12, the Treaty of Pelindaba. AFCONE is responsible for: (i) collating reports and the exchange of information; (ii) arranging consultations; (iii) convening conferences; (iv) reviewing the application to peaceful nuclear activities of safeguards by the IAEA; (v) the complaints procedure; (vi) encouraging regional and sub-regional cooperation programs for peaceful uses of nuclear science and technology; and (vii) promoting international cooperation.

decides that the Party complained of is in breach of its obligations under this Treaty, States Parties to the Treaty shall meet in extraordinary session to discuss the matter. The States Parties convened in extraordinary session may make recommendations to the Party held to be in breach of its obligations and to the African Union. The African Union may, if necessary, refer the matter to the UN Security Council.

Protocol I call on the NWS not to use or threaten to use a nuclear explosive device against any Party to the Treaty and any territory within the Pelindaba NWFZ. **Protocol II** calls on the NWS not to test or assist or encourage the testing of any nuclear explosive device anywhere within the Pelindaba NWFZ.[45] Protocol III, by which parties agree to apply key provisions of the treaty to their territories and situated within the Pelindaba NWFZ zone has been ratified by all eligible states other than Spain.

V. The Central Asian Nuclear-Weapon-Free Zone Treaty

The idea of a Central Asian Nuclear-Weapon-Free Zone (CANWFZ) dates back to the 1992 initiative by Mongolia declaring itself a nuclear-weapon-free zone (NWFZ), in which Mongolia also called for a regional NWFZ. The first formal CANWFZ proposal was made by Uzbek President Islam Karimov at the UN General Assembly in 1993. Additional proposals by Uzbekistan and Kyrgyzstan followed in 1994-1996, but none made any headway owing to a lack of regional consensus on the issue. However, the crucial step was taken on February 27, 1997, when the five presidents of the Central Asian states issued the Almaty Declaration endorsing the creation of a CANWFZ. Experts from all five Central Asian states agreed on the text of a treaty establishing a CANWFZ at a meeting held in Samarkand in Uzbekistan from 25-27 September 2002. The agreement concluded five years of talks that began in 1997. On February 8, 2005, the five Central Asian states adopted a final draft of the treaty text at a meeting in Tashkent, Uzbekistan.

The CANWFZ Treaty was signed on September 8, 2006, at the former Semipalatinsk nuclear test site in Kazakhstan, hence the Treaty is also known as the 'Semipalatinsk Treaty'. The treaty has been ratified by all five Central Asian states--the Republic of Kazakhstan, the Kyrgyz Republic, the

45 Protocol I was signed and ratified by China (September 6, 1996), France (July 31, 1997), the UK (February 27, 2001) and the Russian Federation (March 11, 2011). Protocol II was signed and ratified by China (September 6, 1996), France (July 31, 1997), the UK (February 27, 2001) and the Russian Federation (March 11, 2011). The US is yet to ratify Protocols I and II.

Republic of Tajikistan, Turkmenistan, and the Republic of Uzbekistan. It entered into force on March 21, 2009.[46]

The Treaty in Article 1(b) defines "Nuclear weapon or other nuclear explosive device" as "any weapon or other explosive device capable of releasing nuclear energy, irrespective of the military or civilian purpose for which the weapon or device could be used. The term includes such a weapon or device in unassembled or partly assembled forms, but does not include the means of transport or delivery of such a weapon or device if separable from it." This term encompasses so-called "peaceful nuclear devices."[47] "Nuclear material" is defined in Article 1(d) to mean any source material or special fissionable material as defined in Article XX of the Statute of the International Atomic Energy Agency (lAEA) and as may be amended by the IAEA. Article 1(e) defines "radioactive waste" as "any radioactive material, i.e., any substance containing radio-nuclides that will be or has already been removed and is no longer utilized, at activities and activity concentrations of radio-nuclides greater than the exemption levels established in international standards issued by the IAEA." The term "facility has been defined under Article 1(f) as a reactor, critical facility, conversion plant, fabrication plant, reprocessing plant, isotope separation plant, or separate storage installation, or any location where nuclear material in amounts greater than one effective kilogram is customarily used.

Basic Obligations: The Central Asian States Article 3 of the Treaty, undertake not to conduct research on, develop, manufacture, stockpile or otherwise acquire, possess or have control over any nuclear weapon or other nuclear explosive devices "by any means anywhere." These obligations constitute the core commitments under the treaty. They are not limited to the territory of a state party or to the Central Asian Nuclear-Weapon-Free Zone; they are global commitments undertaken by each states party. The states parties also undertake not to seek or receive any assistance in, or to take any action to assist or encourage, such activities. Each states party undertakes not to allow in its territory: (i) the production, acquisition,

46 The Treaty is guided by the Almaty Declaration of the Heads of State of the Central Asian States adopted on February 28, 1997; the Statement of the Ministers of Foreign Affairs of the five States of the region adopted at Tashkent on September 15, 1997; the UN General Assembly resolutions and decisions 52/38S of December 9, 1997, 53/77 A of December 4, 1998, 55/33W of December 20, 2000, 57/69 of November 22, 2002, 58/518 of December 8, 2003, 59/513 of December 3, 2004 and 60/516 of December 8, 2005, entitled "Establishment of a nuclear-weapon-free zone in Central Asia."

47 Article 1(a), the CANWFZ Treaty.

stationing, storage or use, of any nuclear weapon or other nuclear explosive devices; (ii) the receipt, storage, stockpiling, installation, or other forms of possession of or control over any such weapon or device; and (iii) any actions, by anyone, to assist or encourage the development, production, stockpiling, acquisition, or possession of or control over any nuclear weapon or other nuclear explosive devices. The states parties pledge not to allow the disposal of radioactive waste of other states in their respective territories.[48]

The term "stationing" has been defined in Article 1(c) as implantation, emplacement, stockpiling, storage, installation, and deployment. The prohibition on stationing in Article 3(d)(i) does not alter the sovereign right of each Treaty Party to allow "transit through its territory by air, land or water, including visits by foreign ships to its ports and landing of foreign aircraft at its airfields." "Stationing" does not include transit through territorial waters or airspace, or port visits, by vessels carrying nuclear explosive devices.

Under Article 5, states party have an obligation not to undertake any nuclear weapon test explosion or any other nuclear explosion. They are to prohibit and prevent any such nuclear explosion at any place under its jurisdiction or control; and refrain from causing, encouraging, or in any way participating in the carrying out of any nuclear weapon test explosion or any other nuclear explosion. The states parties are to assist inthe environmental rehabilitation of territories contaminated as a result of past activities related to the development, production or storage of nuclear weapons or other nuclear explosive devices.[49] The states parties retain the right to use nuclear energy for peaceful purposes. For this, the states need to conclude and bring into force an agreement with the IAEA for the application of safeguards following the NPT and an Additional Protocol (AP) thereto.[50]

The states are to maintain measures of physical protection of nuclear material, facilities and equipment to prevent its unauthorized use or handling or theft. The states must ensure physical protection of nuclear material in domestic use, transport and storage, to nuclear material in international transport, and to nuclear facilities within its territory

48 Article 3, the CANWFZ Treaty.

49 Article 6, the CANWFZ Treaty.

50 Article 7 and 8, the CANWFZ Treaty.

as envisaged under the Convention on Physical Protection of Nuclear Material of 1987 and the guidelines developed by the IAEA.[51]

Like other NWFZ treaties, the Treaty also has a Protocol, which is open for signature by China, France, Russia and the UK and the US.[52] Under the Protocol, the signatories are not to use or threaten to use a nuclear weapon or other nuclear explosive devices against any Party to the Treaty (called negative security assurance) and also not to contribute to any act that constitutes a violation of the Treaty or Protocol by the Parties to them. Three NWS (France, the UK and the US) do not recognize the zone. They argue that Article XII of the Treaty, which says that the treaty "does not affect the rights and obligations of the Parties under other international treaties which they may have concluded prior to the date of the [treaty's] entry into force," would allow the stationing of Russian nuclear weapons in Central Asia if the Tashkent (Collective Security Organization) Treaty is invoked.

The CANWFZ Treaty does not establish any institution to implement the denuclearized status of Central Asia, nor are there any pre-existing regional cooperation institutions or mechanisms that could serve as a secretariat for CANWFZ. States Parties have agreed, however, to hold annual consultative meetings of their representatives "to review compliance with the Treaty or other matters related to its implementation."

51 Article 9, the CANWFZ Treaty.

52 All five States have signed the Protocol in New York on May 6,2014. The Treaty meets each of the seven criteria that the US has established for supporting any proposed nuclear-weapon-free zone. The criteria are as follows: (i) The initiative for the creation of the zone should come from the States in the region concerned; (ii) All States whose participation is deemed important should participate; (iii) The zone arrangement should provide for adequate verification of compliance with its provisions; (iv) The establishment of the zone should not disturb existing security arrangements to the detriment of regional and international security or otherwise abridge the inherent right of individual or collective self-defense guaranteed in the Charter of the United Nations; (v) The zone arrangement should effectively prohibit its Parties from developing or otherwise possessing any nuclear explosive device for whatever purpose; (vi) The establishment of the zone should not affect the existing rights of its Parties under international law to grant or deny other States transit privileges within their respective land territory, internal waters, and airspace to nuclear-powered and nuclear-capable ships and aircraft of non-Party nations, including port calls and overflights; and (vii) The zone arrangement should not seek to impose restrictions on the exercise of rights recognized under international law, particularly the high seas freedoms of navigation and overflight, the right of innocent passage of territorial and archipelagic seas, the right of transit passage of international straits, and the right of archipelagic sea lanes passage of archipelagic waters.

The meetings are usually hosted and organized by the current chair of the zone, on a rotating basis.

The existing NWFZs and prohibited activities under these treaties are shown in Table 5.2.

Table 5.2: Key Features of Existing NWFZ

<table>
<tr><th rowspan="2">Agreement</th><th rowspan="2">Year in Force</th><th rowspan="2">Zone</th><th colspan="4">Prohibited Activities Related to Nuclear-Weapons</th></tr>
<tr><th>Manufacture/ Test/ Storage/ basing</th><th>Transit</th><th>Waste</th><th>Peaceful Exploitation</th></tr>
<tr><td>Latin American NWFZ</td><td>1968</td><td rowspan="3">Member Territories and Ocean</td><td rowspan="5">Yes</td><td rowspan="5">No</td><td>No</td><td>No</td></tr>
<tr><td>South Pacific NWFZ</td><td>1986</td><td>Yes</td><td>Yes</td></tr>
<tr><td>Southeast Asia NWFZ</td><td>1997</td><td>Yes</td><td>Yes</td></tr>
<tr><td>African NWFZ</td><td>2009</td><td rowspan="2">Member Territories</td><td>Yes</td><td>Yes</td></tr>
<tr><td>Central Asia NWFZ</td><td>2009</td><td>Yes</td><td>Yes</td></tr>
</table>

Mongolia's Nuclear-Weapon-Free Status

Following the withdrawal of Russian troops from its territory in 1992, Mongolia was no longer an ally of a nuclear-weapon state. In the new circumstances based on its own national and broader regional interests, the President of Mongolia in an address to the United Nations[53] declared his country's territory a nuclear-weapon-free zone.[54]In September 1992,

53 The President of Mongolia announced before the 47th session of the United Nations General Assembly in 1992 that Mongolia's territory would be a nuclear weapons free zone.

54 A comprehensive study conducted in 1976, in accordance with the Resolution 3261 F of the UN General Assembly in 1974, provided for the possibility of a single-State nuclear-weapon-free zone (SS-NWFZ). The study concluded that "obligations relating to the establishment of nuclear-weapon-free zones may be assumed not only by groups of States, including entire continents or large geographical regions, but also by small groups of States and even individual countries."

Mongolia confirmed that it was fully compliant with its obligations as a non-NWS party to the NPT and that it had in place laws giving it "the domestic legal status of being free of nuclear weapons." In 1998, the General Assembly adopted a resolution entitled "Mongolia's international security and nuclear-weapon-free status" in which the Assembly welcomed Mongolia's declaration of its nuclear-weapon-free status and expressed conviction that the internationally recognized status of Mongolia would contribute to enhancing stability and confidence-building in the [Northeast Asian] region. The General Assembly also invited the five nuclear-weapon States, to cooperate with Mongolia in taking the necessary measures to consolidate and strengthen Mongolia's independence, sovereignty and territorial integrity, the inviolability of its borders, its economic security, its ecological balance and its nuclear-weapon-free status, as well as its independent foreign policy.[55]

The "Law of Mongolia on Its Nuclear-Weapon-Free Status" (LOMNWFS), having nine articles, entered into force on February 3, 2000. The legislation on Mongolia's nuclear-weapon-free status consists of the "Constitution of Mongolia", the "LOMNWFS" and other legislative acts adopted in conformity with them. Article 2.2 of the LOMNWFS provides that in case an international treaty to which Mongolia is a party contains provisions different from those provided for in the LOMNWFS, the provisions of the international treaty shall prevail. The law covers the territory of Mongolia in its entirety, including its air space, land, waters, and sub-soil.

An individual, legal person or any foreign State shall be prohibited on the territory of Mongolia from committing, initiating, or participating in the following acts or activities relating to nuclear weapons: (i) developing, manufacturing, or otherwise acquiring, possessing, or having control over nuclear weapons; (ii) stationing or transporting nuclear weapons by any means; and (iii) dumping or disposing of nuclear weapons-grade radioactive material or nuclear waste. Transportation through the territory of Mongolia of nuclear weapons, parts, or components thereof, as well as of nuclear waste or any other nuclear material designed or produced for weapons purposes shall be prohibited.[56] Article 3 of the LOMNWFS defines "nuclear weapon" as "any explosive device that is capable of releasing nuclear energy uncontrollably and that can be used for hostile

55 UN document A/RES/53/77 D dated December 4, 1998.

56 Article 4, the LOMNWFS.

purposes;" and "nuclear-weapon-free status" means "a legal status of being free from nuclear weapons."

The Mongolian government has the right to gather information, stop, detain, and search any suspected aircraft, train, vehicle, individual, or group of persons. The central administrative authority in charge of foreign relations shall be entrusted with monitoring compliance with the present law and the international commitments assumed by Mongolia in connection with the nuclear-weapon-free status. Non-governmental organizations or individuals may, within the mandate provided for by the legislation, exercise public oversight of the implementation of the legislation on the nuclear-weapon-free status and submit proposals thereon to the relevant State authority. International Verification: Mongolia shall conduct international verification of the implementation of the present law in cooperation with the relevant international organizations or by concluding special international agreements thereon. In case of violation or suspected violation of the present law by a foreign State, Mongolia shall officially notify the State concerned with a violation or suspected violation, request an explanation, and peacefully resolve any question that may arise. If deemed necessary, the International Atomic Energy Agency (IAEA) and other relevant bodies could be asked for assistance. In case of a dispute, the issue could be submitted to the relevant international court or arbitration.

In September 2012, the five NWS and Mongolia signed "parallel political declarations regarding Mongolia's self-declared nuclear-weapon-free status." The five nuclear-weapon states, who have not recognized a single-country NWFZ earlier, reaffirmed security assurances made in connection with Mongolia's nuclear-weapon-free status at the UN General Assembly in October 2000 and agreed "to respect the nuclear-weapon-free status of Mongolia and not to contribute to any act that would violate it." It has been suggested that Mongolia's nuclear-weapon-free status, as discussed above, does not and cannot have a legal standing conferred by a treaty or convention, since it traces its origins to a unilateral declaration of policy, not to a treaty.[57] However, Mongolia does have an internationally recognized nuclear-weapon-free status.

Other Proposals

Mongolia's case cannot be considered exceptional, even by the definition given by the General Assembly in 1975 or the guidelines adopted in 1999.

57 TuyaNyamosor, Mongolia's Nuclear-Weapon-Free Status: Recognition vs Institutionalization, Washington DC: The Brookings Institution, 2012, pp. 24

On July 13,1999, the Austrian Parliament passed the "Constitutional Law in favour of a Nuclear-Free Austria." This law prohibits the testing, production, storage, or transport of nuclear weapons within Austrian territory. Transport, as defined by this law, includes fissile material. In addition, nuclear power plants may not be constructed or operated in Austria. Iceland, Denmark and Norway further prohibit the passage of nuclear-laden ships through their ports (despite all states having membership in NATO). In addition to being a member of the Southeast Asian NWFZ, in 1987, the Philippines amended its constitution to establish itself as a nuclear-weapon-free zone.[58]

In Bangladesh, a draft bill to establish there an NWFZ had been submitted to its parliament. The draft legislation refers to principles and goals of the United Nations Charter, the NPT and other international instruments aimed at nuclear disarmament, the 1996 ICJ Advisory Opinion, UNSC resolution 1540 and other relevant international documents. Bearing the above in mind, ideas are being flagged to have Nepal declare itself an SS-NWFZ declaring reflecting that status in the country's Constitution. A similar idea of establishing a single-State zone or a limited NWFZ is flagged in Sri Lanka.[59]

Among the various proposals to establish NWFZs that followed the end of the Cold War, the prominent ones are from South Asia, Northeast Asia, and West Asia. In September 1972, a Pakistani representative to the IAEA called for a treaty between the South Asian countries along the lines of the Treaty of Tlatelolco. Each year from 1974 to 1997 there were General Assembly resolutions on the establishment of an NWFZ in South Asia. When voting occurred, Pakistan supported the resolutions—but they were rejected by India because such a zone would not address its security concerns about Chinese nuclear weapons. The proposal of the Northeast Asia NWFZ arose out of a series of meetings that began in 1991 between retired diplomats and officers from South Korea, Russia, Japan, China, and the US. Today, the proposal for an NWFZ in Northeast Asia is being promoted in a limited way and through a Track-II level process i.e., through non-official channels. In July 2011 a conference was held in Brussels on West Asia Weapon of Mass Destruction Free Zone. All

58 MacDonald Alexander, The Theory and Evolution of Nuclear-Weapon-Free Zones: Could the Arctic Be Next? North American and Arctic Defence and Security Network (NAADSN), February 1, 2021, pp. 28.

59 Enkhsaikhan Dr., Mongolia's experience in promoting the concept of single-State NWFZs, July 6, 2020.

states of West Asia, apart from Iran, later proposed to continue working towards the establishment of an NWFZ in West Asia. The UN General Assembly, on December 2, 2011, adopted without a vote a resolution on the establishment of NWFZ in West Asia.[60] Israel, in an explanation of the vote, stated that it remained committed to a vision of West Asia developing eventually into a zone free of Chemical, Biological, and Nuclear weapons as well as ballistic missiles. In December 2012, Israel again joined consensus on the resolution stating the fragility of regional security and the absence of a mechanism for regional dialogue, without which it was not possible to build confidence and defuse tension. Given the fragile security environment, weakening of governance in some of the states in the regions and ongoing conflicts, the establishment of a new regional NWFZ is only a remote possibility.[61]

Conclusion

The NWFZs provide an important example of pro-active efforts by non-nuclear-armed states to establish a prohibition on nuclear weapons. They give confidence at a regional level that states are not seeking nuclear weapons. Whilst all of the NWFZ treaties are framed slightly differently, all provide strong contributions towards the rejection and stigmatization of nuclear weapons. The treaties generally prohibit such acts as possession, testing, use, production or acquisition of nuclear weapons, as well as prohibitions on assistance or encouragement toward such acts. Such agreements have been encouraged and supported by the international community. The establishment of NWFZ depends on four conditions: the security interest of regional states in avoiding nuclear threats, pre-existing regional institutions and regional economic cooperation, leadership by a core of regional powers and shared interest in spreading non-proliferation norms. Democracy is not a necessary condition, but democratization can help overcome barriers presented by unsure regional governments.

The NWFZs serve the purposes of nonproliferation and disarmament, thereby achieving security from nuclear weapons through institutionalized

60 Resolution A/RES/66/25 dated December 13, 2011 adopted by the General Assembly on December 2, 2011, 'Establishment of a nuclear-weapon-free zone in the region of the Middle East,' Resolution invited all parties to consider the appropriate means that may contribute towards the goal of general and complete disarmament and the establishment of a zone free of weapons of mass destruction in the region of the Middle East.

61 Kane Chen, The role of civil society in promoting a WMDFZ in the Middle East, *Disarmament Forum*, Vol. 2, 2011, pp. 51-62.

mutual restraint. They are an important contribution to the nuclear disarmament regime. States parties to existing zones can contribute to sharing expertise and experience to make the zones stronger and more effective, especially in the areas of verification and compliance. There is a strong need to expand the reach of NWFZs, particularly in areas of the world where nuclear threats are increasing, and where regional conflicts could unleash a nuclear war through escalation of a conventional war, miscalculation or deliberate pre-emptive attack. However, the proposals for new NWFZs will be much more challenging, because they would directly impact nuclear weapon states—restricting their basing, deployment, and transit of nuclear weapons.

Chapter VI

The Treaty on the Prohibition of Nuclear Weapons

The United Nations (UN) emerged at the time of the immense trail of death and destruction resulting from the Second World War including the devastation caused by the detonation of two nuclear bombs over Japanese cities of Hiroshima and Nagasaki. In the words of Dr Marcel Junod, an International Committee of the Red Cross (ICRC) delegate and the first foreign doctor in Hiroshima in 1945 to assess the effects of the atomic bombing and to assist its victim, "At twelve o'clock, we flew over Hiroshima. We… witnessed a site totally unlike anything we had ever seen before. The centre of the city was a sort of white patch, flattened and smooth like the palm of a hand. Nothing remained. …. Thousand of human beings in the streets and garden in the town centre, struck by a wave of intense heat, died like flies. Others lay withering like worms, atrociously burned. All private houses, warehouses, etc., disappeared as if swept away by supernatural power. Trains were flung off the rails. Every living thing was petrified in an attitude of acute pain."[1] Those who survived suffered many difficulties. Even today, there are several hibakushas (atomic bomb survivors) living in Japan, who are suffering from thyroid, breast, lung and other cancers at higher than normal rates. The effects of the bombings have also been passed down through generations to children and grandchildren.

The use of nuclear weapons raised serious denigration, with many governments calling for an outright ban, arguing the very existence of such weapons as a threat to future generations and the survival of humanity. Several of the scientists involved in the development claimed it was a weapon so destructive that there could be no defence against a large-scale

1 The Hiroshima disaster – a doctor's account, ICRC, available at: https://www.icrc.org/en/doc/resources/documents/misc/hiroshima-junod-120905.htm.

attack. The morality of using it on innocent civilians, plus the immediate necessity for arms control, had both become widespread subjects of popular discussion.

Background

After World War II, it was apparent that the development of nuclear capabilities by the states[2] could enable them to divert technology and materials for weapons purposes. Thus the problem of preventing such diversions became a central issue in discussions on peaceful uses of nuclear energy. Nuclear disarmament was the subject of the first resolution adopted by the UN General Assembly in 1946. On January 24, the General Assembly adopted the very first Resolution 1 (I), which sought the elimination from national armaments of atomic weapons and of all other major weapons adaptable to mass destruction.[3] The resolution specifically identified the goal of eliminating nuclear weapons and what it called other weapons adaptable to mass destruction. These were widely understood to include chemical and biological weapons.[4] At the same time, the world community also recognized the need for the states to have the means to defend themselves and to contribute to international peacekeeping efforts—so conventional arms would not be outlawed per se, but limited and regulated to serve these legitimate ends. The common goal was to strengthen international peace and security, through both the elimination

2 In the years immediately after the World War II, the US had a monopoly on specific knowledge of and raw materials for nuclear weaponry. American leaders hoped that their exclusive ownership of nuclear weapons would be enough to draw concessions from the Soviet Union, but this proved ineffective. Just six months after the UN General Assembly, the US conducted its first post-war nuclear test named Operations Crossroads. The purpose of this operation was to test the effect of nuclear explosions on ships. These tests were performed at Bikini Atoll in the Pacific on 95 ships, including German and Japanese ships that were captured during World War II. One plutonium implosion-type bomb was detonated over the fleet, while the other one was detonated underwater.

3 UN General Assembly, Establishment of a Commission to Deal With the Problems Raised by the Discovery of Atomic Energy, A/RES/1(I), January 24, 1946.

4 The General Assembly in those early years clarified that "disarmament" involved the elimination of weaponry, while "regulation" focused on some of the classic functions of arms control, namely, limits on numbers, production, export, and use. The distinction is very important, because literally from the start, the UN has sought not just to "regulate" WMD, but to eliminate them outright. The goal was and remains universal and nondiscriminatory in scope—in a WMD--disarmed world, there would be only "havenot" States, with no exception. Duarte Sergio, Disarmament and Non-proliferation: A Historical Review, Paper presented at seminar on Disarmament and Non-proliferation, March 28, 2011, p. 8.

of WMD and the limitation of conventional arms.

The General Assembly Resolution also created the UN Atomic Energy Commission (UNAEC) and charged it with responsibility for the use of atomic energy "only for peaceful purposes." The resolution, however, was not considered a forceful document by many who supported the complete elimination of atomic weapons. The United States (US) crafted its language to avoid a nuclear ban. Moreover, by placing the UNAEC under the direction of the UN Security Council, the resolution helped to consolidate an unequal global nuclear order.

The US nuclear monopoly was short-lived. In the year 1949, the former Soviet Union tested its first nuclear weapon,[5] and thereafter the US and Soviet Union governments spent massive amounts to increase the quality and quantity of their nuclear arsenals. The rising tensions of the Cold War led to proliferation; and in 1952, the UK did its first nuclear weapon test, followed by France in 1960 and China in 1964.

There have been several attempts, as discussed in the previous chapter, to limit the spread or possession of nuclear weapons, such as the Treaty on the Non-Proliferation of Nuclear Weapons (NPT), negotiated in 1968. It came into legal effect in 1970.[6] The NPT includes a commitment by all countries—including the Nuclear Weapons States (NWS) —to negotiate in good faith toward nuclear disarmament. The Treaty on the Prohibition of Nuclear Weapons goes beyond the NPTs commitment from 1968. The new treaty is the result of mounting global frustration with the failure of

5 While American experts had predicted that the Soviet Union would not have nuclear weapons until the mid-1950s, the first Soviet nuclear bomb was detonated on August 29, 1949. The bomb, named "First Lightning" by the West, was more or less a copy of "Fat Man", one of the bombs the US had dropped on Japan in 1945.

6 As of December 2021, eight countries have declared that they have nuclear weapons. According to Article IX-3 of the Nuclear Non-Proliferation Treaty (NPT), a nuclear-weapon State is one which has manufactured and exploded a nuclear weapon or other nuclear explosive device prior to January 1, 1967. China, France, Russia, the UK, and the US meet this requirement, and have acceded to the NPT as nuclear-weapon states (NWS) as defined by the treaty. The three other countries that have tested nuclear weapons and declared having them are India, Pakistan and North Korea. India and Pakistan have never been parties to the NPT. Israel, a non-NPT state, has maintained a policy of ambiguity by neither confirming nor denying having nuclear weapons, although it is widely considered that it possesses them. In 2003, North Korea declared withdrawal from the NPT, and acquisition of nuclear weapons. The five NWS that have signed the NPT—China, France, Russia, the US and UK—have been strongly criticized by a majority of States for failing to live up to that obligation of their disarmament commitment under NPT.

the Nuclear Weapons States to get rid of their weapons of mass destruction (WMD). Even though it is over 50 years since the NPT came into force, and despite a wave of force cuts in the 1980s, 1990s and early 2000s, progress on nuclear disarmament has all but stopped. For the majority of UN Member States, their nuclear arsenals represent a broken promise to disarm, a violation of basic international normative principles, a source of enormous frustration, and a basic threat to their security.

The treaty on banning nuclear weapons has its origins in the Humanitarian Initiative, a group of non-nuclear weapons states (NNWS) that have sought to push nuclear disarmament forward by focusing on the severe humanitarian consequences of nuclear war.[7]The Austrian government's pledge in 2014 to "stigmatize, prohibit and eliminate nuclear weapons in light of their unacceptable humanitarian consequences andassociated risks" was subsequently adopted as a General Assembly resolution.[8] The General Assembly decided to include in the provisional agenda of its seventy-first session, under the item entitled "General and complete disarmament", a sub-item entitled "Humanitarian pledge for the prohibition and elimination of nuclear weapons".[9]

7 The origins of the TPNW lie in the Final Document of the 2010 NPT Review Conference, which noted the deep concern of all States Parties with "the catastrophic humanitarian consequences of any use of nuclear weapons". Prompted by this, Norway hosted an international conference in Oslo, in March 2013 to explore these humanitarian consequences. Further international conferences followed in Nayarit, Mexico (February 2014), and Vienna, Austria (December 2014), which drew further attention to the subject. Yasmin Afina, et.al., Negotiation of a Nuclear Weapons Prohibition Treaty: Nuts and Bolts of the Ban, The New Treaty: Taking Stock, The United Nations Institute for Disarmament Research (UNIDIR), 2017, p. 11.

8 United Nations General Assembly, "Humanitarian Pledge for the Prohibition and Elimination of Nuclear Weapons", A/RES/70/48, December 7, 2015.

9 The General Assembly recalledthe three international conferences convened, respectively, by Norway in March 2013, Mexico in February 2014 and Austria in December 2014 on the humanitarian impact of nuclear weapons. It urged all States parties to the Treaty on the Non-Proliferation of Nuclear Weapons to renew their commitment to the urgent and full implementation of their existing obligations under article VI, and calls upon all States to identify and pursue effective measures to fill the legal gap for the prohibition and elimination of nuclear weapons and to cooperate with all stakeholders to achieve this goal. The General Assembly requested all States possessing nuclear weapons, pending the total elimination of their nuclear weapon arsenals, to take concrete interim measures to reduce the risk of nuclear weapon detonations, including by reducing the operational status of nuclear weapons and moving nuclear weapons away from deployment and into storage, diminishing the role of nuclear weapons in military doctrines and rapidly reducing all types of nuclear weapons. A/RES/70/48, December 7, 2015.

As the movement gained support among the international community, backers of the Humanitarian Initiative had high hopes that the 2015 Review Conference on the NPT would achieve substantial progress toward nuclear disarmament. Although 160 states endorsed the Humanitarian Initiative at the 2015 NPT Review Conference, the conference failed to adopt a consensus final document. Many countries were dissatisfied with this outcome and sought to shift efforts to advance the disarmament agenda to an open-ended working group (OEWG) on nuclear disarmament within the UN General Assembly. For many advocates of nuclear disarmament, the General Assembly was a preferable negotiating forum, as it decides by a majority vote of member states rather than consensus.

At the three open-ended working group meetings in Geneva in 2016, participating states discussed strategies for moving the nuclear disarmament agenda forward. Many states, such as Algeria, Brazil, Indonesia, and South Africa, spoke in favour of opening negotiations for a ban treaty. Nuclear-reliant states present opposed this fast-tracked approach, speaking in favour of a progressive approach towards disarmament. The proponents of a ban were successful, and at the third session of the OEWG, States voted to adopt the final report recommending the General Assembly convene a conference in 2017 to prohibit nuclear weapons. The vote was 68-22, with 13 countries abstaining. All nine states possessing nuclear weapons boycotted the OEWG, and all dissenting votes came from US allies. The US, which did not attend the OEWG sessions, rejected the final report, calling such efforts to ban nuclear weapons unrealistic. On October 27, 2016, the First Committee of the General Assembly adopted a Resolution to "convene in 2017, a United Nations conference to negotiate a legally binding instrument to prohibit nuclear weapons, leading towards their total elimination."[10] After two rounds of negotiations,[11] on July 7, 2017, a special meeting of the General Assembly passed a resolution endorsing the newly negotiated Treaty on the Prohibition of Nuclear Weapons (TPNW).

10 United Nations General Assembly Resolution A/C.1/71/L.41 proposed by: Austria, Brazil, Chile, Costa Rica, Democratic Republic of the Congo, Ecuador, El Salvador, Guatemala, Honduras, Indonesia, Ireland, Jamaica, Kenya, Liechtenstein, Malawi, Malta, Mexico, Namibia, Nauru, New Zealand, Nigeria, Palau, Panama, Paraguay, Peru, Philippines, Samoa, South Africa, Sri Lanka, Swaziland, Thailand, Uruguay, Venezuela (Bolivarian Republic of) and Zambia. Vide para 12 of the Resolution, the General Assembly called upon States participating in the conference to make their best endeavours to conclude as soon as possible a legally binding instrument to prohibit nuclear weapons, leading towards their total elimination.

11 Opening negotiations took place in New York from 27-31 March 2017 and from 15 June – 7 July 2017.

Both rounds were boycotted by all nuclear weapons possessing states, most NATO countries, and many military allies of nuclear weapons states.The voting on the UN General Assembly Resolution introducing the TPNE was contentious. A total of 122 UN Member States voted yes, one voted no (Netherlands), and one abstained (Singapore). The other 69 Member States did not vote, including all nine nuclear-weapon states. Under the treaty, 50 ratifications were required for the treaty to enter into force, to make the document binding international law.

The TPNW was opened for signature on September 20, 2017 at United Nations Headquarters in New York.[12] Under established international practice, only Heads of State, Heads of Government or Ministers for Foreign Affairs are empowered, by their functions, to sign multilateral treaties on behalf of States without having to produce full powers to that effect. Other representatives wishing to sign the Treaty must have appropriate full powers signed by one of these authorities. States wishing to sign the Treaty should, as necessary, provide the required full powers in advance to the United Nations Secretariat, Office of Legal Affairs. By signing the Treaty on the Prohibition of Nuclear Weapons, a State signals its intention to become a party to it in the future. Once it has signed the Treaty, a State must not take any action that would undermine its object and purpose.[13] Signing the Treaty does not make the State a party to it.[14] States that have not signed a treaty may also consent to be bound by the treaty through the act of accession.

On October 26, 2020, Honduras became the 50th state to ratify or accede to TPNW. The treaty thus entered into force on January 22, 2021, i.e., 90 days after the 50th ratification.[15] For any State that deposits its

12 Signature does not legally bind the signatory State or require it to begin to implement the provisions of the Treaty. To become legally bound by a multilateral treaty, a signatory State must subsequently deposit its instrument of ratification, acceptance or approval. That State will then become a party in accordance with the entry into force provisions of the treaty in question.

13 Article 18, Vienna Treaty on the Law of Treaties, 1969.

14 For constitutional reasons, certain States use the terms 'acceptance' or 'approval' to describe their adherence to multilateral treaties. These terms have the same legal effect as ratification and consequently express a signatory State's consent to be bound by a treaty. Some States can ratify treaties immediately, if their domestic procedures so permit. Nothing prohibits a State from depositing its instrument of ratification, acceptance or approval for the Treaty on the Prohibition of Nuclear Weapons on the same day as it signs the Treaty.

15 Article 15, para 1 (a), The Treaty on the Prohibition of Nuclear Weapons, 2017.

instrument of ratification, acceptance, approval or accession after the date of the deposit of the fiftieth instrument of ratification, acceptance, approval or accession, this Treaty shall enter into force 90 days after the date on which that State has deposited its instrument of ratification, acceptance, approval or accession. The TPNW is the first multilateral treaty to clearly define the possession, use or threatened use of nuclear weapons as illegal under international law.

The International Campaign to Abolish Nuclear Weapons (ICAN) was instrumental in creating the Treaty on the Prohibition of Nuclear Weapons. ICAN was awarded the Nobel Peace Prize in December 2017.[16]

The Treaty on the Prohibition of Nuclear Weapons

The Treaty on the Prohibition of Nuclear Weapons (TPNW) is a landmark international agreement prohibiting a range of nuclear weapon-related activities. It has been hailed by supporters as a historic achievement.[17] The treaty essentially builds on the principles of the UN Charter. It states in the preamble that in accordance with the Charter of the United Nations, States must refrain in their international relations from the threat or use of force against the territorial integrity or political independence of any State, or any other manner inconsistent with the Purposes of the United Nations and that the establishment and maintenance of international peace and

16 Norway (under a social democratic government) funded ICAN from 2010 to 2013 (when a conservative government was elected). ICAN grew into a well-organized, global organization with an international steering committee. In 2013, Norway invited ICAN to help prepare a conference in Oslo on the humanitarian consequences of nuclear war. While the organizers did not offer proposals for action, participants assessed the dangers presented by nuclear weapons as requiring action. The second conference in Nayarit, Mexico, that took place in February 2014, highlighted a "legal gap": the failure to prohibit nuclear weapons like biological and chemical weapons, antipersonnel mines, and cluster munitions despite their much higher destructivity. Tilman Ruff, Negotiating the UN Treaty on the Prohibition of Nuclear Weapons and the Role of ICAN, *Global Change, Peace & Security*, Vol. 30 (2), 2018, pp. 233–241.

17 In the words of the Hiroshima atomic bombing survivor Setsuko Thurlow, "the treaty recognizes that women and girls are more susceptible to the effects of radiation — that there are gendered implications to radioactive violence. I am moved to acknowledge the positive obligations of the treaty as well — such as victims assistance and environmental remediation which will be a hallmark for taking responsibility for the inter-generational effects of radiation." Statement by Setsuko Thurlow, survivor of the atomic bombing of Hiroshima and long time campaigner for nuclear-weapons abolition, as the UN Treaty on the Prohibition of Nuclear Weapons reached 50 state parties required for its entry into force, Available at: https://www.icanw.org/setsuko_thurlow_statement_on_tpnw_entry_into_force.

security are to be promoted with the least diversion for armaments of the world's human and economic resources.

The preamble to the TPNW sets out some of the general principles and policies that inform the treaty. The preamble specifically acknowledges the risks posed by the continued existence of nuclear weapons, including from any nuclearweapon detonation by accident, miscalculation or design, and emphasizes that these risks concern the security of all humanity and that all States share the responsibility to prevent any use of nuclear weapons. The preamble acknowledges the disproportionate impact of nuclear-weapon activities on indigenous peoples and the impact of nuclear weapons on women and girls. The preamble in paragraph 9, reiterates the principles and rules of international humanitarian law, in particular the principle that the right of parties to an armed conflict to choose methods or means of warfare is not unlimited,[18] the rule of distinction, the prohibition against indiscriminate attacks, the rules on proportionality and precautions in attack, the prohibition on the use of weapons of a nature to cause superfluous injury or unnecessary suffering, and the rules for the protection of the natural environment. In its last paragraph, the preamble stresses "the role of public conscience in the furthering of the principles of humanity as evidenced by the call for the total elimination of nuclear weapons" while recognizing the important role played by civil society, NGOs, religious leaders, parliamentarians and the International Red Cross and Red Crescent Movement in advancing the cause of nuclear disarmament. The preamble also makes specific reference to the NPT noting that it "serves as the cornerstone of the nuclear disarmament and non-proliferation regime." The preamble reaffirms the conviction that,

> " ... the establishment of the internationally recognized nuclear-weapon-free zones on the basis of arrangements freely arrived at among the States of the region concerned enhances global and regional peace and security, strengthens the nuclear non-proliferation

18 In addition to a general reference to international law, paragraph 9 of the preamble emphasizes that parties to an armed conflict do not have complete autonomy to choose their "methods or means of warfare". This principle was already contained in Article 22 of the Regulations concerning the Laws and Customs of War on Land, signed in The Hague on October 18, 1907, and in Article 35 of the 1977 Additional Protocol I to the Geneva Conventions (AP I). This principle has become rule of customary law (with a slightly different wording). Paragraph 9 of the preamble is significant as it tries to resolve reservations formulated during the ratification and signing of the AP I. when Belgium, Canada, France, Germany, Italy, the Netherlands, Spain and the UK deposited their instruments of ratification, they formulated a reservation that effectively excluded nuclear weapons from the scope of the AP I.

regime and contributes towards realizing the objective of nuclear disarmament."

Article 1

Article 1, defining the Treaty's prohibitions is the essence of the TPNW. These prohibitions apply at all places and in all circumstances, including during armed conflict. Each State Party undertakes never under any circumstances to:

(a) Develop, test, produce, manufacture, otherwise acquire, possess or stockpile nuclear weapons or other nuclear explosive devices;

(b) Transfer to any recipient whatsoever nuclear weapons or other nuclear explosive devices or control over such weapons or explosive devices directly or indirectly;

(c) Receive the transfer of or control over nuclear weapons or other nuclear explosive devices directly or indirectly;

(d) Use or threaten to use nuclear weapons or other nuclear explosive devices;

(e) Assist, encourage or induce, in any way, anyone to engage in any activity prohibited to a State Party under this Treaty;

(f) Seek or receive any assistance, in any way, from anyone to engage in any activity prohibited to a State Party under this Treaty;

(g) Allow any stationing, installation or deployment of any nuclear weapons or other nuclear explosive devices in its territory or at any place under its jurisdiction or control.

The development, production, manufacture, and any other forms of acquisition of a nuclear weapon or other nuclear explosive device are prohibited under Article 1(1)(a) of the TPNW. The prohibited 'development' of a nuclear weapon or other nuclear explosive device encompasses any of the actions and activities intended to prepare for its production. This covers relevant research, computer modelling of weapons, and the testing of key components, as well as sub-critical testing (i.e. experiments simulating aspects of nuclear explosions using conventional explosives and without achieving uncontrolled nuclear chain reactions). The concepts of 'production' and 'manufacture' overlap significantly, covering the processes that are intended to lead to a completed, useable weapon or device. In general parlance, 'production' is a broader term than 'manufacture': manufacture describes the use of machinery to transform inputs into outputs. Taken together, these concepts encompass not only any factory processes but also any improvisation or adaptation of a nuclear explosive device.[19]

The prohibition on 'otherwise acquiring' a nuclear weapon or other nuclear explosive device is a catch-all provision that encompasses any means of obtaining nuclear weapons or other nuclear explosive devices other than through production. This could be through import, lease, or borrowing from another source or, in theory, by recovering a lost nuclear weapon or capturing or stealing one. This prohibition overlaps with the one in Article 1(1)(c) not to receive control over nuclear weapons or other nuclear explosive devices.[20]

The prohibition on development, production, manufacturing and acquisition also covers key components. It is widely accepted that the missile, rocket, or other munition, including both the container and any means of propulsion, are key components in a nuclear weapon.[21] Delivery platforms such as bombers and submarines are not key components of nuclear weapons as such and are not captured by the prohibitions in Article 1, though they may be integral to a nuclearweapon system. Key components include the fissile material (plutonium or highly enriched uranium) and the means of triggering the nuclear chain reaction.[22]

19 Grethe Lauglo Ostern (ed.), 2021, *Nuclear Weapons Ban Monitor 2020: Tracking progress towards a world without nuclear weapons*, Norwegian People's Aid, pp. 300.

20 As is the case with the NPT, the TPNW does not define 'nuclear weapons' or 'other nuclear explosive devices'. There is, though, a settled understanding among states of these terms. A nuclear explosive device is an explosive device whose effects are derived primarily from nuclear chain reactions. A nuclear weapon is a nuclear explosive device that has been weaponised, meaning that it is contained in and delivered by, for example, a missile, rocket, or bomb. Thus, all nuclear weapons are a form of nuclear explosive device but not all nuclear explosive devices are nuclear weapons. Grethe Lauglo Ostern (ed.), 2021, *Nuclear Weapons Ban Monitor 2020: Tracking progress towards a world without nuclear weapons*, Norwegian People's Aid, p. 31.

21 Test launches of missiles that are either specifically designed to deliver nuclear warheads or which are 'nuclear-capable' constitute prohibited development of nuclear weapons under Article 1(1)(a) of the TPNW (unless the purpose of the launch is to test the conventional capability of the missile). Ibid, p. 32.

22 Fissile material – plutonium or highly enriched uranium (HEU) – is essential in all nuclear weapons. Both military and civilian stocks of HEU and plutonium must be secured and reduced and further production limited, in order to achieve nuclear disarmament, halt proliferation of nuclear weapons and ensure that terrorists do not

Production or procurement of fissile material constitutes prohibited development when this is done with the intent to produce nuclear weapons or other nuclear explosive devices. To research, produce, and use nuclear energy for peaceful purposes is permitted both under the NPT and the TPNW.

The development and production of dual-use components, such as navigation or guidance systems, which could be used in both nuclear and conventional weapons, would only be prohibited under the TPNW when they were intended to be used in nuclear weapons. Under Article II of the NPT, a similar obligation is imposed not to manufacture or otherwise acquire nuclear weapons or other nuclear explosive devices, but this applies only to non-nuclear-weapon states and does not prohibit nuclear-weapon states from continuing to develop, produce, and manufacture nuclear weapons or other nuclear explosive devices.

Today, the US and Russia together possess about 90 percent of the world's nuclear arsenal. The world's nuclear stockpiles pose several threats to human life and national and international security. In addition to the possible intentional or unauthorized use of nuclear weapons, their existence entails a risk of accidental detonations. They could also serve as targets for terrorists or be seized by other parties. The prohibition on possession of any nuclear weapon or other nuclear explosive devices under Article 1(1)(a) makes it illegal to have a nuclear weapon or other nuclear explosive devices. Possession does not require ownership. One nuclear weapon or other nuclear explosive device is sufficient to constitute a stockpile. The prohibition on possession comprises activities such as maintenance and deployment of nuclear weapons or other nuclear explosive devices. Indirectly, it also acts to render deterrence practices unlawful.

Since the first nuclear test explosion on July 16, 1945, at least eight states have conducted more than 2050 nuclear test explosions at dozens of test sites around the world.[23] The prohibition on testing in Article 1(1)(a) of the TPNW bans the detonation of a nuclear weapon or other nuclear explosive devices. It is therefore limited to explosive testing. All non-explosive forms of testing are covered by the prohibition on development in the TPNW. All explosive testing also contravenes the CTBT (a treaty not yet in force) and under customary international law. The preamble of the

acquire them. Production or procurement of fissile material constitutes prohibited development under the TPNW when this is done with the intent to produce nuclear weapons or other nuclear explosive devices. Ibid.

23 Arms Control Association, 'The Nuclear Testing Tally', updated July 2020.

TPNW recognizes the importance of the CTBT and its verification regime as a core element of the nuclear disarmament and non-proliferation regime.

The transfer of any nuclear weapon or other nuclear explosive device or control over them 'to any recipient whatsoever' is prohibited under Article 1(1)(b) of the TPNW.[24] This is so whether this occurs 'directly or indirectly'. This also makes it illegal to transmit possession or ownership to any other state or to any natural or legal person (e.g. a company or organization) of key components of any nuclear explosive device in separate instalments or via intermediaries or third parties where there is a knowledge they will be used to produce a nuclear weapon or other nuclear explosive devices. Unlawful transfer does not necessarily involve payment or other forms of consideration. Under Article I of the NPT, the five nuclear-weapon states parties have committed never to transfer nuclear weapons 'to any recipient whatsoever'. The NPT does not include a corresponding prohibition on non-nuclear-weapon states to transfer nuclear weapons or other nuclear explosive devices or to assist in a transfer.82 These important lacunae are addressed by Article 1(1) (b) and (e) of the TPNW.

Under the TPNW, the provision of uranium to any other state is prohibited where it is not subject to appropriate Safeguards Agreements or if the state party transferring the uranium knows that the material in question will, or is likely to, be used to develop a nuclear weapon or other nuclear explosive devices. Otherwise, states parties to the TPNW are permitted to transfer uranium, including nuclear-armed states and states not a party to the TPNW. If a state exports uranium to a nuclear-armed state or any other state on the understanding that the uranium would be used exclusively for peaceful purposes, the exporting state could not be considered to violate either the TPNW or the NPT if the importing state unexpectedly decided to use the uranium for weapons development instead.

Article 1(1)(c) of the TPNW prohibits receiving the transfer of or control over any nuclear weapons or other nuclear explosive devices directly or indirectly. To 'receive' a nuclear weapon or other nuclear

24 For instance, the UK's nuclear-weapon system is in large measure imported from the US: its nuclear warhead design (built in the UK) is based directly on the US W76; the Trident submarine-launched ballistic missile (SLBM) guidance system and a number of Trident warhead components are imported directly from the US; the Trident detonator is designed and built in the US; and the UKs Trident II SLBMs are on lease from the US. Grethe Lauglo Ostern (ed.), 2021, *Nuclear Weapons Ban Monitor 2020: Tracking progress towards a world without nuclear weapons*, Norwegian People's Aid, p. 39.

explosive device is to take possession or control over it. This broad notion does not require that ownership also passes to the recipient. The prohibition on indirect receipt covers accepting the key components of any nuclear weapon or other nuclear explosive devices as well as an assembled version. This extends to transfers made through intermediaries. Article 1(1)(c) of the TPNW follows a similarly worded provision in Article II of the NPT, but the corresponding prohibition in that Treaty applies only to those states that are designated as non-nuclear-weapon states.

Under Article 1(1)(d) of the TPNW, states parties undertake never under any circumstances to use nuclear weapons or other nuclear explosive devices. Preventing the use of nuclear weapons is a central aim of the Treaty. To use a nuclear weapon or other nuclear explosive device is to launch, release, deliver, or detonate it with hostile intent or for so-called 'peaceful' use, such as in civil engineering. Intent can be discerned from the circumstances and does not have to be publicly declared. Possession or deployment of nuclear weapons for 'deterrence' does not amount to their use under the TPNW but is caught by the prohibition on possession in Article 1(1)(a).

Threatening to use a nuclear weapon or other nuclear explosive device is prohibited under Article 1(1)(d) of the TPNW. This is the case whether such use would itself be a violation of international law or whether the device would be used in legitimate self-defence against foreign aggression. It is, therefore, broader in scope than the prohibition on threat of force within Article 2(4) of the UN Charter. To violate the TPNW, a threat of use must be credible in the circumstances. This means that the threat must emanate from a person in a position to either effect or direct the use of a nuclear explosive device. Therefore, such a threat made by a senior government official in a nuclear-armed state would be prohibited TPNW. The narrow wording in Article 1(1)(d) of the TPNW with the active verb 'threaten to use' also requires that any signalled intention by a state to use nuclear weapons be specific as to the target of possible use. Prohibited threats may, however, be implicit as well as explicit. A stated threat does not, therefore, have to refer to the use of nuclear weapons, though it would be more likely to violate the TPNW should it do so. In certain circumstances of tension, a show of force employing missile testing, an explosive test of a nuclear weapon, or a nuclear strike exercise, could amount to unlawfully threatening to use nuclear weapons under the TPNW.

The prohibition on assisting,[25] encouraging,[26] or inducing[27] prohibited activities is also covered in detail. States parties to the TPNW can remain in alliances and military cooperation arrangements with nuclear-armed states and can continue to execute all operations, exercises, and other military activities together with them in so far as they do not involve nuclear weapons. Any participation in 'nuclear burden-sharing and other nuclear-related military activities, however, would need to be discontinued. Participation in exercises that involve the simulated use of nuclear weapons would also contravene Article 1(1)(e). According to Casey-Maslen, Article 1(1)(e) of the Treaty is likely to be one of the most contested provisions in terms of interpretation and application because its precise scope is unclear—especially for acts such as transit and financing, but also 'whether knowledge or intent is required on the part of the state party to amount to a violation'.[28]

25 **Assistance:** In order for a conduct to constitute assistance there must be a causal link between the conduct and a prohibited activity, where the conduct contributes significantly to this activity, even if it is not essential to its occurrence. Insignificant contributions would not constitute assistance. Inherent in the requirement that the contribution is significant, is that the prohibited activity which is assisted must be ongoing or temporally proximate. This means that it need not have happened or be ongoing, but cannot just be a theoretical possibility. The state must have acted with the knowledge that the conduct would, in the ordinary course of events, assist a prohibited activity. The forms of assistance that are unlawful can be, among others, financial (such as through economic assistance for nuclear-weapon production); technological (for example, by the export of equipment/components for such production); operational (for instance, by conventional military support for nuclear bombing); technical (through the provision of expert information); or human (such as by seconding nuclear scientists to assist in another state's nuclear-weapon programme).

26 **Encouragement:** Encouraging in the context of the TPNW means persuading or seeking to persuade any other state or any legal or natural person to carry out a prohibited activity or continue an ongoing violation of any of the Article 1 prohibitions. The prohibited activity which is encouraged does not need to materialize as it is the act of encouragement that is prohibited and not the result. Encouragement could take the form of verbal, written, material, or institutional support, both from governments as a whole (such as by adoption of a particular policy) and from pertinent senior government or military officials. Where such support has been given, the encouragement is understood to be ongoing until the point at which it is clearly withdrawn.

27 **Inducement:** Inducing a prohibited activity means offering someone something in exchange for the performance of that activity. Thus, inducing will always involve encouragement.

28 Casey-Maslen, S., 2019, *The Treaty on the Prohibition of Nuclear Weapons: A Commentary*, Oxford Commentaries on International Law, Oxford: Oxford University Press, p. 158.

Under Article 1(1)(f) of the TPNW, states parties undertake never under any circumstances to 'seek or receive assistance, in any way, from anyone to engage in any activity prohibited to a State Party' under the Treaty. In contrast to Article 1(1)(e) of the TPNW, which prohibits states from assisting prohibited acts by others, Article 1(1)(f) prohibits states from seeking or receiving assistance to violate the Treaty themselves. This precludes any state party from asking any other state or any legal or natural person to help it to develop, possess, stockpile, test, produce, use, transfer, or receive nuclear weapons or other nuclear explosive devices. A similar prohibition, imposed only on non-nuclear-weapon states, is contained in Article II of the NPT, though it onlyapplies to manufacture: the undertaking is to 'not to seek or receive any assistance in the manufacture of nuclear weapons or other nuclear explosive devices.

Accordingly, article 1(1)(g) of the TPNW outlaws a particular form of assistance or encouragement of prohibited action: allowing any stationing, installation, or deployment of any nuclear weapons or other nuclear explosive devices in a state party's territory or at any other place under its jurisdiction or control.[29] The TPNW's prohibition against such hosting of nuclear weapons applies at all times, including during escalating tension or armed conflict. There is no corresponding prohibition in the NPT. Five states, Belgium, Germany, Italy, the Netherlands, and Turkey, host approximately 150 American B61 nuclear gravity bombs between them on their metropolitan territories. All parties to NWFZ treaties have committed not to allow the stationing of nuclear weapons on their territories.

Article 2

Positive obligations are key elements of humanitarian disarmament treaties, which seek to prevent and remediate the human suffering and environmental harm inflicted by weapons. Article 2(1) of the TPNW imposes a duty on each state to submit a declaration to the UN Secretary-General within 30 days of becoming a party to the Treaty. The declaration must clarify whether the state party has ever owned, possessed, or controlled

29 The concept of jurisdiction refers primarily to a state's sovereign territory, while control extends to areas that the state party occupies or otherwise controls extraterritorially. This is irrespective of the legality of this control under international law. Deployment is the broadest of the three types of prohibited conduct. A violation would not require any prolonged duration, agreement, or infrastructure. Thus, although transit of nuclear weapons is not explicitly prohibited by the TPNW, if movement into the sovereign territory of a state party is not swiftly followed by exit, this might amount to assistance and encouragement to possess nuclear weapons as well as a violation of 1(1)(g) of the TPNW.

nuclear weapons or other nuclear explosive devices. If it has, it must further declare whether it has already eliminated its nuclear-weapon programme, including by destroying or irreversibly converting all nuclear-weapons-related facilities, or whether it still owns, possesses, or controls any such devices. Finally, the declaration must state whether foreign weapons or devices are located – stockpiled, stationed, deployed, or installed – either in its territory or in any other place under its jurisdiction or control.

Article 3

Article 3 of the TPNW requires States Parties that do not possess nuclear weapons to maintain their current International Atomic Energy Agency (IAEA) safeguards, and where they have not done so to bring into force a comprehensive safeguards agreement with the IAEA.[30] The safeguard requirements set out in the TPNW has attracted a certain amount of criticism, as it does not provide for the highest standard of verification that is set out in the Model Additional Protocol to the IAEA Comprehensive Safeguards. It has also been suggested that the lesser verification requirements are insufficient to prevent clandestine nuclear activity and may result in the undermining of efforts to encourage States to introduce Additional Protocol agreements with the IAEA.

Article 4

Article 4 sets out the disarmament requirements of nuclear weapon possessing States. Article 4 contains both "destroy and join" and "join and destroy" options. Article 4(1) relates to a situation where a State Party has owned, possessed or controlled nuclear weapons after July 7, 2017, and eliminated its nuclear weapons programme before the TPNW came into force. This provides for such a State Party to cooperate with a competent international authority to verify the elimination of its nuclear weapons programme. Such a State Party is also required to negotiate a safeguards agreement with the IAEA and at a minimum, maintain these safeguards obligations in the future.

Article 4(2) relates to a situation where a State Party joins the TPNW while still in possession of its nuclear weapons. Such a State Party is required to immediately remove its nuclear weapons from operational

30 Article 3, para 2 of the TPNW: Negotiation of such agreement shall commence within 180 days from the entry into force of this Treaty for that State Party. The agreement shall enter into force no later than 18 months from the entry into force of this Treaty for that State Party. Each State Party shall thereafter maintain such obligations, without prejudice to any additional relevant instruments that it may adopt in the future.

status and destroy them as soon as possible thereafter, but "not later than a deadline to be determined by the first meeting of States Parties." Such a State Party is also required to negotiate a safeguards agreement with the IAEA that is: "sufficient to provide credible assurance of the non-diversion of declared nuclear material from peaceful nuclear activities and of the absence of undeclared nuclear material or activities in the State as a whole."

The TPNW is not a simple "weapon-ban" treaty, since it provides much more substantial detail regarding the elimination and verification of weapons than would normally be expected of a ban treaty. Article 4 provides for a time-bound plan for both the elimination and verification of a State party's nuclear weapons programme, but the actual details are left for negotiation. The States Parties are to designate a competent international authority to negotiate and verify the irreversible elimination of nuclear weapons programmes, including the elimination or irreversible conversion of all nuclear weapons-related facilities following Article 4(1), (2) and (3) of the treaty.[31]

Article 5

Under Article 5, each State Party is to adopt the necessary measures to implement its obligations under the Treaty. They are to take all appropriate legal, administrative and other measures, including the imposition of penal sanctions, to prevent and suppress any activity prohibited to a State Party under the Treaty undertaken by persons or on territory under its jurisdiction or control.

The use [32]and testing of nuclear weapons [33] have caused large-scale deaths, horrific injuries, long-term illnesses, socio-economic exclusion,

31 Article 4, para 6 of the TPNW.

32 The 1945 atomic bombings of Hiroshima and Nagasaki together killed an estimated total of 213,000 people instantaneously or within five months due to the combined effects of blast wind, radiant heat and ionizing radiation. More than 210,000 remaining victims survived the first five months and became hibakusha. Many of them had horrific burns, experienced higher rates of cancer and other illnesses, and endured psychological trauma and socioeconomic marginalization.

33 Nuclear testing, while far less well publicized, has harmed communities in many other parts of the world. At least 2,050 nuclear test explosions were carried out on the territories of 15 states and in a number of seas and oceans in 1945–2017. The list of countries affected by atmospheric and underground nuclear-weapon tests includes: Algeria, Australia, China, North Korea, French Polynesia, India, Kazakhstan, Kiribati, Marshall Islands, Pakistan, Russia, Turkmenistan, Ukraine, United States, and Uzbekistan. These tests caused immediate and long-term health problems including

displacement, and environmental damage. To address the ongoing suffering inflicted by use and testing, the TPNW includes an obligation to assist affected individuals. The TPNW is the latest treaty in the series which has included the provision on victim assistance. The positive obligation to assist the victims has not just been mentioned comprehensively in the substantive provisions but also elaborated in length under the preamble of the TPNW. The preamble together with the provisions of the TPNW forms the legal basis for the victim assistance.[34]Obligations are found in Articles 6 and 7, stipulating that each State Party in a position to do so shall assist the victims of the use or testing of nuclear weapons and to endeavour to clean up the environment in the areas contaminated by the detonation of nuclear weapons. They also permit State Parties to request and receive assistance from other State Parties.

Article 6

Article 6(1) of the TPNW concerns the duty of each state party to provide 'adequate' assistance to any victim of nuclearweapons use or testing under its jurisdiction. Assistance includes, but is not limited to, medical care, rehabilitation, and psychological support, as well as support for social and economic inclusion.[35] Assistance under Article 6(1) must be provided

---

thyroid cancer and birth defects. They displaced whole communities that had traditionally resided on the test sites, and many of those still cannot return. Lingering environmental contamination has interfered with food security and sustainable development.

34 There are some concerns raised by activists over the whole concept of "victim assistance" under the TPNW. They argue that the inclusion of victim assistance clause would unfairly raise the expectations of nuclear weapons use or testing's survivors, and imply that contaminated environments could be fully remediated, even when this is not the case. Furthermore, it is also highlighted that the inclusion of victim assistance in the TPNW would undermine the core and evidenced argument that there could be no full or adequate humanitarian response to a nuclear detonation. Singh Nidhi, Victim Assistance under the Treaty on the Prohibition of Nuclear Weapons: An Analysis, *Journal for Peace and Nuclear Disarmament*, Vol. 3, No. 2, 2020, pp. 265-282.

35 The provision of victim assistance should be guided by the principle of inclusivity. States parties should involve affected individuals and their representatives during the design, implementation, evaluation, and monitoring of victim assistance. Those individuals can describe the harm they have experienced, articulate their current needs, and offer expert insights on how best to address those needs. Inclusivity is a widely accepted principle of victim assistance in humanitarian disarmament and has been codified in the Convention on Cluster Munitions (CCM), which requires affected states parties to 'closely consult with and actively involve cluster munition victims and their representative organizations'. Grethe Lauglo Ostern (ed.), 2021, *Nuclear Weapons Ban Monitor 2020: Tracking progress towards a world without nuclear*

under international human rights law and, where applicable, international humanitarian law. In all cases, assistance must be age-appropriate and gender-sensitive. It must be provided to all based on need without discrimination.

Like victim assistance under Article 6(1), environmental remediation of areas affected by nuclear weapons use and testing is crucial to protecting affected populations from unnecessary suffering and to securing their rights. It also benefits the environment by helping to restore damaged ecosystems and promoting biodiversity. Article 6(2) of the TPNW obligates states parties to remediate any areas in territory under their jurisdiction or control that have been contaminated as a result of activities related to the testing or use of nuclear weapons or other nuclear explosive devices. Article 6(2) builds on the obligations in earlier disarmament treaties to clear landmines and explosive remnants of war but adapts them to nuclear contamination. Given that nuclear fallout causes significant levels of contamination that spread across time and space, the TPNW recognizes that environmental remediation is a long-term commitment. While the earlier treaties imposed specific deadlines for clearing landmines and cluster munition remnants, it is difficult, and often impossible, to return areas affected by nuclear weapons to their pre-detonation condition. Therefore, Article 6(2) specifies that affected states parties must take 'necessary and appropriate measures towards the environmental remediation of [contaminated] areas'. The obligations under Article 6(1) and (2) shall be without prejudice to the duties and obligations of any other States under international law or bilateral agreements.

The drafters of the TPNW were firm on naming those responsible for the humanitarian and environmental situations related to nuclear weapons. This is why section 6 stipulates that "State Party that has used or tested nuclear weapons or any other nuclear explosive devices shall have a responsibility to provide adequate assistance to affected States Parties, for victim assistance and environmental remediation." The TPNW recognizes the principle of "the polluter pays."This is the first time that "an accusing finger" has been pointed at nuclear powers in a treaty on nuclear weapons and that, secondly, the international community has required them to make reparations for their actions.[36]

weapons, Norwegian People's Aid, p. 74.

36 Collin Jean-Marie and Patrice Bouvert, Radioactivity Under the Sand:The Waste From French Nuclear Tests in Algeria, Analysis with regard to the Treaty on the Prohibition of Nuclear Weapons, Heinrich Boll Foundation, July 2020, pp. 53.

Article 7

An affected state party does not have to bear the responsibility of victim assistance alone. Article 7 of the treaty entitles an affected state to ask for and receive assistance from other states parties, and all states parties in a position to do are mandated to help it fulfil its obligations to victims. Assistance may be provided through the United Nations system, international, regional or national organizations or institutions, non-governmental organizations or institutions, the International Committee of the Red Cross, the International Federation of Red Cross and Red Crescent Societies, or national Red Cross and Red Crescent Societies, or on a bilateral basis.[37] Since assistance can take a variety of forms – including financial, material, and technical assistance – every state party should be in a position to provide some sort of aid. Such assistance may be delivered directly to the affected state or indirectly through international and non-governmental organizations. States parties that have used or tested nuclear weapons are specifically identified as having to assist affected states parties.

The term "future generations" appears indirectly several times in the preamble and the articles of the TPNW. The treaty is the latest in a series of treaties termed humanitarian disarmament, aiming to regulate and prohibit entire classes of weapons. As a result of the long-term impact of these weapons and the awareness of the need to protect future generations, it was logical that the TPNW should introduce legal considerations on this subject. The concept of "future generations" is thus directly linked with articles 6 and 7 which concern the positive obligations. There was certainly a wish on the part of the authors to guarantee that people now and in future can again live in a healthy environment, without suffering from the radioactive contamination found in nuclear test zones throughout the world.[38]

Several principles have emerged, however, from the victim assistance provisions in the other humanitarian disarmament treaties. These principles need to be considered while implementation of the victim assistance provisions under the TPNW:

- Human rights-based approach: Victim assistance is not only a medical or rehabilitation issue; it is also a matter of human rights.

37 Article 7, para 5, the TPNW.

38 Collin Jean-Marie and Patrice Bouvert, Radioactivity Under the Sand:The Waste From French Nuclear Tests in Algeria, Analysis with regard to the Treaty on the Prohibition of Nuclear Weapons, Heinrich Boll Foundation, July 2020, pp. 53.

A rights-based approach seeks to address the needs of victims and alter the physical, legal and social environment that prevents the full realization of their human rights. Victim assistance should, therefore, respond to victims' physical and psychological needs and enable victims' full participation in society.

- Victim Inclusive: Victims are the experts on their needs. Their views should be heard and addressed in decision-making that affects their lives.

- The age and gender-sensitive tailored assistance: Services for victims should be tailored to victims' needs and take into account the age and gender of the victim. Barriers to recovery and inclusion in society can differ among groups; for example, women and children may face greater obstacles because they are disproportionately affected by nuclear weapons. States have an active duty to ensure that victim assistance achieves substantive equality.

- Non-discriminatory: Victim assistance programmes should not discriminate against or between victims for any reason.

- Development of laws, policies, national plan, budget, and focal point: To meet its victim assistance obligations, an affected state party should, at a practical level, develop, implement, and enforce any necessary national laws and policies. It should also incorporate relevant guidelines and good practices in the delivery of victim assistance, adopt a national plan and budget for victim assistance activities and designate a government focal point to coordinate implementation.

- Obligations to Report: An affected state party should report on the status and progress of implementation of its victim assistance obligations and update that information regularly.

The principles enumerated above apply broadly to victim assistance under humanitarian disarmament treaties. The challenges presented by nuclear weapons, however, differ in some ways from those presented by other inhumane and indiscriminate weapons, such as antipersonnel landmines and cluster munitions. TPNW states parties should take into account the following three issues when implementing their victim assistance obligations: (i) Intergenerational nature of the harm since harm from nuclear weapons is not limited to one lifetime. The children and grandchildren of survivors can also suffer health impacts and stigma. (ii) Disproportionate impact on indigenous communities: Nuclear weapon testing has disproportionately taken place on indigenous lands, resulting in cultural harm such as forced displacement from homelands and disconnection from indigenous ways of life. (iii) Close link between environmental damage and harm to people: The harm to people from nuclear weapons is closely linked to harm to the environment. Long-term environmental contamination adversely affects human health and several human rights, such as the right to water and the right to freedom of movement.

Article 8

Article 8 of the TPNW provides for regular meetings of states parties. The first meeting of the states parties is to be held within one year of the Treaty's entry into force.[39] Subsequent meetings will be convened every two years unless the states parties agree otherwise, with a review conference to be held after five years and then every six years thereafter. Extraordinary meetings of states parties will be convened if one-third of the state parties support a written request by any state party. The scope of work of the meetings is broad, with each meeting of states parties effectively mandated to consider any matters 'pursuant to and consistent with the provisions of' the TPNW, including its status and implementation.

Other Key Articles

The cost of the meeting of the States Parties and review conferences, etc, to be borne by the States Parties and States not a party to TPNW participating as observers, as per the United Nations scale of assessment adjusted appropriately. The cost related to the implementation of verification measures required under Article 4 of the treaty, as well as the costs related to the destruction of nuclear weapons or other nuclear explosive devices, and the elimination of nuclear-weapon programmes, including the elimination or conversion of all nuclear-weapons-related facilities, should be borne by the States Parties to which they apply.[40]

The provisions for undertaking amendments in the text of TPNW are outlined in article 10 of the treaty.A meeting of States Parties or a review

39 The First Meeting of States Parties to the TPNW will be hosted by Austria. At this meeting, the states parties will start taking important decisions that will shape the long-term implementation, institutionalization, and universalization of the Treaty.

40 Article 9, the TPNW.

conference may agree upon amendments which shall be adopted by a positive vote of a majority of two-thirds of the States Parties.

When a dispute arises between two or more States Parties relating to the interpretation or application of the Treaty, the parties concerned shall consult together with a view to the settlement of the dispute by negotiation or by other peaceful means of the parties' choice following Article 33 of the UN Charter.[41]

Article 12 of the Treaty obligates each state party to encourage states, not a party to sign or ratify the Treaty, with the goal of universal adherence. The manner and frequency of the actions to be taken are not set out in the provision and are therefore left to the discretion of the state party.

The Treaty does not provide for States Parties to make reservations (**Article 16**), and it is of unlimited duration. Each State Party has the right to withdraw from the Treaty if it decides that extraordinary events related to the subject matter of the Treaty have jeopardized the supreme interests of its country. It shall give notice of such withdrawal to the Depositary. Such notice shall include a statement of the extraordinary events that it regards as having jeopardized its supreme interests. Withdrawal will take effect twelve months after the receipt of notification of withdrawal by the Depository. If the withdrawing State Party is involved in an armed conflict, it will remain bound by the obligations of the Treaty until it is no longer involved in the conflict.[42]

The TPNW reflects a different view, insisting that nuclear weapons *can* be eliminated from world politics without a wholesale transformation of the current system of states in an era of complex global interdependence. Borne of a movement focused on the humanitarian impact of nuclear weapons use, the treaty commits its states-parties to conduct environmental remediation and provide assistance to victims of nuclear weapons use or testing under their jurisdiction. The treaty establishes the responsibility of states that use or test nuclear weapons to assist other affected parties. Further, the treaty mandates the destruction of nuclear arsenals, with a view that the details of nuclear weapons elimination would be negotiated at a later date. Dismissed by the nuclear-armed states and their allies, the impact of the treaty will become evident only over time. The treaty's negotiators do not have illusions that the new instrument will produce immediate results in reducing nuclear risks or nuclear weapons. Instead,

41 Article 11, the TPNW.

42 Article 17, the TPNW.

the aim is to delegitimize nuclear weapons and make it more difficult for states to continue to rely on nuclear weapons as part of their military and foreign policy strategies.

The link to the NPT is provided in Article 18 of the TPNW, which deals with the TPNW's relationship with other agreements. It reads: "The implementation of this Treaty shall not prejudice obligations undertaken by States Parties concerning existing international agreements, to which they are a party, where those obligations are consistent with the Treaty." Such 'savings clauses' are used in many international agreements. In this case, the existing international agreements that are meant to be protected would include the NPT.

States' Riposte to the TPNW

Five NWS

The TPNW was adopted on July 7, 2017, after two rounds of negotiations at the UN General Assembly. Both rounds were boycotted by all nuclear weapons possessing states, most NATO countries, and many military allies of nuclear weapons states including Japan. 122 countries voted in favour of the treaty; The Netherlands was the only country to vote against the treaty and Singapore abstained from the vote. Immediately following the vote, the US, the UK, and France released the following joint statement declaring that they "do not intend to sign, ratify or ever become a party" to the treaty.[43]

Joint Press Statement from the Permanent Representatives to the United Nations of the United States, United Kingdom, and France Following the Adoption

> France, the United Kingdom and the United States have not taken part in the negotiation of the treaty on the prohibition of nuclear weapons. We do not intend to sign, ratify or ever become party to it. Therefore, there will be no change in the legal obligations on our countries with respect to nuclear weapons. For example, we would not accept any claim that this treaty reflects or in any way contributes to the development of customary international law. Importantly, other

43 Joint statement issued by the United States Mission to the United Nations, 7 July 2017, available at: https://usun.usmission.gov/joint-press-statement-from-the-permanent-representatives-to-the-united-nations-of-the-united-states-united-kingdom-and-france-following-the-adoption/.

states possessing nuclear weapons and almost all other states relying on nuclear deterrence have also not taken part in the negotiations.

This initiative clearly disregards the realities of the international security environment. Accession to the ban treaty is incompatible with the policy of nuclear deterrence, which has been essential to keeping the peace in Europe and North Asia for over 70 years. A purported ban on nuclear weapons that does not address the security concerns that continue to make nuclear deterrence necessary cannot result in the elimination of a single nuclear weapon and will not enhance any country's security, nor international peace and security. It will do the exact opposite by creating even more divisions at a time when the world needs to remain united in the face of growing threats, including those from the DPRK's ongoing proliferation efforts. This treaty offers no solution to the grave threat posed by North Korea's nuclear program, nor does it address other security challenges that make nuclear deterrence necessary. A ban treaty also risks undermining the existing international security architecture which contributes to the maintenance of international peace and security.

We reiterate in this regard our continued commitment to the Treaty on the Non-Proliferation of Nuclear Weapons (NPT) and reaffirm our determination to safeguard and further promote its authority, universality and effectiveness. Working towards the shared goal of nuclear disarmament and general and complete disarmament must be done in a way that promotes international peace and security, and strategic stability, based on the principle of increased and undiminished security for all.

We all share a common responsibility to protect and strengthen our collective security system in order to further promote international peace, stability and security.

The TPNW is deeply inspired by humanitarian ideals and the conviction that the use of nuclear weapons has disastrous consequences for human beings and the environment.[44] The treaty is the third one in a series of arms control instruments prohibiting the entire category of weapons.[45]

44 Rietiker Danniel, New Hope for Nuclear Disarmament or "Much Ado About Nothing?": Legal Assessment of the New "Treaty on the Prohibition of Nuclear Weapons" and the Joint Statement by the USA, UK, and France Following its Adoption, *Harvard International Law Journal*, Volume 59, Fall 2017, pp. 23-32.

45 The other two treaties are: The 1997 Ottawa Convention on anti-personnel mines

The joint statement by the US, the UK and France aims at preventing the establishment of a customary rule called "persistent objector." According to this rule, a State which persistently objects to a rule of customary international law during the formative stages of that rule will not be bound by it when it comes into existence. A persistent objector cannot hinder a customary norm to be established, but only avoid the application of the norm on its behalf.[46]

Nuclear weapons are considered critical to Russia's security and influence in the existing and foreseeable international environment. Russia's reaction to the signing of the TPNW has been negative. It matches the reaction of the other four nuclear-weapon states (NWS) who claim that implementation of Article VI of the NPT is proceeding at a reasonable pace and in good faith. They all argue that fast-track nuclear disarmament could undermine international security rather than strengthen it. Yet the Russian attitude is different to that of the other NWS in many ways. Russia insists that the right path toward a world free of nuclear weapons is through gradual reductions that will eventually reach zero. In the First Committee of the 2020 UN General Assembly Russia delivered a statement attacking the TPNW for potentially 'destroying' the non-proliferation regime, asserting that it is not based on the principles of the NPT and 'cannot' achieve nuclear disarmament.It is believed that Russia will most likely remain silent and pretend that the ban treaty does not exist. It will try to stay away from public debates and will not openly oppose the measure itself nor the non-nuclear states which promote it.[47]

China was the only P5 country that did not vote against the TPNW negotiations at the UN General Assembly in 2016 and Foreign Ministry

---

(also known as the Mine Ban Treaty) and the 2008 Convention on Cluster Munitions (CCM), or Oslo Convention.

46 If the customary rule to be created concerns a peremptory norm of international law (*jus cogens*), it is applicable to all States and no State can pretend to be a persistent objector. The use of nuclear weapons can affect such norms and breach fundamental human rights that cannot be derogated from even in situation of emergency, such as the right to life, the prohibition of inhuman and degrading treatment or the prohibition of genocide. The legal effect of the joint statement issued by the USA, UK and France is therefore limited. Rietiker Danniel, New Hope for Nuclear Disarmament or "Much Ado About Nothing?": Legal Assessment of the New "Treaty on the Prohibition of Nuclear Weapons" and the Joint Statement by the USA, UK, and France Following its Adoption, *Harvard International Law Journal*, Volume 59, Fall 2017, pp. 27-28.

47 Sokov Nikolai, "Russsia and the Nuclear Ban Treaty," in Shatabhisha Shetty and Denista Raynova (ed.), *Breakthrough or Breaking Point? Global Perspectives on the Nuclear Ban Treaty*, Global Security: Special Report, December 2017, pp. 13-17.

spokesperson Hua Chunying stated on March 20, 2017, that the Chinese goal of a "final comprehensive ban on and total destruction of nuclear weapons" was "fundamentally in line with the purposes of negotiations on the nuclear weapons ban treaty."[48] There is a view that the treaty does not negatively affect China's existing nuclear policies as a non-State Party. For these reasons, China does not need to respond harshly to the TPNW and should develop a forward-looking policy to further promote nuclear disarmament.[49]

NATO and the other European States

NATO has maintained a strong unified position in opposition to the TPNW. NATO partner countries have decided not to join, citing the potential effect on their security and ongoing cooperation with NATO as grounds for this decision.[50] On September 20, 2017, when the TPNW was opened for signature at UN Headquarters in New York; the North Atlantic Council (NAC), the NATO Alliance's governing body composed of representatives of all Allies, met in Brussels and issued a statement announcing that the then 29 Allies could not support the new treaty. The statement was adopted based on consensus, invited other states that might be willing to do so to 'seriously reflect on its implications for international peace and security.[51] Since then, the Alliance has maintained its unified position in opposition to the TPNW. NATO Allies have levelled several criticisms against the TPNW; however, one of the main has been that the TPNW is not compatible with their political, military and legal commitments related to the Alliance. On December 15, 2020, the NAC adopted a further statement on the TPNW:[52]

---

48 Foreign Ministry Spokes person Hua Chunying's Regular Press Conference on March 20, Ministry of Foreign Affairs of the PRC, March 20, 2017. Available at: http://www.fmprc.gov.cn/mfa_eng/xwfw_665399/s2510_665401/t1447146.shtml.

49 Raymond Wang & Dr Tong Zhao, "China and the Nuclear Ban Treaty," in Shatabhisha Shetty and Denista Raynova (ed.), *Breakthrough or Breaking Point? Global Perspectives on the Nuclear Ban Treaty*, Global Security: Special Report, December 2017, pp. 27-31.

50 Hill Steven, NATO and the Treaty on the Prohibition of Nuclear Weapons, Research Paper, The Royal Institute of International Affairs, Chatham House, London, January 2021, p. 32.

51 North Atlantic Council Statement on the Treaty on the Prohibition of Nuclear Weapons, dated September 20, 2017, available at: https://www.nato.int/cps/en/natohq/news_146954.htm.

52 North Atlantic Council Statement as the Treaty on the Prohibition of Nuclear Weapons Enters Into Force, December 15, 2020, available at: https://www.nato.int/cps/en/natohq/news_180087.htm.

> We reaffirm our commitment to the preservation and strengthening of arms control, disarmament, and non-proliferation. As the Treaty on the Prohibition of Nuclear Weapons, or ban treaty, nears entry into force, we collectively reiterate our opposition to this treaty, as it does not reflect the increasingly challenging international security environment and is at odds with the existing non-proliferation and disarmament architecture.
>
> We continue to support the ultimate goal of a world without nuclear weapons, in full accordance with all provisions of the NPT, including Article VI, in an ever more effective and verifiable way that promotes international stability and is based on the principle of undiminished security for all. The NPT remains the only credible path to nuclear disarmament.
>
> NATO is a defensive Alliance. The fundamental purpose of NATO's nuclear capability is to preserve peace, prevent coercion, and deter aggression. A world where the states that challenge the international rules-based order have nuclear weapons, but NATO does not, is not a safer world. As long as nuclear weapons exist, NATO will remain a nuclear alliance. Allies are determined to ensure that NATO's nuclear deterrent remains safe, secure, and effective, and reject any attempt to delegitimize nuclear deterrence.

As a multilateral institution, NATO itself has limited power to affect nuclear disarmament. Regardless of the tenacity with which NATO maintains its opposition to the TPNW, the reality is that the treaty will now be here to stay. It is in the best interests of NATO to continue to support the development of revived and innovative approaches to nuclear disarmament generally while continuing to maintain the Alliance's principled opposition to the TPNW. [53]

53 While NATO as an alliance remains firmly opposed to the TPNW, there is strong and growing support for it within many NATO states.Opinion polls in 11 NATO states have shown overwhelming public support for joining the Treaty on the Prohibition of Nuclear Weapons. More than 50 former leaders, foreign ministers, and defence ministers – including two who served as NATO secretaries general – have implored current leaders to "show courage and boldness" and join the treaty. Much of the opposition to the TPNW, including from NATO states, is based on myths and misconceptions, as well as deliberate falsehoods. While total elimination of nuclear weapons may remain a distant goal, envisioning and planning for NATO as a "non-nuclear alliance" should begin now – in line with the new global norm. Report: Why NATO members should join the nuclear weapon ban treaty, ICAN, available at: https://www.icanw.org. Also see: Hill Steven, NATO and the Treaty on the Prohibition of Nuclear Weapons, Research Paper, The Royal Institute of International Affairs,

The Italian parliament in September 2017 adopted a resolution committing the government to pursue a nuclear-weapon-free world and 'in a way compatible with its NATO obligations and with the positioning of allied states, to explore the possibility of becoming a party to the legally binding treaty prohibiting nuclear weapons. Italy, however, boycotted the TPNW negotiations in 2017. As an umbrella state and host of foreign nuclear weapons, it is not in compliance with the prohibitions in Article 1 of the Treaty. The former Italian prime minister Enrico Letta and former foreign minister Franco Frattini were among the signatories to an open letter in September 2020 calling on current leaders in umbrella states to 'show courage and boldness' and join the TPNW.

The Netherlands was the only umbrella state (NATO) to participate in the negotiations of the TPNW in 2017 and the only state that voted against the adoption of the Treaty on July 7, 2017. As an umbrella state and host of foreign nuclear weapons, it is not in compliance with the prohibitions in Article 1 of the Treaty. The Netherlands voted against the UN General Assembly resolutions on the TPNW in 2018, 2019, and 2020.[54]Norway started the initiative on the humanitarian consequences of nuclear weapons, which resulted in a majority of states negotiating and adopting the TPNW. But Norway boycotted the negotiations in 2017 and has not adhered to the Treaty.

A few European states like Germany, Ireland, the Netherlands, Norway, Sweden, Switzerland and the UK have conducted reviews of the TPNW within their national frameworks.[55] These national reviews present a wide range of arguments from both a legal and a policy perspective relating to nuclear weapons. The House of Lords inquiry concludes that the TPNW has little chance of achieving its goal in the short or medium-term and

---

Chatham House, London, January 2021, pp. 32.

54 However, in November 2018, the Dutch House of Representatives adopted a series of motions calling on the government to intensify its advocacy for nuclear disarmament, including championing the TPNW within NATO and examining the compatibility of the TPNW with existing Dutch legislation. In January 2019, the Dutch foreign and defence ministers informed the Dutch House of Representatives that there are no legal obstacles within Dutch law preventing the Netherlands from joining the TPNW. An opinion poll conducted in April 2019 shows that a large majority of Dutch citizens want the Netherlands to sign the TPNW.

55 One EU member state is a nuclear weapon state (France), other four are having United States nuclear weapons on their territory (Belgium, Germany, Italy and the Netherlands) and a majority of EU member states' security policies are closely connected to cooperation with nuclear weapon states, given that they are members of the NATO and as such benefit from the nuclear umbrella.

that while it may not undermine the NPT, it could exacerbate polarization and increase the division between the nuclear-weapon states and the non-nuclear-weapon states. The House of Lords at the same time also suggests that the British Government 'adopt a less aggressive tone about this treaty and seek opportunities to work with its supporters towards the aims of Article VI of the NPT'.[56] The Swedish review follows a similar line, arguing that the nuclear disarmament process is stagnating and fragmentation must be avoided.[57] In this regard, the review foresees that Sweden's accession to the TPNW could prevent it from playing a facilitating role in global nuclear disarmament, while also damaging the perception of Sweden in Europe. However, the Swedish review also acknowledges that the TPNW has helped to increase awareness of the need for nuclear disarmament.[58]

The German review states that the TPNW is part of common nuclear disarmament architecture,[59] whereas the Irish review interprets it as a way to highlight the international community's concern at the slow pace of nuclear disarmament within the NPT framework.[60] The German review acknowledges that the government's official position is that the lack of a verification standard makes the NPT and the TPNW incompatible. The Swiss review stresses that the TPNW could, over time, reinforce the

56 British House of Lords, Select Committee on International Relations, 'Rising nuclear risk, disarmament and the Nuclear Non-Proliferation Treaty', 7th Report of Session 2017–19, 24 Apr. 2019; and British Minister of State, Foreign, Commonwealth and Development Office, Lord Ahmad of Wimbledon, 'Prohibition of Nuclear Weapons', vol. 809, 21 Jan. 2021.

57 Sweden voted in favour of adopting the TPNW at the Diplomatic Conference in 2017, but subsequently abstained on the General Assembly resolutions on the TPNW in 2018, 2019, and 2020. In July 2019 the Swedish government announced that it would 'refrain from signing or pursuing ratification of the TPNW at the present time.' The Swedish Ministry of Foreign Affairs has confirmed that it will seek to become an observer state once the TPNW enters into force, to actively follow its further development. The government has also indicated that Sweden might reassess its position following the NPT review conference, now postponed to 2021.

58 Lundin, L., Inquiry into the consequences of a possible Swedish accession to the Treaty on the Prohibition of Nuclear Weapons, January 2019.

59 German Parliament, Report on the Legal Relationship between the Treaty on the Prohibition of Nuclear Weapons and the Non-Proliferation Treaty, 19 Jan. 2021.

60 Hurley, D., 'The Treaty on the Prohibition of Nuclear Weapons', Oireachtas Library and Research Service, May 2019. Irish Houses of the Oireachtas, Minister of State at the Irish Department of Foreign Affairs and Trade (Deputy Ciarán Cannon), Dáil Éireann debate, vol. 986, no. 3, 19 Sep. 2019; and Irish Houses of the Oireachtas, Seanad Éireann debate, vol. 268, no. 12, 4 Dec. 2019.

taboo associated with the use of nuclear weapons.[61]The Swiss review notes that it remains to be seen whether future meetings of states parties to the TPNW will allow constructive interaction between the agreements, or will result in duplication, fragmentation or further polarization. According to Norway, a prohibition on nuclear weapons that does not have the support of all the countries that have such weapons will unfortunately not lead to the elimination of a single nuclear warhead. Further, the Norwegian Government will maintain its disarmament and non-proliferation policy to further the implementation of the NPT and will be at the forefront of efforts to implement concrete, effective measures to promote disarmament and disarmament verification at the international level.[62]

Asian Response

North Korea boycotted the TPNW negotiations in 2017. North Korea is the only state to have tested a nuclear weapon in the 21st century. It abstained from the General Assembly resolutions on the TPNW in 2018 and 2019 and voted against in 2020. In 2017, North Korea stated in the First Committee of the UN General Assembly that it consistently supports the total elimination of nuclear weapons and the efforts for denuclearization of the entire world. However, as long as the US who constantly threatens and blackmails the [Democratic People's Republic of Korea] with nuclear weapons rejects the NBT [Nuclear Ban treaty] the DPRK is not in a position to accede to the treaty.

As the only country to suffer the horrors of wartime atomic bombings, it was expected that Japan would eagerly sign any TPNW to ban such weapons. However, Japan's failure to ratify the treaty attracted criticism from numerous pro-disarmament groups and atomic bomb survivors, who said the decision discredits the government's long-standing anti-nuclear position.[63] Earlier, in 2013 at a General Assembly meeting on

---

61 Swiss Federal Department of Foreign Affairs, Report of the Working Group to analyse the Treaty on the Prohibition of Nuclear Weapons, June 30, 2018.

62 Norwegian Ministry of Foreign Affairs, Review of the consequences for Norway of ratifying the Treaty on the Prohibition of Nuclear Weapons, November 28, 2018.

63 Japan has been a long-time advocate for the total elimination of nuclear weapons. However, the decision not to support the treaty is not wholly unexpected. Japan voted against the 2016 UN General Assembly resolution to convene the conference to negotiate the legal prohibition of nuclear weapons. It also refused to participate in the negotiations after delivering a statement on the initial day of the first round in March 2017. In the Japanese government's view, adopting the ban treaty does not represent a practical nuclear disarmament measure, not for the foreseeable future at

nuclear disarmament, then-Prime Minister Abe Shinzo boasted that the elimination of nuclear weapons has been "the Japanese people's unwavering aspiration since World War II." In October 2020, Chief Cabinet Secretary said that the treaty is different from our approach and the government's position not to sign it 'remains unchanged.' Again in January 2021, Prime Minister Suga Yoshihide reiterated that Japan, which remains under the US "nuclear umbrella," has "no intention of signing the treaty" due to the lack of support by nuclear-armed states and non-nuclear states.[64] In Japan, tensions have increased between hibakusha (atomic bombing survivors) and the government. While the hibakusha and their activists remain outraged by Japan's refusal to join, government officials continue to doubt the treaty's effectiveness and call for a realistic approach to disarmament. The government still considers US extended nuclear deterrence as the only strategic option to deal with regional challenges.[65]

South Korea voted against the UN General Assembly resolutions on the TPNW in 2018, 2019, and 2020. In the words of the South Korean delegation to the 2018 NPT Preparatory Committee, the TPNW, 'crafted without the participation of nuclear-weapon states cannot but bear intrinsic limitation.' Ban Ki-moon, a former foreign minister of South Korea and a former UN secretary-general, was among the signatories to an open letter in September 2020 calling on current leaders in umbrella states to 'show courage and boldness' and join the TPNW.

India and Israel, both nuclear-armed states boycotted the TPNW negotiations in 2017. Both the states voted against the General Assembly resolutions on the TPNW in 2018, 2019, and 2020. In the First Committee of the 2019 General Assembly, India said that it did not participate in the TPNW negotiations and therefore will not join the Treaty or be bound by its obligations. It further said that the TPNW does not constitute or contribute to customary international law.In the First Committee of the

least. It believes that the treaty is unlikely to bring about the reduction in numbers and salience of nuclear weapons, or even small disarmament concessions from nuclear-armed states. Until appropriate means of dealing with nuclear threats are found, Tokyo will not be able to renounce its reliance on US extended nuclear deterrence. Tosaki Hirofumi, "Japan and the Nuclear Ban Treaty," in Shatabhisha Shetty and Denista Raynova (ed.), *Breakthrough or Breaking Point? Global Perspectives on the Nuclear Ban Treaty*, Global Security: Special Report, December 2017, pp. 33-36.

64 Siripala Thisanka, Japan's Dilemma Over Nuclear Disarmament, *The Diplomat*, February 10, 2021.

65 Sayuri Romei, Nuclear ban treaty offers rare chance for Japan, *The Asahi Shimbun*, April 28, 2021. Available at: https://www.asahi.com/ajw/articles/14330097.

2019 UN General Assembly, Israel said it did not participate in the TPNW negotiations and has deep reservations about this initiative.

Pakistan, a nuclear-armed state, also boycotted the TPNW negotiations in 2017. In the First Committee of the 2020 UN General Assembly, Pakistan explained that it voted against the TPNW resolution because progress on nuclear disarmament and arms control cannot be divorced from security challenges.

Sri Lanka has consistently voted in favour of the General Assembly resolutions on the TPNW in 2018, 2019, and 2020. Sri Lanka aligned itself with the Non-Aligned Movement (NAM) statement in the First Committee of the 2020 UN General Assembly, which said: 'NAM welcomes multilateral efforts towards nuclear disarmament and the total elimination of nuclear weapons. Moreover, NAM takes note of the adoption of the Treaty on the Prohibition of Nuclear Weapons on July 7, 2017. It is hoped that, when entered into force, the Treaty would contribute to furthering the agreed global objective of total elimination of nuclear weapons.'

Singapore participated in the TPNW negotiations in 2017 but was the only state to abstain from the vote when the Treaty was adopted and has not adhered to it. The government has also consistently abstained from the UN General Assembly resolution on the TPNW, in 2018, 2019, and 2020. Singapore maintains policies and practices that are compliant with all of the prohibitions in Article 1 of the Treaty and can therefore sign and ratify it without making changes to existing practices or policies.[66]

The United Arab Emirates (UAE) voted in favour of adopting the TPNW at the UN Diplomatic Conference in 2017 but has not yet adhered to the Treaty. The UAE has consistently voted in favour of the UN General Assembly resolutions on the TPNW in 2018, 2019, and 2020. In the First Committee of the 2020 UN General Assembly, the UAE said that it 'supports all international efforts aimed to support progress in achieving the common goal of establishing a world free of nuclear weapons and other weapons of mass destruction. We also express our concern regarding the

66 In First Committee of the 2020 General Assembly, Singapore stated, "The TPNW is a historic agreement. It contributes towards global nuclear disarmament and complements other existing nuclear disarmament and non-proliferation instruments. There is an increasing number of instruments of ratifications and accessions to the Treaty. ... We believe that once entered into force, the TPNW will contribute further to the goal of the total elimination of nuclear weapons. It is hoped that, when entered into force, the Treaty would contribute to furthering the agreed global objective of total elimination of nuclear weapons."

lack of progress in nuclear disarmament and the continuous instances of noncompliance with the regime of nuclear nonproliferation.'

National Review of the TPNW

One of the arguments in favour of the adoption of the TPNW was to close the so-called legal gap related to the use of nuclear weapons. The ICJ in the 1996 Advisory Opinion on Nuclear Weapons suggested that the use of nuclear weapons can be lawful under international law, albeit in very limited circumstances: i.e., in self-defence of a state--when its survival is at stake. The TPNW seeks to close this gap with the argument that nuclear weapons should be made illegal. From a legal standpoint, there seems to be a consensus that the TPNW and the NPT are compatible. From a policy standpoint, however, states are divided on whether the TPNW reinforces or fragments the NPT framework.[67]

Conclusion

The 2017 TPNW is the result of mounting global frustration with the failure of the Nuclear Weapons States (NWS) to get rid of their weapons of mass destruction (WMD). Despite massive progress with chemical and biological weapons, nuclear weapons remain integral to their arsenals. Even though it is almost 50 years since the NPT came into force, and despite a wave of force cuts in the 1980s, 1990s and early 2000s, progress on nuclear disarmament has all but stopped. The TPNW represents a fearless act of self-empowerment. The non-nuclear-weapons states (NNWS) have invented an international disarmament treaty without the involvement of the NWS or their allies. The TPNW is the result of mounting global frustration with the failure of the Nuclear Weapons States to get rid of their weapons of mass destruction (WMD). Despite massive progress with chemical and biological weapons, nuclear weapons remain integral to their arsenals. Even though it is almost 50 years since the NPT came into force, and despite a wave of force cuts in the 1980s, 1990s and early 2000s, progress on nuclear disarmament has all but stopped. For the majority of UN Member States, their nuclear arsenals represent a broken promise to disarm, a violation of basic international normative principles, a source of enormous frustration, and a basic threat to their security.

67 Michal Onderco and Andrea Farres Jimenez, A Comparison of National Review of the Treaty on the Prohibition of Nuclear Weapons, *Non-proliferation and Disarmament Papers*, No. 76, June 2021, pp. 13.

The treaty is short. It leaves important subjects like verification and responses to defection by states that abandon the treaty to return to nuclear weapons, for future negotiations. This makes the treaty primarily an agreement on principles for eliminating nuclear weapons, not a list of detailed procedures. The new TPNW will not, by itself, immediately eliminate any nuclear weapons, the treaty can, over time, help to further delegitimize nuclear weapons and strengthen the legal and political norm against their use. Every step aimed at reducing the risk of disastrous nuclear weapons use are necessary and should be welcomed. The perception of critics that the TPNW is of no value in the absence of the participation of nuclear-armed States because they hold the key to nuclear disarmament, may not be realistic. To treaty supporters, the NWS are trying to preserve an illegal and immoral tool of power, based on no norm or principle accepting to world opinion. While nuclear weapons have not been used to destroy enemy targets since 1945, they are deployed widely and used continuously for nuclear deterrence. Preventing nuclear war, according to this logic, requires nuclear weapons. That is what most nuclear forces are in hardened silos or submarines on ready alert. The world's nuclear-armed states must now forestall a new nuclear arms race and rediscover the path to a world free of nuclear weapons. The UN Member States should ensure that the treaty becomes the backbone of a strong new international normative principle against nuclear weapons.

Chapter VII

Nuclear Weapons and Humanity: What is the Future of Nuclear Weapons?

Since the bombing in Japan in 1945, nuclear weapons have not been used in any armed conflict or otherwise. Russia and the US still possess 11,755 nuclear weapons, nearly 90 percent of the world total. In addition to the US and Russia, there are seven more nuclear-weapon states: the UK, France, China, India, Israel, Pakistan and North Korea. Nuclear weapons are unique in their destructive power. Once the US developed nuclear weapons in 1945, the Soviet Union had to respond. China also cited US nuclear threats for its decision to build the bomb and later added the threat from the Soviet Union. According to India, China's test forced them to consider its nuclear options. Once India tested weapons in 1998, Pakistan followed within days. The reasons advanced by Israel and North Korea can be added to this web. From this perspective, nuclear proliferation is inevitable. As one state goes nuclear another state is forced to do so, and then another and another. In short, "proliferation begets proliferation.[1]

In recent years, the overall numbers of nuclear weapons have declined; however, the US, Russian, the UK and France are now on a new kind of nuclear arms race--- an extensive modernization programme to enhance their nuclear targeting capabilities. The US and Russia are specifically modernizing their triad composed of long-range bombers, land-based ICBMs and SSBNs to serve as a survivable first- and a second-strike capability. China and India are also expanding their range of delivery platforms to include nuclear-powered ballistic missile submarines (SSBNs), intercontinental ballistic missiles (ICBMs) armed with multiple

1 Cirincione Joseph, 2007, *Bomb Scare: The History and Future of Nuclear Weapons*, New York: Columbia University Press, p. 53.

independently targetable re-entry vehicles (MIRVs), dual-capable cruise missiles and hypersonic glide vehicles.[2] The number of nuclear weapons with Pakistan has also increased in the recent few years.[3]

Technological Advancement and Nuclear Weapons

The world is undergoing a new industrial revolution that is characterized by rapid and converging advances in many technological areas. There is a concern that applications of new technologies like artificial intelligence (AI)[4] could increase nuclear risks. The adoption or perceived adoption of new AI capabilities by any state could make a nuclear-armed state fear for the survivability and reliability of its nuclear deterrent. For instance, AI could fail or be misused in ways that could trigger an accidental or inadvertent escalation of a crisis or conflict into a nuclear conflict.[5] The

2 China Power: Does China have an effective sea-based nuclear deterrent, Centre for Strategic and International Studies, May 2, 2019, available at: https://chinapower.csis.org/ssbn/; Kile, S. N. and Kristensen, H. M., 2019, World Nuclear Forces: Overview, *SIPRI Yearbook 2019: Armaments, Disarmament and International Security*, Oxford: Oxford University Press, pp. 319–20.

3 The developing military cooperation between China and Pakistan is contributing to India's security concerns. In fact, the nuclear competition between China and India and between India and Pakistan has gained momentum recently. China is modernizing and increasing the size of its nuclear arsenal, and India and Pakistan are expanding their nuclear warhead stockpiles and developing new delivery systems. Topychkanov Petr, Enhancing South Asian Nuclear Dialogue: The Implications of Covid-19, SIPRI Policy Brief, September 2021, p. 12.

4 The term Artificial Intelligence (AI) refers to a wide set of computational techniques that allow computers and robots to solve complex, seemingly abstract problems that had previously yielded only to human cognition—for example, observing the world through vision, processing natural language and learning. *Focus on Computational Methods in the Context of LAWS*, Focus on Computational Methods in the Context of LAWS, International Panel on the Regulation of Autonomous Weapons (iPRAW), November 2017, p. 9. Available at: https://www.ipraw.org/wp-content/uploads/2017/11/2017-11-10_iPRAW_Focus-On-Report-2.pdf.

5 On November 9, 1979 computers from three different United States nuclear command posts showed that a massive Soviet strike was underway. Senior officers from the three posts immediately convened a threat-assessment conference. In the meantime, the intercontinental ballistic missile (ICBM) force received a preliminary warning and the entire North American air defence interceptor force was put on alert. The officers reviewed the raw data from the satellites and radars spread around the country. The data showed that there was no sign that an attack was underway, so the alert was cancelled. It was later determined that the false alarm had been caused by a software simulation of a Soviet missile attack that had been 'inexplicably transferred' into the normal early-warning display at the command headquarters. Boulanin Vincent, Lora Saalman, et. al., Artificial Intelligence, Strategic Stability and Nuclear Risk, Stockholm:

incorporation of AI into military systems also pose new challenges as far as a nuclear risk reduction is concerned, as it could increase the risk of escalation into a nuclear conflict accidentally due to technical failure or unauthorized use.[6] In politically sensitive situations, such as an intentional or unintentional collision at sea, increasing reliance on AI systems could become problematic since it could lead human operators to take premature or misguided decisions that could trigger an armed conflict or even the release of nuclear weapons.

There are many pathways through which a malicious actor may infiltrate a nuclear weapons system without a state's knowledge. Human error, system failures, design vulnerabilities, and susceptibilities within the supply chain all represent common security issues in nuclear weapons systems. Cyber-attack methods such as data manipulation, digital jamming and cyber spoofing could jeopardize the integrity of communication, leading to increased uncertainty in decision-making. The likelihood of attempted cyber-attacks on nuclear weapons systems is relatively high and increasing from advanced persistent threats from states and non-state groups.[7]

Hypersonic Weapons. Speed is a key factor in a nuclear attack. Several modern militaries[8] are currently working to develop hypersonic weapons which

---

SIPRI, June 2020, p. 20.

6 On September 26, 1983, at about 00.30, the Soviet early-warning system Oko detected that a US attack was underway. The computer display showed that five missiles originating from the USA were heading towards the USSR. Within minutes, Lieutenant Colonel Stanislav Petrov, who was in charge of supervising the operation of early-warning system, and his team cross-checked the intelligence information, but they could not determine with certainty whether it was a false alarm. Petrov nonetheless decided to report the incident as a false alarm to his superiors. He reportedly trusted his gut instinct. He knew the technical limitation of the systems and it seemed to him that the US attack would not make sense: 'when people start a war, they don't start it with only five missiles; you can do little damage with just five missiles. He was right. The satellite had wrongly identified the missiles. Petrov's decision to rely on his common sense was later hailed as having saved the world from a nuclear war. Ibid, p. 20.

7 UnalBeyza and Lewis Patricia, Cybersecurity of Nuclear Weapons Systems: Threats, Vulnerabilities and Consequences, International Security Department, Chatham House, January 2018, p. 23.

8 Although the US, Russia, and China are most aggressively pursuing hypersonic technology, other nations like Australia, France, Germany, India, Israel, Norway, South Korea, Spain, Sweden and the UK are also following hypersonic technology. Speier Richard H. George Nacouzi, Carrie A. Lee, and Richard M. Moore, Hypersonic Missile Nonproliferation: Hindering the Spread of a New Class of Weapons, Rand

can travel at speeds above Mach 5 (five times the speed of sound), or above around 6,100 km per hour. [9] There are two primary categories of hypersonic weapons: (i) Hypersonic glide vehicles (HGV) are launched from a rocket before gliding to a target; and (ii) Hypersonic cruise missiles are powered by high-speed, air-breathing engines, or "scramjets," after acquiring their target.[10] These hypersonic weapons may be designed to carry nuclear warheads.[11] Unlike normal ballistic missiles, hypersonic weapons do not follow a ballistic trajectory after their initial ballistic boost phase but travel typically in the higher atmosphere.[12] They are significantly harder to track than ICBMs because their lower flight path and the curvature of the Earth delay their detection by ground-based radar.[13] Hypersonic weapons are expected to combine significantly higher speeds with enhanced manoeuvrability. They would enable offensive missile strikes to destroy targets at great distances. They are designed to operate at altitudes that make them particularly difficult to detect, either from the ground, because of the limited viewing angle, or from space because of background clutter and therefore may circumvent advanced defence systems built to intercept ballistic missiles. Therefore, hypersonic weapons may provide less time to respond, compared to existing cruise and ballistic missiles. Hypersonic

Corporation, 2017, p. 123.

9 'Hypersonic' is generally understood to refer to any vehicle or flight which goes faster than five times the speed of sound. Hypersonic Weapons, Discussion paper for the Convention on Certain Conventional Weapons (CCW), Article 36, Geneva, February 2019, p. 6.

10 Sayler Kelley M., Hypersonic Weapons: Background Issues for Congress, Congressional Research Service, R45811, October 19, 2021, p. 2.

11 In March 2021, the US announced that it has successfully tested an unarmed prototype of a hypersonic missile, a nuclear-capable weapon that could accelerate the arms race between superpowers. The Pentagon said a test glide vehicle flew at hypersonic speeds -- more than five times the speed of sound, or Mach 5 -- to a designated impact point. The test followed the first joint US Army and Navy flight experiment in October 2017, when the prototype missile demonstrated it could glide in the direction of a target at hypersonic speed. US successfully tests nuclear-capable hypersonic missile, *The Economic Times*, March 21, 2021.

12 Wilkening Dean, Hypersonic Weapons and Strategic Stability, *Survival*, Vol. 61, Issue 5, October-November 2019, pp. 129-148.

13 Unlike ballistic missiles, which follow a parabolic trajectory, hypersonic weapons glide or fly at a relatively constant height, which has the potential to reduce warning times and make them harder to detect. Futter Andrew, Explaining the Nuclear Challenges posed by Emerging and Disruptive Technology: A Primer for European Policy Makers and Professionals, Non-Proliferation and Disarmament Papers, No. 73, March 2021, p. 15.

weapons are likely to increase the risk of pre-emptive strikes, accidents, miscalculations, conflict instability and rapid conflict escalation owing to their potential to shorten decision times. Some analysts are of the view that the US should use hypersonics to achieve strategic advantages over Russia and China; others believe that hypersonic weapons could present a threat to strategic stability or inspire an arms race.[14]

With the rapid technology changes nuclear weapons modernization, a new era of power rivalry is emerging. Global power shifts have propelled China's rise and enhanced its military threat to the US and its allies. However, in the sphere of strategic nuclear weapons, Russia remains the US' only competitor.[15] At a time when the entire world is fighting against the Covid-19 pandemic, we have to rethink on investments not only in nuclear weapons modernization but the necessity of having such weapon systems in military arsenals of a few. It is in the interest of the nuclear-weapon states to avoid an expensive nuclear arms race.[16]

Today, many developed nations are struggling hard to fight the Covid-19 pandemic. A large number of states, besides coping up with the pandemic losses, are trying to overcome the effects of poverty and lack of education to realize their aspirations of life with dignity. Today no state, not even the most developed one, can address adequately the immediate humanitarian emergency or long-term consequences caused by a nuclear weapon detonation in a populated area, nor provide adequate assistance to those affected. Such capacity is unlikely ever to exist. Under these appalling circumstances, we remain vulnerable to the major threat of nuclear arsenals and fissile materials used for their production. Despite the common obligation to achieve disarmament, nuclear deterrence continues to be a part of the defence doctrines of the five nuclear powers recognized by the Treaty on the Non-proliferation of Nuclear Weapons (NPT). The list must also include those that did not accede to the NPT: India, Pakistan, Israel

14 Sayler Kelley M., Hypersonic Weapons: Background and Issues for Congress, Congressional Research Service, R45811, August 25, 2021, p. 28.

15 Lissner Rebecca, The Future of Strategic Arms Control, Discussion Paper Series on Managing Global Disorder No. 4, Council on Foreign Relations, April 2021, p. 42.

16 Arms control can entail either freezes or reductions, and it can limit certain categories of nuclear weapons, delivery systems, or behaviors, or it can eliminate them entirely. Such limitations benefit arms race stability directly: by imposing freezes or reductions, arms control can reduce incentives for states to undertake costly arms buildups. Lissner Rebecca, The Future of Strategic Arms Control, Discussion Paper Series on Managing Global Disorder No. 4, Council on Foreign Relations, April 2021, p. 4.

and North Korea. In such a scenario, what US President Barack Obama said in Berlin is worth remembering:[17]

> This is the moment when we must renew the goal of a world without nuclear weapons. The two superpowers that faced each other across the wall of this city came too close too often to destroying all we have built and all that we love. With that wall gone, we need not stand idly by and watch the further spread of the deadly atom. It is time to secure all loose nuclear materials; to stop the spread of nuclear weapons; and to reduce the arsenals from another era. This is the moment to begin the work of seeking the peace of a world without nuclear weapons.

Terrorism and Nuclear Weapons

There is a serious threat that secrets from a scientist in Pakistan could help build a bomb that detonates in any other country. Terrorist groups have declared their intent to obtain fissile materials to create a nuclear threat device (NTD), which can be anything from a crude, homemade nuclear device, an improvised nuclear device (IND), a radiological dispersal device (RDD), a radiological exposure device (RED), or a weapon acquired from one of the established nuclear states that has fallen out of state control. Terrorists do not share the same goals or need the same capabilities as states. In addition, they are not bound by international law or nuclear treaties and agreements. For a fabricated nuclear device, weight and size constraints may not be important to a terrorist; unsafe designs would be acceptable. Finally, a wide variety of delivery methods could be used, with no regard for collateral damage to civilian populations or the terrorists themselves.[18]

A non-state group could attempt to obtain fissionable material or an intact nuclear weapon from a rogue state's arsenal. Concerning knowledge that is needed for the creation of crude nuclear weapons, such information is widespread and no longer limited to an exclusive club of scientists. The fear of proliferation of facilities, equipment and techniques required for the production of highly enriched uranium is increased by the uncovering of the Khan network, in which Dr Khan had sold weapon designs and centrifuge technology to several unpredictable regimes, including Iran, North Korea and Libya. Even after uncovering the Khan network, control of dual-use goods remains challenging because it can always be claimed

17 Obama Speech in Berlin on July 24, 2008, *The New York Times*, July 24, 2008. Available at: https://www.nytimes.com/2008/07/24/us/politics/24text-obama.html.

18 Nuclear Matters Handbook 2020, The Office of the Deputy Assistant Secretary of Defence for Nuclear Matters, USA, pp. 179-180.

that they are for civilian, non-nuclear use.[19] If a non-State actor has been able to find sufficient financial support, assembled a network of dedicated and skilled individuals, and acquired the necessary knowledge, equipment and raw materials, it may attempt to build a nuclear weapon. The use of even a single nuclear weapon with a relatively small destructive power in or near a populated area is likely to produce humanitarian needs that will be difficult or impossible to address.[20] The devastation inherent in nuclear weapons outweighs any justification for their existence.

n some states, nuclear material stocks remain insecure. There is a risk that additional countries may utilize peaceful nuclear technologies to produce fissile material for nuclear bombs. Pakistan is a permanent base of numerous armed non-state militant/terrorist groups.[21] The fear of nuclear weapons or fissile material reaching in their hand cannot be ruled out. States must secure nuclear weapons, materials, related technology, and knowledge to prevent their malicious use by non-state actors. Few analysts believe that terrorists would find it extremely difficult to design or assemble a nuclear weapon,[22] but we should never rule out such possibilities. No analyst would have ever imagined that fully occupied passenger airliners would be used by the terrorists to demolish 415 meters tall Twin Towers of the World Trade Centre in 2001. The states must prevent non-state actors/terrorists from obtaining nuclear weapons or weapons-usable materials, and technology. [23]

19 David Albright, Paul Brannan and Andrea Scheel Stricker, Detecting and Disrupting Illicit Nuclear Trade after A. Q. Khan, *Washington Quarterly*, April 2010, pp. 85–106.

20 Meulenbelt Stephanie E and Maarten S. Nieuwenhuizen, Non-State actors' pursuit of CBRN weapons: From motivation to potential humanitarian consequences, *International Review of the Red Cross*, Vol. 97, No. 899, 2015, pp. 831–858.

21 The US officials have identified Pakistan as a base of operations and/or target for numerous armed, non-state militant groups, some of which have existed since the 1980s. Notable terrorist and other groups operating in and/or launching attacks on Pakistan are of five broad, but not exclusive types: (i) globally-oriented; (ii) Afghanistan-oriented; (iii) India- and Kashmir-oriented; (iv) domestically-oriented; and (v)) sectarian (anti-Shia). Twelve of the fifteen groups are designated as Foreign Terrorist Organizations (FTOs) under US law and most, but not all, are animated by Islamist extremist ideology. "Terrorist and Other Militant Groups in Pakistan," the Congressional Research Service, September 23, 2021, p. 3.

22 Carson Mark, Theodore Taylor, Eugene Eyster, William Maraman, Jacob Wechsler, Can Terrorists Build Nuclear Weapons? Nuclear Control Institute, Washington DC, available at: https://www.nci.org/k-m/makeab.htm.

23 In April 2004, the UN Security Council adopted Resolution 1540, which requires all states to "criminalize proliferation, enact strict export controls and secure all sensitive materials within their borders." Resolution 1540 called on states to enforce effective

There are a number of the treaty and customary law provisions which outlaw the use of nuclear weapons. Many activists and organizations are of the view that Article VI of the NPT should be considered part of customary international law, which must be respected by all states, whether a party to the NPT or not.[24] The 2021 Nuclear weapons ban treaty has further instituted a set of legal measures related to the manufacture, possession and use of nuclear weapons. If we accept the premise that the development, deployment, and use of nuclear weapons represent a threat to the continued existence of mankind and thus to the life of the international community, and if we further accept that the function of international law is to facilitate the self-preservation of the international community; then the conclusion is inescapable that the existence of nuclear weapons is inconsistent with international law and order.[25]

The bombing of Hiroshima and Nagasaki: A War Crime?

In 1945, a handful of US political and scientific elites made the irreversible decision to use the atom bombs. Neither Hiroshima nor Nagasaki was a significant military target. Hiroshima and Nagasaki bombings are raising new questions after 75 Years. Was the bombing necessary to end the war? Whether the atomic bombing of Hiroshima and Nagasaki would be illegal today? Whether it would amount to a 'War Crime' today? Can nuclear war be ever justified?

After the bombing of Hiroshima, US President Harry Truman's official statement proclaimed: "It is an atomic bomb. It is a harnessing of the basic power of the universe. The force from which the sun draws its power has been loosed against those who brought war to the Far East." In his first radio address after the bombing of Hiroshima, President Truman claimed that "the world will note that the first atomic bomb was dropped on Hiroshima, a military base. That was because we wished in this first

---

domestic controls over WMD and WMD-related materials in production, use, storage, and transport; to maintain effective border controls; and to develop national export and trans-shipment controls over such items, all of which should help interdiction efforts.

24 The regime of nuclear arms control and non-proliferation set by the NPT, particularly in its Article VI, is especially important because it is the only legally binding commitment on nuclear disarmament contained in a multilateral treaty. Lima Sergio Eduardo Moreira, 2017, *The Universal Obligation of Nuclear Disarmament*, Alexandre de Gusmao Foundation, Ministry of Foreign Affairs, Brazil, p. 224.

25 Bleimaier John Kuhn, Nuclear Weapons and Crimes against Humanity under International Law, *Catholic Lawyer*, Vol. 33, No. 2, 2017, pp. 161-172.

attack to avoid, insofar as possible, the killing of civilians. …. Having found the bomb we have used it. We have used it against those who attacked us without warning at Pearl Harbor, against those who have starved and beaten and executed American prisoners of war, against those who have abandoned all pretence of obeying international laws of warfare." The statement that President Truman made is incorrect and also misleading."[26] Truman's speech exposes his retributive instincts and raised Japanese violations of international law as a justification for dropping the bomb.[27]

Hiroshima is neither the capital of Japan nor one of the main cities of Japan. More than 90% of people killed by atom bombs were civilians.[28] The atomic bomb dropped on Hiroshima was deliberately detonated above the residential and commercial centre of the city, and not directly on legitimate military targets, to magnify the shock effect on the Japanese public.[29]The aim of the Target Committee (Robert Oppenheimer and Maj Gen Leslie Groves of the Manhattan Project) and the Higher-level Interim Committee (led by Secretary of War Henry Stimson) was to kill large numbers of Japanese civilians in the attack. Richard Overy, a Professor of History at the University of Exeter, has opined that bombing was immoral and unnecessary. These bombs did not kill people only but caused massive urban destruction.[30]

According to Mark Selden, there were mutually reinforcing factors behind the decision to bomb Hiroshima and Nagasaki: (i) The US had a wartime goal that required Japan's unconditional surrender; (ii) The US' racist belief that the atrocious behaviour of Japanese forces (treachery, brutality, and fanaticism) in the war nullified any humanitarian

26 Truman H. S., Statement by President Truman, Office of the Historian, August 6, 1945. Available at: https://history.state.gov/historicaldocuments/frus1945v06/d401.

27 McKinney Katherine E., Scott D. Sagan & Allen S. Weiner, Why the atomic bombing of Hiroshima would be illegal today, *Bulletin of the Atomic Scientists*, Vo. 76(4), 2020, pp. 157-165.

28 Bernstein, B. J., Reconsidering the 'Atomic General': Leslie R. Groves, *The Journal of Military History*, Vol. 67 (3), 2003, pp. 904–905.

29 McKinney Katherine E., Scott D. Sagan & Allen S. Weiner, Why the atomic bombing of Hiroshima would be illegal today, *Bulletin of the Atomic Scientists*, Vo. 76(4), 2020, pp. 157-165.

30 Throughout 1945, US planners deliberately spared five cities from firebombing. Kyoto, the ancient imperial capital, Hiroshima, Kokura, Niigata, and Nagasaki were reserved by the Atomic Bomb Target Selection Committee to display the power of the atom to Japan and the world. Selden Mark, The United States, Japan, and the atomic bomb, *Bulletin of Concerned Asian Scholars*, Vol. 23 (1), 1991, pp. 3-12.

consideration for the Japanese people; (iii) The US leadership was convinced that the atomic bomb would save the lives of numerous US soldiers by obviating a costly invasion of Japan; and (iv) The commitment to establish US primacy and to check Soviet advance at the outset of a postwar era that would be shaped by Soviet-US conflict.[31] In other words, the US wanted to demonstrate its unique military power – its possession of the atomic bomb –to gain a political and diplomatic advantage over the Soviet Union in the post-war settlement in both Asia and Europe.[32]

According to Martin J Sherwin (a co-recipient of Pulitzer Prize of 2006), those bombings had little to do with the Japanese decision to surrender. The evidence has become overwhelming that it was the entry of the Soviet Union on August 8, into the war against Japan that forced surrender. Truman could have waited for the Soviet Union to enter the war but he did not want the USSR to have a claim to participate in the occupation of Japan. The next, militarily Japan was finished and further blockade and urban destruction would have produced surrender in August or September 1945 at the latest, without the atomic bomb. A second bomb on Nagasaki was just as unnecessary as the first one. The bombs of two different types were used in two cities just to assess the cynical scientific imperative.[33] Thus, there were geopolitical reasons for killing everybody in the two Japanese cities that may have been more persuasive with US leaders than the urgency to end the war.

The most contemporary critique of the US moral position on the atom bomb was voiced by the Indian jurist Radhabinhod Pal, the lone dissenting voice at the Tokyo War Crimes Tribunal.[34] Justice Pal, recalling

31 Selden Mark, The United States, Japan, and the atomic bomb, *Bulletin of Concerned Asian Scholars*, Vol. 23 (1), 1991, pp. 3-12.

32 Hudson Kate, Why the atom bomb was dropped on Japan, Campaign for Nuclear Disarmament, August 5, 2018, https://cnduk.org/why-the-atom-bomb-was-dropped-on-japan-2/.

33 The Hiroshima bomb was made from highly-enriched uranium-235. This was prepared by diffusion enrichment techniques using the very small differences in mass of the two main isotopes: U-235 (originally 0.7% in the uranium) and U-238, the majority. The 21-kiloton explosive charge for the bomb detonated over Nagasaki was provided by about 6.2 kilograms of plutonium-239 (>90% Pu-239), and its preparation depended on the operation of special nuclear reactors built for the purpose. Therefore, an experiment was accomplished on human being to assess the destructive power of U-235, U-238 and U-239.

34 Justice Radhabinod Pal was an Indian judge on the International Military Tribunal for the Far East (IMTFE), which was set up by the Allied powers, post World War II, to try Japanese leaders for "war crimes". The other 10 judges were from the US,

Kaiser Wilhelm II's account of his duty to bring World War I to a swift end-- "everything must be put to fire and sword; men, women and children and old men must be slaughtered and not a tree or house be left standing," observed: "This policy of indiscriminate murder to shorten the war was considered to be a crime. ... If any indiscriminate destruction of civilian life and property is still illegal in warfare, then, in the Pacific War, this decision to use the atom bomb is the only near approach to the directives of the German Emperor during the first World War and of the Nazi leaders during the Second World War." Pal concluded that a victor who destroyed noncombatant populations with weapons ranging from firebombs to atomic bombs had no moral claim to unilaterally brand its enemy as a desecrater of the laws of war.

In addition to these, history indicated that the bomb was made for defence only. The origin of the Manhattan Project was designed to save the US, not to win the war by destroying a part of civilization. From 1949-1991 the Cold War was waged under the shadow of Mutually Assured Destruction (MAD), and even though the US fought major wars in Korea (while Truman was still in office), Vietnam, Iraq, and Afghanistan, nuclear weapons were never again deployed. In other words, not using them in those wars has been an admission that they should never have been used offensively in the first place. In 1945, the Japanese military could not attack the US at that time.

Nuclear weapons raise some concerns under international law. These concerns are primarily related to the impact these weapons can have on civilians and civilian areas, and to their effects on the environment. Their use in Hiroshima and Nagasaki in 1945 and subsequent studies have shown that nuclear weapons have immediate and long-term consequences

---

Canada, Britain, France, the Netherlands, Australia, New Zealand, the Soviet Union, China and the Philippines. Pal was included as a judge after the trial proceedings had started, merely to beef up the Asian presence on the bench. Pal, issued a dissentient opinion paper titled *Dissentient Judgment of Justice Pal*, and asserted that all Japanese Class-A defendants at the trials were criminally innocent. Since the tribunal's language department omitted the word "dissentient," the paper became widely known in Japan as "Pal's Judgment." Justice Pal objected to the introduction of an *ex post facto* law at the tribunal because he believed that by ruling on *ex post facto* law, international society would not be bound by a common understanding against wars, instead it would subscribe to an understanding that the victors of wars were entitled to judge the defeated while disregarding the rules of international law. Nakajima Takeshi, The Radhabinod Pal Dissentient Judgment and Nationalism in Post-War Japan, Hokkaido University, March 25, 2011, available at: https://core.ac.uk/download/pdf/198398648.pdf.

due to the heat, blast and radiation generated by the explosion and, in many cases, the distances over which these forces are spread. The sheer scale of the casualties and destruction resulting from the use of a nuclear weapon in or near a populated area and its long-term effects on health and the environment raises serious questions about the compatibility of this weapon with international humanitarian law. The US knew of the indiscriminate destruction that the bombs would cause and intentionally used them as a way to end the war early. Intentional killing of civilians in an indiscriminate attack for any reason, even to end a war early, is a war crime and violation of IHL.

At the time of World War II, the international laws that applied to wars were the Hague Conventions of 1899 and 1907. These regulations set forth rules regarding attacks on civilian populations.[35] The Conventions did not anticipate air warfare and, therefore, did not contain any specific provisions on-air attacks; instead, it prohibited targeting undefended towns and cities by naval and field artillery. Additionally, the Conventions prohibited using "arms, projectiles, or material calculated to cause unnecessary suffering."[36] The Tokyo District Court supports these assertions.[37]

In September 1938, the League of Nations, "under the recognized principles of international law," issued a unanimous resolution outlawing the intentional bombing of civilian populations, with special emphasis against bombing military objectives from the air. The League warned, "Any attack on legitimate military objectives must be carried out in such a way that civilian populations in the neighbourhood are not bombed through

35 Hague Convention IV Respecting the Laws and Customs of War on Land and its Annex: Regulations Concerning the Laws and Customs of War on Land, 1907.

36 Articles 23(e) and 25, The Hague Convention, 1907.

37 In *Shimoda v. State* (1964), the plaintiffs sued the Japanese government for injuries resulting from the nuclear bombings. The Tokyo District Court found that the United States' use of nuclear weapons during World War II violated the Hague Conventions and customary international law by causing unnecessary suffering. The Tokyo Court decided that the nuclear bombing of Nagasaki and Hiroshima violated international standards at the time. The court noted that the nuclear bomb was a "really cruel weapon" that caused massive destruction and mass casualties. Relying on the Hague Conventions and customary international law, the court distinguished between conventional and nuclear aerial bombings and between defended and undefended cities. The court also ruled that an indiscriminate attack was only legal under international law if it occurred in defended cities. Thus under the *Shimoda* case, the attacks on Hiroshima and Nagasaki violated international law. Vail Christopher, The Legality of Nuclear Weapons for Use and Deterrence, *Georgetown Journal of International Law*, Vol. 48, 2017, pp. 839-872.

negligence." The resolution also reaffirmed that "the use of chemical or bacterial methods in the conduct of war is contrary to international law." Also, the dropping of the atom bomb was partially racially motivated. Opponents of President Truman's decision to use the atomic bomb argue that racism played an important role in the decision; that had the bomb been ready in the time it never would have been used against Germany.[38]

The laws of war regarding aerial bombardment were not well-developed during World War II. The US desire to avoid its military casualties expected in the planned invasion of Japan, combined with a vengeance against the Japanese Emperor and military, overwhelmed legal concerns and morality about killing a large number of civilians including women and children.[39] Such a nuclear attack would be illegal today on three counts: (i) intentionally attack against civilians (the principle of distinction); (ii) excessive collateral damage disproportionate to the direct military advantage (the principle of proportionality); taking all feasible precautions to reduce collateral damage against civilians (the precautionary principle). Today military operations in several states are reviewed by the judicial branch of the military (or by the members of the Judge Advocate General's Corps).

The US government has long accepted that the principles of distinction, proportionality, and precaution as codified in the 1977 Additional Protocol I (AP I) and has referred to them as part of binding customary international law.[40] The 2018 Nuclear Posture Review (NPR) issued by President Trump

---

38 The US-British bombing of Dresden, an undefended German city with no significant war industry, remains the single best known and most widely condemned example of firebombing and the deliberate annihilation of civilian populations in the history of war. On February 13, 1945, 1,400 British aircraft followed by 1,350 US bombers destroyed Dresden and unleashed a firestorm visible 200 miles away. The destruction of Dresden killing 35,000 Germans was the prelude to the wave of US B-29 firebomb and napalm attacks that sowed destruction across virtually every major Japanese city and exacted a heavy toll in human life in the spring and summer of 1945. Selden Mark, The United States, Japan, and the atomic bomb, *Bulletin of Concerned Asian Scholars*, Vol. 23 (1), 1991, pp. 3-12.

39 McKinney Katherine E., Scott D. Sagan & Allen S. Weiner, Why the atomic bombing of Hiroshima would be illegal today, *Bulletin of the Atomic Scientists*, Vo. 76(4), 2020, pp. 157-165.

40 A nuclear attack deliberately aimed at the centre of a city to maximize civilian casualties would clearly violate the principle of distinction, enshrined in Article 48 of API, which requires governments to distinguish between the civilian population and combatants and between civilian objects and military objectives and then direct "operations only against military objectives." The proportionality principle expressed in Article 51(5)

has reaffirmed that the US is committed to adhering to the law of armed conflict in any initiation and conduct of nuclear operations.[41]

The 2019 United States' Nuclear Operations (Joint Publication 3-72) categorically states:[42]

> The law of war governs the use of nuclear weapons, just as it governs the use of conventional weapons. For example, nuclear weapons must be directed against military objectives. In addition, attacks using nuclear weapons must not be conducted when the expected incidental harm to civilians is excessive compared to the military advantage expected to be gained. US policy on the use of nuclear weapons complies with all law of war requirements. Combatant commander (CCDRs), and other subordinate commanders responsible for the conduct of nuclear operations, must ensure their staff judge advocate is involved in nuclear operations planning and targeting processes.

A nuclear strike against a legitimate military target could be legal only if it met all three criteria: no intentional targeting of civilians, absence of disproportionate collateral damage, and with all feasible precautions made to reduce collateral damage. According to Gabriella Blum, the use of an atom bomb over Hiroshima would be considered a war crime today.[43]

The historical debate over the morality, legitimacy, and necessity of the bombings is still as contentious today as global nuclear politics. The US completely disregarded the rule of distinction--between the Japanese military and the civilian population, comprising predominantly of

---

prohibits attacks which may be expected to cause incidental loss of civilian life, injury to civilians, damage to civilian objects, or a combination thereof, which would be excessive in relation to the concrete and direct military advantage anticipated. Article 52 (2) also clearly limits legitimate military objectives "to those objects which by their nature, location, purpose or use make an effective contribution to military action and whose total or partial destruction, capture or neutralization, in the circumstances ruling at the time, offers a definite military advantage." See: Matheson Michael J., The United States Position on the Relation of Customary International Law to the 1977 Protocols Additional to the 1949 Geneva Conventions, *American University Journal of International Law and Policy*, Vol. 2, 1987, p. 426.

41 Nuclear Posture Review: 2018, The US Department of Defence, Washington, DC, p. 23.

42 Nuclear Operations: Joint Publication 3-72, The Chairman of the Joint Chiefs of Staff, June 11, 2019, p. III-4. This publication provides fundamental principles and guidance to plan, execute, and assess nuclear operations.

43 Blum Gabriella, The Laws of War and the "Lesser Evil", *The Yale Journal of International Law*, Vol. 35, Issue 1, 2010, pp. 1-69.

women, children, and the elderly. In the end, it was precisely the women and children of Hiroshima and Nagasaki who bore the brunt of the atomic attack. Based on the analyses under the Hague Conventions of 1899 and 1907 and customary rules of international humanitarian law contained in AP I, the bombing of Hiroshima and Nagasaki violated international law both at the time of the attacks and under current international law.[44]

On May 27, 2016, Barack Obama, the then US President paid his respect to the Japanese people at Hiroshima Peace Memorial. He said:

> Seventy-one years ago, on a bright, cloudless morning, death fell from the sky and the world was changed. A flash of light and a wall of fire destroyed a city and demonstrated that mankind possessed the means to destroy itself. ... There are many sites around the world that chronicle this war -- memorials that tell stories of courage and heroism; graves and empty camps that echo of unspeakable depravity. Yet in the image of a mushroom cloud that rose into these skies, we are most starkly reminded of humanity's core contradiction; how the very spark that marks us as a species -- our thoughts, our imagination, our language, our tool-making, our ability to set ourselves apart from nature and bend it to our will -- those very things also give us the capacity for unmatched destruction. The very spark that marks us as a species – our thoughts, our imagination, our language, our tool-making, our ability to set ourselves apart from nature and bend it to our will – those very things also give us the capacity for unmatched destruction... Technological progress without an equivalent progress in human institutions can doom us. The scientific revolution that led to the splitting of the atom requires a moral revolution as well.[45]

The evidence of the immediate and longer-term impacts of the use and testing of nuclear weapons has been the subject of scientific investigation since 1945. The World Health Organization in a 1987 report has reported that the blast wave, thermal wave, radiation and radioactive fallout generated by nuclear explosions have devastating short- and long-term effects on the human body, and that existing health services are not

44 Vail Christopher, The Legality of Nuclear Weapons for Use and Deterrence, *Georgetown Journal of International Law*, Vol. 48, 2017, p. 852.

45 Remarks by President Obama and Prime Minister Abe of Japan at Hiroshima Peace Memorial, The White House Office of the Press Secretary, available at: https://obamawhitehouse.archives.gov/the-press-office/2016/05/27/remarks-president-obama-and-prime-minister-abe-japan-hiroshima-peace.

equipped to alleviate these effects in any significant way. A nuclear weapon detonation in or near a populated area would – as a result of the blast wave, intense heat, and radiation and radioactive fallout – cause massive death and destruction, trigger large-scale displacement [46] and cause long-term harm to human health and well-being, as well as long-term damage to the environment, infrastructure, socioeconomic development and social order.[47] The scale of destruction and contamination after a nuclear detonation in or near a populated area could cause profound social and political disruption as it would take several decades to reconstruct infrastructure and regenerate economic activities, trade, communications, health-care facilities and schools.[48]

At the 2015 NPT Review Conference a "humanitarian pledge" to "stigmatize, prohibit and eliminate" nuclear weapons was supported by a large majority of states. In a working paper submitted by Austria during the conference, it was stated:

> The impact of a nuclear weapon detonation, irrespective of the cause, would not be constrained by national borders and could have regional and even global consequences, causing destruction, death and displacement as well as profound and long-term damage to the environment, climate, human health and well-being, socioeconomic development, social order and could even threaten the survival of humankind.
>
> The use and testing of nuclear weapons have demonstrated their devastating immediate, mid- and long-term effects. Nuclear testing in several parts of the world has left a legacy of serious health and environmental consequences. Radioactive contamination from these tests disproportionately affects women and children. It contaminated food supplies and continues to be measurable in the atmosphere to this day. As long as nuclear weapons exist, there remains the possibility of a nuclear weapon explosion. The risk increases over time."[49]

46 Simon Bagshaw, Population Displacement: Displacement in the Aftermath of Nuclear Weapon Detonation Events, ILPI-UNIDIR, 2014.

47 Economic impact of a nuclear weapon detonation, Article 36, 2015.

48 Neil Buhne, Social and economic impacts: Structural restoration of lives and livelihoods in and around affected areas, presentation to the Conference on the Humanitarian Impact of Nuclear Weapons, Oslo, 2013, available at: https://www.regjeringen.no/globalassets/upload/ud/vedlegg/hum/hum_buhne.pdf.

49 The Vienna Conference on the Humanitarian Impact of Nuclear Weapons (8-9 December 2014) and the Austrian Pledge: Input for the NPT 2015 Review Conference,

The *Nuclear Weapons Case* (Obligations Concerning Negotiations Relating to the Cessation of the Nuclear Arms Race and on Nuclear Disarmament) was brought before the International Court of Justice by the Marshall Islands.[50] Public hearings were held in three cases in 2016. The case did not succeed due to the lack of jurisdiction and admissibility under Article 36, paragraph 2 of the statute of the ICJ. It has been observed by some commentators that the ICJ has avoided taking decisive action on matters regarding international security, particularly in regards to nuclear armament in cases that involve the interest of the big powers.[51]

On March 2, 2020, the International Committee of the Red Cross (ICRC) convened a meeting of experts on the humanitarian impacts and risks of the use of nuclear weapons. The report concludes, "The evidence of the humanitarian impacts of nuclear weapons is essential to assess the legality of their use under international humanitarian law and it gives a fact-based entry point for discussions about nuclear disarmament and nuclear non-proliferation. ... The only way to guarantee that nuclear weapons are never used again is by prohibiting and eliminating them."[52]

The bombing of Japan violated the Hague Conventions of 1907 because the US bombed undefended cities and the attack itself was indiscriminate, causing disproportionate casualties and destruction beyond the military establishments. The UN and the ICJ have maintained their stand against the use of nuclear weapons; their stockpiles should be eliminated. Despite the NPT-based international consensus on the need for disarmament and non-proliferation of nuclear weapons, several countries claim a right to possess and threaten to use such weapons to deter aggression. These countries also

---

Working paper submitted by Austria, NPT/CONF.2015/WP.29 dated April 21, 2015.

50 On April 24, 2014, the Republic of the Marshall Islands filed Applications against nine States (China, N. Korea, France, India, Israel, Pakistan, Russia, UK and US), accusing them of not fulfilling their obligations with respect to the cessation of the nuclear arms race at an early date and to nuclear disarmament.

51 Lima Sergio Eduardo Moreira, 2017, *The Universal Obligation of Nuclear Disarmament*, Alexandre de Gusmao Foundation, Ministry of Foreign Affairs, Brazil, p. 37.

52 In addition to scientific experts from Sciences Po, Columbia University, Rutgers University, the Federation of American Scientists, Chatham House, the Gender and Radiation Impact Project and the United Nations Institute for Disarmament Research, representatives from approximately 45 states and a range of UN agencies and civil society organizations took part in the meeting. Humanitarian impacts and risks of use of nuclear weapons, 10th Review Conference of the Parties to the Treaty on the Non-Proliferation of Nuclear Weapons, August 29, 2020, available at: https://www.icrc.org/en/document/humanitarian-impacts-and-risks-use-nuclear-weapons.

perceive nuclear deterrence to be essential for maintaining international stability.8 However, the concept of nuclear deterrence has become stale. Today, neither the US nor the Russian Federation are in a position to fight and win a nuclear war. Instead, they should pursue a policy of 'minimal nuclear deterrence focused on a nuclear no-first-use (NFU) policy—it may lead towards comprehensive nuclear disarmament.[53] Any further reliance on nuclear deterrence is dangerous as it may lead to nuclear weapon use after 75 years.[54]

Most national leaders have repeatedly expressed their hope that these weapons will never be used. Despite this, several states have attempted to develop or acquire nuclear weapons. Cirincione (2007) has advanced five reasons for this: (i) to enhance national security; (ii) prestige—states see weapons as a prerequisite for great power status to protect their sovereignty;[55] (iii) domestic politics—competing for bureaucratic and military actors within the state; (iv) technological triumph—capable of developing nuclear weapons; and (v) economics—nuclear weapon is considered chapter option than a conventional defence. At the same time, because of these five reasons states decide not to build nuclear weapons. The states consider that the security benefits are greater without nuclear weapons, that prestige is enhanced by non-nuclear-weapon status, because domestic politics convinces leaders not to pursue these programmes, or because the technological and economic barriers are too significant to overcome.[56]

53 ErastoTytti, New Technologies and Nuclear Disarmament: Outlining a Way Forward, Stockholm: SIPRI, May 2021, p. 25.

54 Successful nuclear deterrence requires leaders to have accurate and comprehensive technical information. If decision-makers believe incorrectly that their adversary has launched a nuclear attack, and so launches a counterattack, then for all practical purposes deterrence has failed. For instance, the missile flight time between India and Pakistan can be as little as five minutes. Even if each country has highly sophisticated early-warning systems, how does a state record and transmit the news of an incoming attack, and how does the leader make an informed decision, within a timescale of just five minutes? Rublee Maria Rost, "Nuclear Deterrence Destabilized," Perspectives on Nuclear Deterrence in the 21st Century, Chatham House, April 2020, pp. 14-18.

55 For instance the US Joint Chiefs of Staff publication, "Nuclear Operations" June 11, 2019 (JP 3-72) states: "US nuclear forces serve the national objective of maintaining peace through strength. Credible nuclear capabilities are important, as the President must have the means to respond appropriately to an attack on the US, its allies, and partners. ... No nation should doubt the strength of our deterrence commitments or the strength of US and allied capabilities to deter and, if necessary, defeat any threat's nuclear or nonnuclear aggression."

56 Cirincione Joseph, 2007, *Bomb Scare: The History and Future of Nuclear Weapons*, New

Nuclear Weapon Elimination and India

India has played a leading role in global efforts towards nuclear disarmament. India was the first country to call for a ban on nuclear testing in 1954 and a non-discriminatory treaty on the non-proliferation of nuclear weapons, as distinct from non-dissemination, in 1965. India is committed to the goal of a nuclear-weapons-free world and complete elimination of nuclear weapons, consistent with the highest priority accorded to nuclear disarmament by the Final Document of the First Special Session of the UN General Assembly on Disarmament (SSOD-I). India, as a responsible nuclear weapon State, has a nuclear doctrine outlining credible minimum deterrence with the posture of no-first-use and non-use against non-nuclear-weapon States.[57]Indian Foreign Secretary on the International Day for the Total Elimination of Nuclear Weapons at the 76th UN General Assembly recently stated:[58]

> India welcomes the convening of the High-Level Plenary meeting to commemorate the International Day for Total Elimination of Nuclear Weapons. It provides a valuable opportunity for the international community to reaffirm its commitment to global nuclear disarmament and to enhance public awareness about the objectives of the total elimination of nuclear weapons. ... India is committed to the goal of universal, non-discriminatory, and verifiable nuclear disarmament, leading to the complete elimination of nuclear weapons, consistent with the highest priority accorded to nuclear disarmament. India believes that the goal of nuclear disarmament can be achieved through a step-by-step process, underwritten by a universal commitment and an agreed multilateral framework that is global and non-discriminatory.

York: Columbia University Press, pp. 205, at pp. 47-48.

57 India conducted its first nuclear test in 1974. In May 1998, however, India conducted a series of publicized nuclear tests which established its status as a self-declared nuclear weapon state. Subsequently, Prime Minister Vajpayee made a statement in the Parliament that India does not intend to use these weapons for aggression or for making threats against any country; these are weapons of self-defence, to ensure that India is not subjected to nuclear threats or coercion.

58 Indian Foreign Secretary's Statement on the International Day for the Total Elimination of Nuclear Weapons at the 76th United Nations General Assembly, September 28, 2021.

Conclusion

The detonation of even one nuclear weapon in a highly-populated area such as a city is likely to cause human harm on a large scale. Beyond the instantaneous death and injury caused, one of the most significant and immediate costs and sources of lasting disruption from a nuclear weapon detonation will be the displacement of people from their homes and communities, with all of its downstream consequences in terms of human misery and economic loss. The spread of radioactive fallout would be a significant factor influencing displacement patterns and any humanitarian response. These displaced people will urgently need shelter, uncontaminated food and water, adequate specialized healthcare, as well as protection from violence, abuse, and discrimination, both in the short term and in the longer term. Meeting these needs, while maintaining ongoing humanitarian operations throughout the world, would pose a fundamental challenge for global humanitarian response, with potentially catastrophic consequences.[59]

Nuclear weapons pose a continuing threat to the world. New weapon technologies pose possible challenges to international stability and peace and security. In the face of the growing automation of weaponry, as discussed earlier, new measures are necessary to ensure humans always maintain control over the use of force. Recent developments have raised serious concerns for the maintenance of international peace and security, the upholding of humanitarian principles, and the preservation of human rights. Since its inception, the United Nations has sought the global elimination of nuclear weapons and all other weapons of mass destruction. Today, approximately 13,000 nuclear weapons remain in the stockpiles of nine countries, and hundreds remain on high alert, ready to be launched within minutes. The growing awareness of the catastrophic humanitarian consequences that would result from limited use of nuclear weapons has prompted new initiatives aimed at their prohibition and complete elimination.[60] The States that possess nuclear weapons must take steps to reduce all types of nuclear weapons, reduce their role in security doctrines, and work together to achieve concrete and irreversible steps to prepare for a world free of nuclear weapons. The atomic bombing of Hiroshima

59 Bagshaw Simon, Population Displacement: Displacement in the aftermath of nuclear weapon detonation events, ILPI-UNIDIR Vienna Conference Series, Paper No. 4, 2014, p. 8.

60 Securing Our Common Future: An Agenda for Disarmament, United Nations: Office for Disarmament Affairs, New York, 2018, p. 73.

and Nagasaki had no moral or military justification; it was a crime against humanity and will continue to be so if such weapons are used in future.

The major international legal regime applicable to nuclear weapons elimination now includes Article VI of the Nuclear Non-proliferation Treaty (NPT) and the Treaty on the Prohibition of Nuclear Weapons (TPNW). The UN member states must ensure that the treaty regime becomes the backbone of a strong new international normative principle against nuclear weapons. In this regard following is recommended:

- The obligation to pursue effective measures towards nuclear disarmament is a shared responsibility of all the members States of the United Nations. They must condemn the development, testing, production, stockpiling, transfer, deployment, threat and use of nuclear weapons.
- In response to the global appeal for nuclear disarmament, the United States, Russia and China should concurrently launch intensive trilateral strategic dialogues to increase transparency and mutual understanding in security policies that do not rely on nuclear weapons. Other states having nuclear weapons should follow the approach.
- For the gradual elimination of nuclear weapons, nuclear weapons states must develop their military strategies and tactics which do not dependent on nuclear deterrence.
- Every state must exercise strict governmental control (non-military) over the operations relating to producing the nuclear material that could be used in any form in weapon making. The United Nations must establish enforcement arrangements under an international legal regime to ensure that any state breaching its obligations is effectively penalized.
- Every state must ensure that all nuclear and radiological material is kept secure with the governmental authorities (non-military) so that it is out of the reach of non-state actors.[61] The five "Ds"

61 The Global Initiative to Combat Nuclear Terrorism (GICNT) is an innovative, multi-pronged action aimed at enhancing the domestic capacities of a state, as well as its ability to interconnect internationally and to deal with the risk of a terrorist attack involving nuclear or radioactive materials. The Global Initiative to Combat Nuclear Terrorism (GICNT) is a voluntary partnership of 89 nations. They have endorsed a set of core nuclear security principles across the full spectrum of nuclear terrorism

of nuclear security: deter, detect, delay, deny, and defeat must be strictly followed.

Upon receiving the 2005 Nobel Peace Prize, Mohamed ElBaradei,[62] the director-general of the International Atomic Energy Agency, said, "As long as some of us choose to rely on nuclear weapons, we continue to risk that these same weapons will become increasingly attractive to others. ….. if we hope to escape self-destruction, then nuclear weapons should have no place in our collective conscience, and no role in our security."[63] The only assurance against the risk of future detonation of nuclear weapons is their total elimination from the military arsenal.

deterrence, prevention, detection, and response objectives. Its eight guiding principle, in brief, are: (i) Improve accounting, control, and protection of nuclear/radiological material; (ii) Enhance security of civilian nuclear facilities; (iii) Detect and suppress illicit trafficking of nuclear/radiological material; (iv) Improve ability to search for, confiscate, and establish safe control of nuclear/radiological material; (v) Assure denial of safe haven and resources from terrorists seeking to acquire or use nuclear/radiological material; (vi) Ensure adequate legal frameworks to combat activity related to nuclear terrorism; (vii) Respond to and mitigate the consequences of nuclear terrorism; and (viii) Promote information sharing to prevent and respond to acts of nuclear terrorism.

62 The Norwegian Nobel Committee decided that the Nobel Peace Prize for 2005 is to be shared, in two equal parts, between the International Atomic Energy Agency (IAEA) and its Director General, Mohamed ElBaradei, for their efforts to prevent nuclear energy from being used for military purposes and to ensure that nuclear energy for peaceful purposes is used in the safest possible way.

63 Mohamed ElBaradei, Remarks at IAEA Nobel Peace Prize Ceremony 2005, December 10, 2005, available at http://www.iaea.org/NewsCenter/Statements/2005/ebsp2005n020.html.

Bibliography

Alex-Martin Becky et.al., Addressing the Humanitarian and Environmental Consequences of Atmospheric Nuclear Weapon Tests: A Case Study of UK and US Test Programs at Kiritimati (Christmas) and Malden Islands, Republic of Kiribati, *Global Policy*, Vol. 12, Issue 1, February 2021, pp. 106-121.

Alilat Farid, Algeria: France urged to reveal truth about past nuclear tests, *The Africa Report*, September 10, 2020.

Bhumitra Chakma, 2009, *Pakistan's Nuclear Weapons*, Routledge, pp. 208.

Blechman Barry M. and Alexander K. Bollfrass, 2010, *National Perspectives on Nuclear Disarmament*, Washington DC: Stimson Centre, pp. 382.

Bleimaier John Kuhn, Nuclear Weapons and Crimes against Humanity under International Law, *Catholic Lawyer*, Vol. 33, No. 2, 2017, pp. 161-172.

Blix Hans, 2008, *Why Nuclear Disarmament Matters*, Cambridge: The MIT Press, pp. 95.

Bolton Matthew, Humanitarian and Environmental Action to Address Nuclear Harm, Background Paper, International Disarmament Institute Pace University, October 2017, pp. 36.

Bolton Matthew, et. al., Fall out on Countries Downwind from French Pacific Nuclear Weapons Testing, Aotearoa New Zealand, Australia, Cook Islands, Fiji, Niue, Samoa, Tokelau, Tonga and Tuvalu, International Disarmament Institute, Pace University, 2018, pp. 30.

Borrie John, Tim Caughley, et. al., 2016, *A prohibition on Nuclear Weapons: A guide to the issues*, United Nations Institute for Disarmament Research (UNIDIR) and International Law and Policy Institute (ILPI), pp, 60.

Borrie John and Tim Caughley, 2014, An Illusion of Safety: Challenges of Nuclear Weapon Detonations for United Nations Humanitarian Coordination and Response, Geneva: United Nations Institute for Disarmament Research, pp. 88.

Borrie John, A Hramful Legacy: The lingering humanitarian impacts of nuclear weapons testing, ILPI-UNIDIR Vienna Conference Series, Paper No. 2, pp. 7.

Boulanin Vincent, Lora Saalman, et. al., Artificial Intelligence, Strategic Stability and Nuclear Risk, Stockholm: SIPRI, June 2020.

Bridges, Paul W. II, The Bombs Bursting In Air: A History Of The Effects of Atmospheric Nuclear Weapons Testing On Washington County, Utah, 1951-1963, Unpublished Dissertation, 2014, pp. 136.

Burns John F., India sets 3 nuclear blasts, defying a worldwide ban; tests bring a sharp outcry, *The New York Times*, May 12, 1998.

Burr William, et. al., Blast from the Past, *Foreign Policy*, September 22, 2019.

Casey-Maslen, S., 2019, *The Treaty on the Prohibition of Nuclear Weapons: A Commentary*, Oxford Commentaries on International Law, Oxford: Oxford University Press, p. 304.

Caurus W. Seth, *Defining "Weapons of Mass Destruction,"* Centre for the Study of Weapons of Mass Destruction Occasional Paper, No. 8, Washington, DC: NDU Press, 2012, pp. 90.

Caves John P. and Carus W. Seth, 2021, *The Future of Weapons of Mass Destruction: An Update*, National Intelligence University Presidential Scholar's Paper, Washington, DC: National Intelligence Press, pp. 110.

Cirincione Joseph, 2007, *Bomb Scare: The History and Future of Nuclear Weapons*, New York: Columbia University Press, p. 224.

Clark Ronald W., 1961, *The Birth f the Bomb: The untold story of Britain's part in the weapon that changed the world*, London: Phoenix House Ltd., pp. 209.

Clarke, R., 1986, *London under attack: the report of the Greater London Area War Risk Study.* Oxford: Blackwell, pp. 397.

Cohen Avner, 1998, *Israel and the Bomb*, New York: Columbia University Press, pp. 470.

Cobo Jose R. Martin, The Tlatelolco: An Update, *IAEA Bulletin*, Vol. 26, No. 3, 1984, pp. 25-30.

Collin Jean-Martin and Patric Bouveret, Radioactivity Under the Sand; The Waste From French Nuclear Tests in Algeria: Analysis with regard to the Treaty on the Prohibition of Nuclear Weapons, Heinrich Boll Foundation, July 2020, p. 53.

Complex Cleanup: The Environmental Legacy of Nuclear Weapons Production, *OTA-O-484*, US Congress, Office of Technology Assessment, Washington, DC: Government Printing Office, February 1991, p.212.

Cooperation among Nuclear-Weapon-Free Zones: History, Challenges and Recommendations, The Vienna Center for Disarmament and Non-Proliferation (VCDNP) Task Force Report, 2018, p. 32.

Corn Geoffrey S. and Shane R Reeves, 2016, *US Military Operations: Law, Policy and Practice*, Oxford: Oxford University Press, p. 862.

Craig Campbell and Sergey Radchenko, 2008, *The Atomic Bomb and the Origins of the Cold War*, London: Yale University Press, p. 200.

Datan Merav and Jürgen Scheffran, The Treaty is Out of the Bottle: The Power and Logic of Nuclear Disarmament, *Journal for Peace and Nuclear Disarmament*, Vol. 2, No. 1, 2019, pp. 114-132.

Delpech Therese, 2012, *Nuclear Deterrence in the 21st Century: Lessons for the Cold War for a New Era of Strategic Piracy*, RAND Corporation, p. 196.

Dimmen Anne Guro, Gendered Impacts: The Humanitarian Impacts of Nuclear Weapons from a Gender Perspective, Paper 5, ILPI-UNIDIR, 2014, p. 7.

Docherty Bonnie, From Obligation to Action: Advancing Victim Assistance and Environmental Remediation at the First Meeting of States Parties to the Treaty on the Prohibition of Nuclear Weapons, *Journal of Peace and Nuclear Disarmament*, Vol. 3, No. 3, 2020, pp. 253-264.

Douple Evan B., Mabuchi Kiyohiko, et. al., Long-term Radiation-Related Health Effects in a Unique Human Population: Lessons Learned from the Atomic Bomb Survivors of Hiroshima and Nagasaki, *Disaster Med Public Heath Prep*, Vol. 5, March 2011, pp. S122-S133.

Duarte Sergio, Disarmament and Non-proliferation: A Historical Review, Paper presented at seminar on Disarmament and Non-proliferation, March 28, 2011, p. 8.

Eamonn McCann, Hiroshima was a crime against humanity, *The Irish Times*, August 6, 2015.

Effects of Nuclear Earth-Penetrator and Other Weapons, National Research Council Washington DC: The National Academies Press, 2005, p. 134.

Erasto Tytti, New Technologies and Nuclear Disarmament, SIPRI, May 2021, p. 25.

Ethical imperatives for a nuclear-weapon-free world, Resolution adopted by the General Assembly on December 7, 2015, A/RES/70/50 dated December 11, 2015.

Ethical imperatives for a nuclear-weapon-free world, Resolution adopted by the General Assembly on 7 December 2020, A/RES/75/73 dated December 17, 2020.

Evans Christopher P., Questioning the Status of the Treaty on the Prohibition of Nuclear Weapons as a 'Humanitarian Disarmament' Agreement, *Utrecht Journal of International and European Law*, Volume 36(1), 2021, pp. 52–74.

Evans Christopher P., Remedying the Limitations of the CTBT? Testing under the Treaty on the Prohibition of Nuclear Weapons, *Melbourne Journal of International Law*, Vol. 21, 2020, pp. 1-43.

Evans Gareth, Tanya Ogilvie and Thakur Ramesh, 2015, *Nuclear Weapons: The State of Play*, Centre for Non-Proliferation and Disarmament, Australian National University, p. 302.

Fehner Terrence R. and F. G. Gosling, Origins of the Nevada Test Site, United States Department of Energy, December 2000, pp. 95.

Fehner Terrence R. and F.G. Gosling, Battlefield of the Cold War, Vol. I, Atmospheric Nuclear Weapons testing: 1951-1963, United States Department of Energy, September 2006, p. 244.

Fitzpatric Mark, 2014, *Overcoming Pakistan's Nuclear Dangers*, International Institute for Strategic Studies, London: Routledge, p. 171.

Frankel Michael J., James Scouras and George W. Ullrich, The Uncertain Consequences of Nuclear Weapons Use, National Security Report, The Johns Hopkins University Applied Physics Laboratory, 2015, p. 38.

Frankel Michael J., James Scouras and George W. Ullrich, Tickling the Sleeping Dragon's Tail: Should We Resume Nuclear Testing? The Johns Hopkins University Applied Physics Laboratory, 2021, p. 48.

Futter Andrew, 2018, *Hacking the Bomb: Cyber Threats and Nuclear Weapons*, Georgetown University Press, p. 197.

Goldblat, Jozef, Nuclear-Weapon-Free-Zones: A History and Assessment, *Nonproliferation Review*, Vol. 4(3), 1997, pp. 18-32.

Gosling David, India's Nuclear Explosion: Its Effects upon Environment, *Economic and Political Weekly*, Vol. 9, No. 26, June 29, 1974, pp. 1002-1004.

Gowin Emmet, 2019, *The Nevada Test Site*, Princeton University Press, p. 160.

Greenwell John, The atom bombing of Hiroshima and Nagasaki: Were they war crimes? *ISAA Review*, Vol. 12 (2), 2013, pp. 35-44.

Grethe Lauglo Ostern (ed.), 2021, *Nuclear Weapons Ban Monitor 2020: Tracking progress towards a world without nuclear weapons*, Norwegian People's Aid, pp. 300.

Herota Deborah, The United States' Nuclear Testing Programme in the Marshall Islands, *Bound Away: The Liberty Journal of History*, Vol. 2, Issue 2, 2018, pp. 11.

Hill Steven, NATO and the Treaty on the Prohibition of Nuclear Weapons, International security Programme, London: Chatham House, January 2021, p. 32.

Homer-Dixon Thomas F., et al., Environmental Change and Violent Conflict, *Scientific American*, Number 268, February 1993, pp. 38-45.

Hurley Daniel, The Treaty on the Prohibition of Nuclear Weapons, Oireachtas Library & Research Service, 2019, pp. 23.

Iaria Adriano, International Humanitarian Law and the UN Nuclear Ban Treaty, *Insitutto Affari Internazionali*, September 14, 2017, pp. 1-4.

ICRC report on the effects of the atomic bomb at Hiroshima, *International Review of the Red Cross*, Vol. 97, No. 899, 2015, pp. 859–882.

Jean-Marie Henckaerts and Louise Doswald-Beck, 2005, *Customary International Humanitarian Law, Vol. 1: Rules*, Cambridge: Cambridge University Press, p. 621.

Johnson Rebecca, Rethinking Security Interests for a Nuclear Weapon-Free Zone in the Middle East, *Disarmament Diplomacy*, Issue No. 86, Autumn 2007.

Jones Vincent C, 1985, *Manhattan: The Army and the Atomic Bomb*, Centre of Military History, US Army, Washington DC, p. 660.

Jose Coleen, Kim Wall and Jan Hinzel, Marshall Island: This dome in the Pacific houses tons of radioactive waste – and it's leaking, *The Guardian*, February 3, 2015.

Kalinowski Martin B., 2004, *International Control of Tritium for Nuclear Nonproliferation and Disarmament*, London: CRC Press, pp. 248.

Kelly Cynthia C. (ed.), 2004, *Remembering the Manhattan Project: Perspectives on the Making of the Atomic Bomb and its Legacy*, New Jersey: World Scientific, p. 187.

Kohlhoff Dean W., 2002, *Amchita and the Bomb: Nuclear Testing in Alaska*, Seattle and London: University of Washington Press, pp. 166.

Koppe Erik, 2008, *The Use of Nuclear Weapons and the Protection of the Environment During International Armed Conflict*, Oregon: Oxford and Portland, p. 446.

Lawrence Michael J. Holly L.J. et.al., The effects of modern war and military activities on biodiversity and the environment, *Environmental Review*, Vol. 23, 2015, pp. 443-460.

Lee Manseok and Natch Michael, Challenges to the Nuclear Non-Proliferation Treaty, *Strategic Studies Quarterly*, Fall 2020, pp. 95-120.

Leigh-Phippard, Helen, Nuclear-Weapon-Free-Zones: Problems and Prospects, *Arms Control*, Vol. 14, No. 2, pp. 93-114.

Levite Ariel E., Lyu Jinghua, et.al., China-US Cyber-Nuclear C3 Stability, Working Paper, Carnegie Endowment for International Peace, Publications Department, 2021, pp. 48.

Lewis Jonathan and Stelle Ben, 2001, *Hell in the Pacific: From Pearl Harbour to Hiroshima and Beyond*, London: Channel 4 Books, p.288.

Lima Sergio Eduardo Moreira, 2017, *The Universal Obligation of Nuclear Disarmament*, Alexandre de Gusmao Foundation, Ministry of Foreign Affairs, Brazil, p. 224.

Linderfalk Ulf, 2007, *On the Interpretation of Treaties: The Modern International Law as Expressed in the 1969 Vienna Convention on the Law of Treaties*, The Netherlands: Springer, pp. 437.

Lodgaard Sverre, 2011, *Nuclear Disarmament and Non-Proliferation: Towards a nuclear-weapon-free world?* London: Routledge, p. 263.

MacDonald Alexander, The Theory and Evolution of Nuclear-Weapon-Free Zones: Could the Arctic Be Next? North American and Arctic Defence and Security Network (NAADSN), February 1, 2021, p. 28.

Maclellan Nic, 2017, *Grappling with the Bomb: Britain's Pacific H-Bomb Tests*, Australian National University Press, p. 383.

Macmillan Nic, 2017, *Grappling with the Bomb: Britain's Pacific H-Bomb Tests*, Australian University Press, p. 383.

Maresca Louis and Eleanor Mitchell, The human costs and legal consequences of nuclear weapons under international humanitarian law, *International Review of the Red Cross*, Vol. 97, No. 899, 2015, pp. 621-645.

Matsick Rob, Shaking the Rust Off the Comprehensive Nuclear- Test-Ban Treaty Ratification Process , *Journal of National Security Law and Policy*, Vol. 10, 2019, pp. 405-428.

McKinney Katherine E., Scott D. Sagan & Allen S. Weiner, Why the atomic bombing of Hiroshima would be illegal today, *Bulletin of the Atomic Scientists*, Vol. 76, No. 4, pp. 157-165.

Mendenhall Elizabeth, Nuclear-Weapon-Free Zones and Contemporary Arms Control, *Strategic Studies Quarterly*, Vol. 14, No. 4, Winter 2020, pp. 122-151.

Michal Onderco and Andrea Farres Jimenez, A Comparison of National Review of the Treaty on the Prohibition of Nuclear Weapons, *Non-proliferation and Disarmament Papers*, No. 76, June 2021, pp. 13.

Military and Security Developments Involving the People's Republic of China 2021, Annual Report to Congress, Office of the Secretary of Defence, USA, pp. 173.

Mohan Pulkit, Ensuring Cyber Security in India's Nuclear Systems, ORF Issue Brief, Issue No. 12, October 2020, pp. 13.

Mount Adam, The case Against Nuclear Weapons, Centre for American Progress, May 2017, pp. 64.

Muller Harald et. al., A Nuclear Weapon-Free Zone in Europe: Concept, Problems, Chances, January 2016, PRIF Working Paper, pp. 80.

Nanda Ved P. and Lowe Jeffrey C., Nuclear Weapons and the Ecology: Is International Law Helpless to Address the Problem, *Denv. Jour of International Law and Policy*, Vol. 19, No. 1, 1990, pp. 87-114.

Naono Akiko., The Origins of '*Hibakusha*' as a Scientific and Political Classification of the Survivor, *Japanese Studies*, Vol. 39(3), 2019, pp. 333-352.

Narang Vipin, 2014, *Nuclear Strategy in the Modern Era: Regional Powers and International Conflict*, Oxford: Princeton University Press, pp. 341.

Nuclear Operations, Joint Publication 3-72, Unied States Joint Force Department. June 11, 2019, pp. 60.

Nuclear Matters Handbook 2020, The Office of the Deputy Assistant Secretary of Defence for Nuclear Matters, USA, pp. 80.

Nuclear Weapon Prohibition Treaty: A Safeguards Debacle, *Trust and Verify*, Autumn 2017, Issue No. 158, pp. 18.

Nystuen Gro, Staart Casey-Maslen and Annie Golden Bersagel (ed.), 2015, *Nuclear Weapons under International Law*, Cambridge: Cambridge University Press, p. 503.

Nystuen Gro, Legal aspects of nuclear weapons: a 'birds-eye view' of international law and nuclear weapons, *ILPI-UNIDIR, Paper 6, 2014*, p. 7.

Perkovich George and James M. Action (ed.), 2009, *Abolishing Nuclear Weapons: A Debate*, Washington DC: Carnegie Endowment, pp. 344.

Podvig Pavel and Ryan Snyder, Watch them go: Simplifying the elimination of fissile materials and nuclear weapons, The United Nations Institute for Disarmament Research (UNIDIR), 2019, p. 56.

Pollock Nancy, Nuclear contamination of food in the Pacific: Lifting the veil of secrecy, *Pacific Ecologist*, Issue 22, Summer 2013, pp. 21.

Poolos J., 2008, *The Atomic Bombings of Hiroshima and Nagasaki*, New York: Chelsea House Publishers, p. 128.

Pravalie Remus, Nuclear Weapons Tests and Environmental Consequences: A Global Perspective, *AMBIO*, Royal Swedish Academy of Sciences,

Vol. 43, 2014, pp. 729-744.

Radioactive Heaven and Earth: The health and environmental effects of nuclear weapons testing in, on, and above the earth, 1991, Report of the IPPNW International Commission to Investigate the Health and Environmental Effects of Nuclear Weapons Production and the Institute for Energy and Environmental Research, New York: The Apex Press, pp. 193.

Reny Col Stephen, Nuclear-Armed Hypersonic Weapons and Nuclear Deterrence, *Strategic Studies Quarterly*, Vol. 14, No. 4, Winter 2020, pp. 47-73.

Rhodes Riachard, 1995, *Dark Sun: The Making of the Hydrogen Bomb*, New York: Simon & Schuster, pp. 731.

Rhodes Riachard, 1986, *The Making of the Atomic Bomb*, New York: Simon & Schuster, pp. 881.

Richard Theodore T., Nuclear Weapons Targeting: The Evolution of Law and U.S. Policy, *Military Law Review*, Vol. 224, Issue 4, 2016, pp. 862-978.

Roff S.R., Mortality and morbidity of members of the British Nuclear Tests Veterans Association and the New Zealand Nuclear Tests Veterans Association and their families, *Medicine, conflict and survival*, Vol. 15(Suppl.1), Jul-Sep 1999, pp. 1-51.

Rogoff Martin A., The International Legal Obligations of Signatories to an Unratified Treaty, Maine Law Review, Vol. 32, 1980, pp. 263-299.

Ruff Tilman A., The humanitarian impact and implications of nuclear test explosions in the Pacific region, *International Review of the Red Cross*, Vol. 97, No. 899, pp. 775–813.

Rust Susanne, How the US betrayed the Marshall Islands, kindling the next nuclear disaster, *Los Angeles Times*, November 10, 2019.

Sandoz Yves, Christophe Swinarski and Bruno Zimmerman (eds), 1987, *Commentary on the Additional Protocols of 8 June 1977*, Geneva: ICRC, pp. 1625.

Sayler Kelley M., Hypersonic Weapons: Background Issues for Congress, Congressional Research Service, R45811, August 25, 2021 and October 19, 2021.

Serrano Monica, 1992, *Common Security in Latin America: The 1967 Treaty of Tlatelolco*, London: Institute of Latin American Studies, pp. 108.

Shetty Shatabhisha and Denitsa Raynova, Breakthrough or Breakpoint? Global Perspectives on the Nuclear Ban Treaty, Global Security: Special Report, December 2017, pp. 70.

Simon Steven L., Andre Bouville and Charles E. Land, Fallout from Nuclear Weapons Tests and Cancer Risks, *American Scientist*, Vol. 94, 2006, pp. 48-57.

Singh Nidhi, Victim Assistance under the Treaty on the Prohibition of Nuclear Weapons: An Analysis, *Journal of Peace and Nuclear Disarmament*, Vol. 3, No. 3, 2020, pp. 265-282.

Siracusa Joseph M., The Eight Pillars of the Nuclear Nonproliferation Regime and the Search for Global Security, Global Policy Essay, September 2012, pp. 17.

SIPRI Yearbook 2021, Armaments, Disarmament and International Security, Oxford: Oxford University Press.

Slade R, Tickner R and Wynn-Pope P, Protecting Humanity from the Catastrophic Consequences of Nuclear Weapons: Reframing the Debate Towards the Humanitarian Impact, *International Review of the Red Cross,* Vol. 97, No. 889, 2015, pp. 7-31.

Smith Shane, Cyber Threats and Weapons of Mass Destruction, Centre for the Study of Weapons of Mass Destruction, June 2021, pp. 4.

Sood Rakesh (ed.), 2019, *Nuclear Order in the Twenty-First Century*, New Delhi: Observer Research Foundation, pp. 157.

Sources and Effects of Ionizind Radiation, Volume I, UN Scientific Committee on the Effects of Atomic Radiation (UNSCEAR), Report to the General Assembly (with Scientific Annexes C), New York: United Nations, 2000, pp.158-291.

Speier Richard H. George Nacouzi, Carrie A. Lee, and Richard M. Moore, Hypersonic Missile Nonproliferation: Hindering the Spread of a New Class of Weapons, Rand Corporation, 2017, p. 123.

Srogosz Tomasz, Possession of nuclear weapons – between legality and legitimization. *International and Comparative Law Review*, Vol. 16, No. 1, 2016, pp. 7–21.

Stoutland Page O. and Samantha Pitts-Kiefer, Nuclear Weapons in the New Cyber Age: Report of the Cyber-Nuclear Weapons Study Group, The Nuclear Threat Initiative, 2018, pp. 29.

Subritzky Monika, An Analysis of the Treaty on the Prohibition of Nuclear Weapons in Light of its Form as a Framework Agreement, *Gottingen Journal of International Law*, Vol. 9, 2019, pp. 367-384.

Susanne Rust, How the U.S. betrayed the Marshall Islands, kindling the next nuclear disaster, Los Angeles Times, 2019.

Tago Atsushi, The Origins of Nuclear Weapons Free Zones: Security Communities or Substitutes for a 'Nuclear Umbrella'? Graduate School of Law, Kobe University, Japan, pp. 28.

Thakur Ramesh (ed.), 1998, *Nuclear Weapons-Free Zones*, New York: Macmillan Press Ltd, pp. 235.

The Commander's Handbook on the Law of Naval Operation, US Nay, US Marine Corps and US Coast Guard, NWP 1-14M/MCTP 11-10B/ COMDTPUB P5800.7A, August 2017.

The Commander's Handbook on the Law of Land Warfare, Headquarters, Department of the Army, US Marine Corps, FM 6-27, August 2019.

Tomonaga M., The atomic bombings of Hiroshima and Nagasaki: A summary of the human consequences, 1945-2018, and lessons for *Homo sapiens* to end the nuclear weapon age, *Journal for Peace and Nuclear Disarmament*, Vol. 2(2), 2019, pp. 1-27.

Topychkanov Petr, Enhancing South Asian Nuclear Dialogue: The Implications of Covid-19, SIPRI Policy Brief, September 2021, p. 12.

Unal Beyza, Patricia Lewis and Sasan Aghlani, The Humanitarian Impacts of Nuclear Testing: Regional Responses and Mitigation Measures, International Security Department, Chatham House, May 2017, pp. 37.

Unal Beyza and Patricia Lewis, Cyber-security of Nuclear Weapons Systems: Threats, Vulnerabilities and Consequences, Chatham House, January 2018, pp. 24.

The Treatment of the Issue of Nuclear Disarmament in Relevant Forums Established by the United Nations, Nuclear Disarmament, OEWG Brief no. 1, UNIDIR, pp. 12.

Tilman Ruff, Negotiating the UN Treaty on the Prohibition of Nuclear Weapons and the Role of ICAN, *Global Change, Peace & Security* , Vol. 30 (2), 2018, pp. 233–241.

Tuya Nyamosor, Mongolia's Nuclear-Weapon-Free Status: Recognition vs Institutionalization, Washington DC: The Brookings Institution, 2012, pp. 24.

United Nations conference to negotiate a legally binding instrument to prohibit nuclear weapons, leading towards their total elimination, A/ CONF.229/2017/NGO/WP.11 dates March 28, 2017.

Vail Christopher, The Legality of Nuclear Weapons for Use and Deterrence, *Georgetown Journal of International Law*, Vol. 48, 2017, pp. 839-872.

Wainstock Dennis D., 2010, *The Decision to Drop the Atomic Bomb: Hiroshima and Nagasaki: August 1945*, USA: Enigma Books, p. 228.

Warren Aiden and Philip M Baxter (ed), 2020, *Nuclear Modernization in the 21st Century*, Routledge, p. 203.

William K. Ris, French Nuclear Testing: A Crisis for International Law, *Denv. Journal of International Law and Policy*, Vol. 4, 1974, pp. 111-132.

Woolf Amy F. et.al., Arms Control and Nonproliferation: A Catalog of Treaties and Agreements, Congressional Research Service Report, March 11, 2011, pp. 68.

Yan Wudan, In the Shadow of Nuclear Sins, *Nature*, Vol. 568, April 4, 2019.

Yasmin Afina, et.al., Negotiation of a Nuclear Weapons Prohibition Treaty: Nuts and Bolts of the Ban, The New Treaty: Taking Stock, The United Nations Institute for Disarmament Research (UNIDIR), 2017, p. 14.

Index

I

K

L

M

N

CPSIA information can be obtained
at www.ICGtesting.com
Printed in the USA
LVHW011943130222
710999LV00004B/101

9 789390 917785